WORLD'S BEST

WEDDING & HONEYMOON

DESTINATIONS

From the Best Selling Wedding Planning Series in America
By WeddingSolutions.com

FREE TRAVEL GUIDE

INTRODUCTION

Hilton Maldives Resort & Spa - The Maldives

Congratulations on your engagement! You must be very excited to have found that special person with whom you will share the rest of your life. And you must be looking forward to what may be one of the happiest times of your life -- your wedding and honeymoon! Planning this special time can be fun and exciting. But it requires hours of research in order to make the right decision. That is why Wedding Solutions, the most renowned wedding publishing and consulting company in America, has created a publication titled The *Ultimate Guide to the World's Best Wedding & Honeymoon Destinations.*

This FREE insert is a condensed version of the *Ultimate Guide to the World's Best Wedding & Honeymoon Destinations.* And it highlights 26 of the most beautiful and romantic resorts in the world. These resorts were selected for their quality of service, ideal location, outstanding facilities and beautiful surroundings.

The *Ultimate Guide to the World's Best Wedding & Honeymoon Destinations* features over 150 of the best wedding and honeymoon hotels and resorts in the world, including detailed descriptions about each hotel and resort, such as contact information, room rates, website, nearby attractions, on-site facilities, wedding services and more.

It also features complete descriptions of the most popular destinations (islands or regions) for an elegant destination wedding or unforgettable honeymoon. Some of the destinations featured in this guide are: Hawaii, Caribbean, Fiji, Thailand, Tahiti, Bora Bora, Moorea, Italy, Greece and many more.

WORLD'S BEST WEDDING & HONEYMOON DESTINATIONS

WRITTEN BY:
Elizabeth and Alex Lluch

PUBLISHED BY:
Wedding Solutions Publishing, Inc.

© Copyright 2004

Cover Photo: Le Méridien Bora Bora - Bora Bora, French Polynesia
Back Cover: Top: Hilton Maldives Resort & Spa - The Maldives
               Middle: Sandals Negril Beach Resort & Spa - Negril, Jamaica
               Bottom: Hilton Maldives Resort & Spa - The Maldives

Range of rates are provided in U.S. dollars unless otherwise noted. Contact location for current rates.
The information provided in this guide is subject to change without notice.

Printed in Korea

TABLE OF CONTENTS

Galley Bay Resort

ANTIGUA

• at a glance
Location: Antigua
Mailing Address: Five Islands P.O. Box 305 St. John's Antigua
Reservations: 954-481-8787 or 1-800- 858-4618
Fax: 954-481-1661
Web Site: www.eliteislandresorts.com
Size of Property: 40 acres
Accommodations: 69 rooms
Range of Rates: $650 - $1,150

about the area
Currency: EC (Eastern Caribbean)
Weather: Tropical
Languages: English
Nearest Airport: VC Bird International

Sink your feet into sugary sand and hold on to your hats as the wind whips through your hair. An extraordinarily exclusive retreat perfect for the discerning traveler, Galley Bay's natural elegance, classic Caribbean charm and Gauguin-inspired Tahitian style sets this all-inclusive haven apart from the rest. Your room is waiting, nestled amidst 40 secluded acres of beachfront tropical gardens, a lagoon & bird sanctuary, and a very private 3/4 mile pristine white-sand beach. All guests are welcomed with consummate Antiguan hospitality and whisked away from our historical sugar mill reception by golf cart to one of our astonishing cottages or beachfront accommodations. Delight in fun-filled activities such as non-motorized water sports (windsurfing, sailing, snorkeling), "Hobie-style" catamarans and kayaking. Or stroll along romantic walking trails around the bird sanctuary lagoon. And at the end of the day relax, rejuvenate and refresh your body and soothe your soul at Galley Bay Salon. ✎

• ROMANTIC FEATURES •

Take a trip to a resort that personifies love and romance in its entirety. Set against a backdrop of greens and browns, the sparkling blue of the pool sets off an iridescent glow that appeals to even the most unromantic of individuals and brings to mind an image of an oasis in the midst of a desert. The sensual feel of the sand beneath your feet, the caress of the wind against your skin and the heat from the Caribbean sun can hypnotize even the strongest of minds. Our honeymoon/romance packages offer something for everyone. Tempt your mind, body and soul with a champagne sunset cruise, aromatic massages, champagne continental breakfast in bed, spa treatments and tours of this island paradise. ✎

• nearby attractions

Find special Caribbean treasures at a variety of Antigua's shops and boutiques. Go diving or snorkeling to explore the beauty of Antigua's waters. Circumnavigate the island on a catamaran cruise or visit a saltwater bird lagoon sanctuary.

• onsite facilities

Eat and drink island style at our 2 restaurants, a lounge and a bar. Enjoy an exotic free-form freshwater swimming pool with cascading waterfall, a game room, table tennis, croquet, bicycles, horseshoes, open-air fitness center, & tennis.

• wedding services

Galley Bay is the perfect place for a romantic and unique wedding at a tropical paradise. With beautiful surroundings and staff who looks forward to making to your special day unforgettable. It is a memorable and joyous occasion for all.

• at a glance
Location: Antigua
Mailing Address: Dickinson Bay P.O. Box 147 St. John's, Antigua
Reservations: 1-866-SANDALS
Fax: 305-668-2775
Web Site: www.sandals.com
Size of Property: 19 acres
Meeting Space: 1,334 square feet
Accommodations: 193 rooms and suites
Range of Rates: $335-$575

about the area
Currency: U.S. Dollars
Weather: Tropical
Languages: English
Nearest Airport: V.C. Bird International

• nearby attractions

Champagne Sunset Cruise • Cades Reef Cruise • Horseback Riding • Jolly Roger Pirate Cruise • Bird Island Cruise • Tropikelly Trails • Circumnavigation Cruise • Shirley Heights Lookout • Estate Safari • Prickley Pear Experience

• onsite facilities

Tennis, fitness center, volleyball, lawn chess, croquet, pool tables, European spa*, scuba, snorkeling, sailing, paddle boats, windsurfing. Butler service for select suites.

• wedding services

Free Wedding with minimum 5 nights. Package includes: document preparation, certified copies of marriage license, wedding reception with champagne and hors d'oeurves for four, wedding cake, honeymoon candlelight dinner, bouquet, and boutonniere.

Sandals Antigua
Caribbean Village & Spa

ANTIGUA

S et on breathtaking Dickenson Bay, the island's best and most famous beach, this 5 Star Diamond awarded resort offers the charm of a quaint Caribbean village accompanied by the refined luxuries of a world-class all-inclusive. Voted World's Leading Honeymoon Resort for eight years in a row, Sandals Antigua offers magnificent gardens, hidden pools, and 193 rooms and suites including exotic cone shaped cottages-in-the-round with 24-hour rooms service. A few steps from the turquoise sea and white sand beach are 5 freshwater pools, 5 whirlpools, and 6 bars serving unlimited premium brand drinks. When it comes to dining, there are four extraordinary restaurants plus a courtyard bistro giving more dining choices than any other resort in Antigua. ❧

· ROMANTIC FEATURES ·

When you want a romantic bath drawn for two, only at Sandals can you say "The Butler did it." Stay in a suite with Butler service and you'll receive a level of luxury that is exclusive to Sandals guests. Trained by the elite *Guild of Professional English Butlers*, these Butlers will pamper you in extraordinary ways from a gourmet meal in-suite prepared expressly for you to unpacking or packing your clothes. There's no limit to the way that a Sandals suite with Butler service will ensure every moment of your stay is perfect. ❧

St. James's Club

ANTIGUA

Location: Antigua
Mailing Address: P.O. Box 63 Mamora Bay, Antigua West Indies
Reservations: 954-481-8787 or 1-800-858-4618
Fax: 954-481-1661
Web Site: www.eliteislandresorts.com
Size of Property: 100 acres
Accommodations: 172 rooms, villas & suites
Range of Rates: $460 - $1,100

about the area
Currency: EC (Eastern Caribbean)
Weather: Tropical
Languages: English
Nearest Airport: VC Bird International

· nearby attractions

Shop at English Harbour's unique shops and boutiques, go diving or snorkeling to explore the beauty of Antigua's waters, circumnavigate the island on a catamaran cruise, go deep-sea fishing, or golf at the nearby Cedar Valley Golf Club.

· onsite facilities

4 Restaurants, 5 Bars, Las Vegas-Style Casino, Jacaranda Lounge, Spa & Beauty Salon, Tennis Complex & Pro Shop, 4 Swimming Pools, Fitness Center & Jacuzzi, On-site Deli, On-Site Tour Desk, Full-Service 18-Slip Marina & Yacht Club.

· wedding services

Experience Love In Tropical Elegance by saying "I do" in an exquisite gazebo or on the beach with the sand under your feet. Then have a private reception and dance to the beat of a steel pan while basking in the glow of your memorable day.

I ndulge in the opulence of our private 100-acre peninsula with its undulating hills yielding panoramic windswept, ocean views and delightfully serene palm-fringed beaches, on Antigua's southeastern coast. World-class amenities and impeccable service pamper you and epicurean delights tempt you. Clear, turquoise waters surround your own private oasis where stretches of white sand are your canvas by day and millions of stars gaze down upon you at nighttime. From its luxuriously well-appointed spa, to its Las Vegas-style casino which adds a touch of sophistication, to its bountiful array of fun activities, St. James's Club will capture your heart, mind, body and soul. Dine waterside, surrounded by majestic yachts, or in the privacy of our 250 guest rooms, suites and villas. Every imaginable amenity is yours for the asking. A certain understated elegance gives St. James's Club its renowned reputation for distinction and provides you the epitome of a blissful Caribbean memory.

· ROMANTIC FEATURES ·

At St. James's Club we are dedicated to ensuring your special occasion is one to remember for all time. Take advantage of the entire 100 acres that the resort sits on. The white sandy beaches are perfect for soaking up the rays of a gorgeous Caribbean sun and sipping on a cold island concoction. Gaze at the breathtaking view of the ocean or the lush, tropical gardens from the privacy of your balcony or take a romantic stroll to experience both first hand. If you are in a quiet reflecting mood, visit the Spa & Beauty Salon or enjoy a poolside massage. Or you can gaze into each others eyes over English-style afternoon tea on the Garden Patio or at a romantic candlelit dinner at Piccolo Mondo.

British Colonial Hilton

N A S S A U , B A H A M A S

Location: Nassau, Bahamas
Mailing Address: Number One Bay Street P.O.Box N-7148 Nassau, Bahamas
Reservations: 242-322-3301
Fax: 242-302-9010
Web Site: www.hiltoncaribbean.com/nassau
Size of Property: 8 acres
Meeting Space: 7,500 square feet
Accommodations: 291 rooms and suites
Range of Rates: $120 - $250

about the area
Currency: USD - Bahamian Dollar
Weather: Tropical. Avg. 80 degrees
Languages: English
Nearest Airport: Nassau Int'l Airport

• nearby attractions

Beautiful white sand beaches; the Straw Market; unlimited duty-free shopping; Fort Fincastle; Adastra Gardens and Zoo; National Arts & Cultural Museum; and the Arawak Cay Fish Fry.

• onsite facilities

Guests can relax on the private beach, in the lush tropical gardens, or in the outdoor freshwater pool. Non-motorized watersports, kayaking and paddleboats available, along with an on-site snorkeling facility and a full service spa and gym.

• wedding services

Our team of on-site wedding coordinators can arrange the ceremony, officiant, flowers, photography, decor, ideal location, and marriage license. The wedding cake, music and styling can be arranged, if needed, as well as airport transfers.

Situated on the site of old Fort Nassau, The British Colonial Hilton is the oldest building in downtown Nassau and an architectural masterpiece, which remains a part of Bahamian history. After its recent $68 million renovation in October 1999, this 291 room oceanfront property has evolved into a classic and luxurious leisure and business hotel that maintains a tropical, Colonial feel. Centrally located in downtown Nassau, it is in close proximity to all the happenings and activities on and off the island, from unlimited duty free shopping on Bay St., golfing and casinos, to diving with the dolphins. Guests can enjoy the dazzling sun and ocean waves at our freshwater pool; and just off our private beach, kayaking and snorkeling are popular diversions.

Each room and suite is beautifully furnished in Colonial decor with modern conveniences. There are 2 restaurants and 3 bars on property, as well as nightly entertainment in the upscale Blue Note Jazz.

· ROMANTIC FEATURES ·

Host an event as picture perfect as the Caribbean! The property offers an intimate and relaxed atmosphere, with private lounge areas throughout the hotel as well as beautiful gardens and private beach areas that are perfect for relaxing or having a wedding. The hotel has an experienced staff of meeting professionals on hand and can cater any number of special themed dinners or receptions, from grand events to small and intimate affairs. They can assist with the little details or help you plan the entire event from decor to location.

Guests can indulge in a variety of services at the Azure Spa, including aromatherapy, couples massages, body wraps, facials, hydrotherapy bath, or simply relaxing in a hammock in our lush tropical gardens.

• **at a glance**
Location: Nassau, Bahamas
Mailing Address: P.O. Box 39-CB-13005
Cable Beach, Nassau, Bahamas
Reservations:1-866-SANDALS
Fax: 305-668-2775
Web Site: www.sandals.com
Size of Property: 16 acres
Meeting Space: 11,000 square feet
Accommodations: 405 rooms and suites
Range of Rates: $405 - $750

about the area
Currency: U.S. Dollars
Weather: Tropical
Languages: English
Nearest Airport: Nassau International

• **nearby attractions**

Botanical Gardens, Dolphin Encounter, Horseback Riding, Submarine Dive, Deep Sea Fishing, Powerboat Adventures, Blue Lagoon Excursion, Shipwreck Adventure, Catamaran Cruise, Hartley's Undersea Adventure.

Sandals Royal Bahamian
Spa Resort & Offshore Island

N A S S A U ,   B A H A M A S

N estled in beautiful Nassau, this Five Star Diamond Resort is

truly a star with winning the vote as the Caribbean's Leading Resort as well as the Top Caribbean Spa Resort by the readers of Conde Nast Traveler.   From the regal elegance of European sophistication to the relaxed, Caribbean charm, every rare pleasure is included in one all-inclusive price. Enjoy eight sumptuous world-class restaurants including and Authentic British Pub, all land and water sports, lavish rooms and suites; some offering 24-hour room service and V.I.P. chauffeured Rolls Royce

transfers and the option of an award winning European Spa.*

Just a short boat ride away from the main resort is Sandals Cay, a romantic private island that offers you two exotic adventures for the price of one. Discover paradise with two secluded pearl-white beaches, a pool with a swim-up bar and Café Goombay, an authentic island fish house.

• **onsite facilities**

Private offshore island includes pool, swim-up pool bar, 2 beaches and seafood restaurant. European spa*, fitness centers, volleyball, basketball, tennis, scuba, snorkeling, sailing, windsurfing. Butler service for select suites.

• **ROMANTIC FEATURES** •

Renowned as the "Pearl of the Caribbean" for it's flawless classic elegance and timeless European luxury, guests can retreat to the Royal Village, an enclave of intimate villa suites amidst exotic gardens and hidden pools for a very private romantic experience. Stay in a suite with Butler service and you'll be spoiled beyond your wildest dreams. Trained by the elite *Guild of Professional English Butlers,* these Butlers will pamper you in extraordinary ways. Imagine a bath drawn scented by lemongrass. Or a gourmet meal designed especially for you. There's no limit to the way that a Sandals suite with Butler service will ensure every moment of your stay is perfect.

Certain spa services additional.

• **wedding services**

Free Wedding with minimum 5 nights. Package includes: document preparation, certified copies of marriage license, wedding reception with champagne and hors d'oeurves for four, wedding cake, honeymoon candlelight dinner, bouquet, and boutonniere.

Long Bay Resort

TORTOLA, BRITISH VIRGIN ISLANDS

• at a glance

Location: Tortola, British Virgin Islands
Mailing Address: Long Bay Beach Resort & Villas PO Box 433
Roadtown, Tortola BVI
Reservations: 954-481-8787 or 1-800-858-4618
Fax: 305-668-2775
Web Site: www.eliteislandresorts.com
Size of Property: 52 acres
Accommodations: 90 rooms & 26 villas
Range of Rates: $460 - $1,300

about the area

Currency: U.S. Dollars
Weather: Sub-tropical
Languages: English
Nearest Airport: Beef Island, BVI (EIS)

• nearby attractions

Visit the famous, romantic, private beach of Smuggler's Cove. Take a trip to the Bomba Shack to party with both locals and tourists. Or go on one of Virgin Adventure's amazing tours in the sun, sand & sea of this Caribbean jewel of an island.

• onsite facilities

Long Bay is equipped with its own mini strip mall, tennis shop run by a famous tennis pro and a Boutique with Columbian Emeralds. Enjoy a full spa, superb pool, gym, innumerable activities, 2 onsite restaurants & an exclusive tour company.

• wedding services

Experience Love In Tropical Elegance. If the thought of a barefoot wedding on a beautiful beach in the shade of gently swaying palm trees, or a ceremony in a beachside gazebo bedecked with bougainvillea is your style, then come to Long Bay.

Lose yourself on this dreamy island of pleasure and paradise.

Let us put you under our spell amidst vibrant green vegetation, rolling hillsides, inviting beaches and our brand of island hospitality. For a few pleasurable days you can live on top of the world in one of our hillside accommodations or live as close as possible to our aquatic wildlife in spectacular beachfront cabanas. When you have had enough of lounging on luxurious sandy beaches, relaxing under the rays of a Caribbean sun and resting in the privacy of your home away from home, you can work off that excess energy by treating your body to the sinful pleasures of our Spa. For some fun in the sun go sailing, swimming, surfing, snorkeling, scuba diving, sport fishing, horseback riding or play tennis. If your perfect getaway brings to mind the following expressions: perfect setting, ideal facilities, warm and inviting atmosphere, exotic surroundings, a caring and courteous staff, fun, sea and sun, then we are right for you.

• ROMANTIC FEATURES •

Long Bay Resort is a place where the pace of daytime entertainment is more along the lines of watching the pelicans dive for fish off the beach, or of drifting laconically through the pool to our swim-up bar. It is a perfect place to begin your married life or spend time with your loved one. Long Bay's special environment is ideal for making your marriage vows and it is a very special place for you to celebrate afterwards. When you think that discovering new places with your partner is always a very special event, beginning your new life together in one is priceless. Delightful places like the beach is exquisite for the sand between-your-toe's castaways and saying 'I love you.'

Palm Island Resort

PALM ISLAND, GRENEDINES

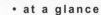

• at a glance

Location: Palm Island, Grenedines
Mailing Address: Palm Island St. Vincent, Grenedines West Indies
Reservations: 954-481-8787 or 1-800-858-4618
Fax: 954-481-1661
Web Site: www.eliteislandresorts.com
Size of Property: 135 acres
Accommodations: 37 rooms & suites
Range of Rates: $700 - $950

about the area

Currency: EC (Eastern Caribbean)
Weather: Tropical
Languages: English
Nearest Airport: Union Island (UNI)

• nearby attractions

Take a boat ride and snorkel at the nearby Tobago Cays. Hike along Cactus Hill Trail, Point Lookout Trail, or Iguana Nature Trail. And cruise the waters of the Caribbean while sipping champagne on a romantic sunset ride on the "Pink Lady."

• onsite facilities

2 Restaurants & 2 Bars, Tennis Court, Fitness Center/Entertainment Room, a 9-hole "putt & pitch" golf course, a Free-Form Swimming Pool, On-Site Tour Desk, Boutique, Land Turtles Sanctuary, 5 exquisite beaches and an array of water sports.

• wedding services

Experience Love In Tropical Elegance, on a private Caribbean island. Palm Island is the perfect place for a romantic and unique wedding. Choose from beautiful surroundings such as the pristine beach overlooking the sea or secluded gardens.

T his exclusive resort is set in pure paradise where tranquility reigns and an unforgettable experience of a lifetime is inevitable. This natural oasis has changed little since it was first discovered. When you arrive, your state of mind is set back decades. A perfect antidote to everyday stresses. Here you reawaken the things that matter most. Fill your senses with serenity amidst lush tropical landscapes embraced by five dazzling white-sand beaches. Sumptuous gourmet dining served oceanfront by award-winning chefs in the most romantic setting of all the Grenadines.

All 40 intimate guest rooms are air-conditioned and feature island motifs, custom rattan furnishings and luxurious amenities. The vantage point from your private balcony or patio provides a sweeping panoramic view at every turn as far as the eye can see. Cycle around the island, dive into the sea or set adrift in a catamaran or sea kayak. Let balmy breezes and Caribbean waves paint the canvas that is your backdrop for fun.

· ROMANTIC FEATURES ·

This private island couples serenity and luxury as seamlessly as its sandy shores dissolves into its impossibly blue waters. Immerse yourself in our unparalleled environment, where service is delicately balanced with an air of privacy for all. Enjoy a private picnic for two on one of our five beaches, or let the gentle sway of a hammock ease away your cares as you await the magnificent color change of the sky as another day in paradise draws to a close. Stay nestled amidst palm trees and tropical gardens alight in the iridescent glow of nature's color. Enjoy the pleasures of our honeymoon packages including massages, romantic dinners, sunset cruises, champagne breakfast in bed and much more.

Raffles Resort

CANOUAN ISLAND, THE GRENADINES

Location: Canouan Island, The Grenadines
Mailing Address: 440 Park Avenue, 5th floor New York, NY 10022 USA
Reservations: 1-877-CANOUAN
Fax: 1-312-565-9930
Web Site: www.raffles.com
Size of Property: 300 acres
Meeting Space: 3,500 square feet
Accommodations: 156 rooms and suites
Range of Rates: $345 - $1365

about the area
Currency: U.S. Dollar,
XCD - Eastern Caribbean Dollars
Weather: Tropical
Languages: English
Nearest Airport: Canouan International

• nearby attractions

Located in The Grenadines, pristine Canouan Island is only 20 miles from Mustique. Day trips to nearby Tobago Keys and other picturesque islands of the Grenadines are easy to arrange.

• onsite facilities

Pamper yourselves at the exotic Amrita Spa, or opt for an in-room treatment. Savor gourmet cuisine in four world-class restaurants. Enjoy excellent watersports, boating and an 18 hole championship-grade golf course.

• wedding services

Canouan Island has a beautiful, reconstructed, non-denominational, 12th Century English church that's ideal for romantic weddings. We have a wedding coordinator on staff to make sure your special day is everything you dreamed it would be.

For a fortunate few, the Caribbean sun is about to shine a little brighter. July 15, 2004 will mark the unveiling of what will be the ultimate convergence of luxury and romance.

On the shores of the Caribbean's pristine Canouan Island, some of the most respected names in luxury and hospitality will come together on 1,200 secluded acres, to create the premiere resort property in the western hemisphere, Raffles Resort at Canouan Island.

Imagine a championship-grade, 18-hole golf course designed by Jim Fazio; European-style gaming at the Villa Monte Carlo managed by Trump; a cliff-side luxury Amrita Spa; private yacht moorings operated by The Moorings, Ltd.; the largest swimming pool in the Southern Caribbean, and seaside recreation on a picture-perfect white sand beach—all brought together by Raffles, an internationally renowned hospitality company whose name is synonymous with the Asian commitment to unparalleled personal service.

ROMANTIC FEATURES

It's hard to imagine a more perfect honeymoon destination than Raffles Resort at Canouan Island. With only 156 ocean-view accommodations, couples have the rare opportunity to retreat into a paradise all their own.

Of course, when you do decide to emerge, the ultimate luxury experience awaits. Four world-class restaurants let you wine and dine as if touring the cuisine capitals of Europe. Pamper yourself with any number of exceptional indulgences at the Amrita Spa—or opt for a special in-room massage for two.

Spend the day basking on an immaculate, crescent white sand beach, then return at night for moonlight stroll, the gentle Caribbean Sea lapping at your feet. It is romantic, indeed.

San Souci Resort and Spa

OCHO RIOS, JAMAICA

• at a glance

Location: Ocho Rios, Jamaica
Mailing Address: Sans Souci Resort, P.O. Box 103, Ocho Rios/St.Anne Jamaica
Reservations: 1-876-994-1206
Fax: 1-876-994-1544
Web Site: www.SansSouciJamaica.com
Size of Property: 27 acres
Meeting Space: 3,000 square feet
Accommodations: 146 suites
Range of Rates: $170 - $320 per person

about the area

Currency: U.S. Dollars
Weather: Tropical
Languages: English
Nearest Airport: Montego Bay

Situated along the majestic emerald cliffs of Jamaica's northern coast, the exclusive, four-diamond, all-inclusive Sans Souci Resort & Spa encompasses a unique 27-acre property unparalleled in natural beauty, history and legend.

Located just a short distance from the fabled town of Ocho Rios, the property where the Sans Souci Resort & Spa now resides has been sought out for centuries by travelers because of its fabled natural mineral spring and pristine beaches. Today this beautiful landscape is coupled with a true world class resort and spa and has aptly been coined the "Jewel of Jamaica."

Sans Souci Resort & Spa is built entirely around a natural mineral spring that has historically been acclaimed with restoring health, wellness, energy, and even love. Legend calls it a "fountain of love." Dating back to the mid-1600's, stories have been told of a Spanish maiden and an English naval officer who shared a forbidden love in the grottos beneath the cliffs. Risking everything, the couple would steal away under a canopy of stars to the spring's bubbling grottos. Because of their unbridled love, said to still linger in the hidden grottos, the legend attests that couples who soak in the mineral spring together will awaken hidden passion.

Local history books also tell of generations of nearby residents who lined up every Sunday to take their turn bathing in the natural mineral spring, believing it to heal minor ailments, skin conditions, and arthritic pains.

• nearby attractions

Ocho Rios is a popular seaport town and stopover for numerous cruise ships, with plenty of native shopping opportunities. Other attractions include horseback riding at Chukka Stables, Dunns River Waterfalls and Blue Mountain Biking Tours.

• onsite facilities

On site facilities include two beaches, 4 pools, tennis courts, full-service spa, fitness/aerobics center, water sports facilities with scuba, snorkeling, sailing and kayaking, four restaurants, three bars, and duty free gift/jewelry shops.

• wedding services

Ceremonies can be performed in a variety of breathtaking locations on the property, including a picturesque gazebo perched atop a lush hillside overlooking the ocean, an intimate tropical garden, and an alcove adorned by fresh-cut flowers.

Today guests at the resort learn that not only is the natural mineral spring at the Sans Souci Resort & Spa without comparison, but also without peer is the individual hospitality and pampering that the staff provides to every guests.

Moreover the scenery is divine. Winding pathways through lush greenery, an elaborate labyrinth of small bridges, breathtaking vistas, four pools, two beaches, outdoor Jacuzzis, hilltop gazebos and secluded hammocks for two barely begin to describe the relaxed beauty of the resort. Thoughtfully arranged activities include sailing, windsurfing, water-skiing, hydra-biking, kayaking, scuba diving, snorkeling, volleyball, basketball, tennis, golf, and bocce ball. Nearby there is also golf at the prestigious Upton Links (green fees are free) and plenty of sightseeing opportunities and recreational pursuits from white water rafting, to mountain biking, shopping and swimming with the dolphins at Dolphin Cove. One beach is even "clothing optional."

A new favorite pastime at the Sans Souci Resort & Spa is getting pampered at the full-service professionally staffed tropical-style spa. Here guests may choose from a long menu of treatments performed in private cabanas perched above the melodic hum of the Caribbean waters. Included in the stay, the resort has handpicked an assortment of services for each guest to ensure everyone receives an ample amount of bodily indulgence. Guests can lounge in the original

grottos of the spring or in the resort's eco-friendly additions.

Whether relishing under the warm sun while listening to the whispering breeze, reinventing oneself in the resort's state-of-the-art fitness pavilion, dining at one of the resort's four award-winning restaurants, or sipping premium cocktails at one of the five distinctively themed bars, every guest at the Sans Souci Resort & Spa will find what they're looking for. And for those who prefer intimate privacy, the resort provides 24-hour in-suite dining in any of the elegant oceanview suites . ✤

· ROMANTIC FEATURES ·

Weddings at the Sans Souci Resort & Spa are nothing short of magical. Couples can practically breeze into their own fairytales. Because each detail of the wedding is virtually free and handled by a complimentary professional wedding coordinator, couples can relax and enjoy every moment of their time together.

Sans Souci Resort & Spa will help each couple to grant each wedding wish. Many couples elope to the Sans Souci Resort & Spa, and more are decidedly choosing the resort to have a destination wedding, surrounded by intimate friends and family. ✤

· wedding utopia

Few places in the world can compare to Sans Souci Resort & Spa as an elegant seaside wedding utopia. A place of great beauty, it has inspired lovers for hundreds of years.

· wedding packages

In addition to providing the most unforgettable and photographically perfect setting, Sans Souci offers complete wedding packages with a wide array of complimentary services.

Royal Plantation

OCHO RIOS, JAMAICA

• **at a glance**
Location: Ocho Rios, Jamaica
Mailing Address: Main Street, P.O. Box 2, Ocho Rios, St. Ann, Jamaica
Reservations: 1-888-48-ROYAL
Fax: 305-668-2775
Web Site: www.royalplantation.com
Size of Property: 8 acres
Meeting Space: 1,848 square feet
Accommodations: 77 suites
Range of Rates: $320 - $1,025

about the area
Currency: U.S. Dollars
Weather: Tropical
Languages: English
Nearest Airport: Sangster International

Secluded and simply exquisite, yet breathtakingly beautiful.

Royal Plantation is rich in British inspired elegance, reminiscent of aristocratic plantation manors. There are seventy-seven magnificent suites, each showcasing Caribbean elegance with Plantation style fabrics and hues, fine Italian bed linens and 100% down duvets. And 24 hour service available to all guests. Beach Butlers are just a nod away servicing a Caribbean cocktail and delicious Jamaican fare.

Dining pleasures begin at one of four restaurants that will captivate all your senses. Be tempted at Jamaica's first Caviar + Champagne bar and retire at the Cognac and Cigar Lounge.

Hundreds of feet above sea level is the picturesque Upton Golf and Country Club. Considered the islands' most elite, this is the most desired course to play while away.

For renewal of the body, mind and spirit, the impressive Spa, recognized as a Leading Spa by The leading Small Hotels of the World takes each to a new level of tranquility - in your suite or on the ocean pier under a gazebo. ෴

• **nearby attractions**

Tour of Dunn's River Falls, Port Antonio River Rafting, Port Antonio Highlight, Luminous Lagoon, Sun Valley / Firefly, Kingston Tour, Martha Brae River Rafting, Black River Safari, Sightseeing & Shopping, Coyaba / Fern Gully, Blue Mountains.

• **onsite facilities**

Tennis, 24-hour state of the art fitness center, scuba diving, freshwater pool and two whirlpools. Complimentary limousine transfers are available for guests staying in Villa Plantana, Prime Minister and Governor Suites. Private car and bus transfers can be arranged upon request for all other guests at an additional charge.

• **wedding services**

Weddings, renewal of vows and special event packages offer exclusive features only available at Royal Plantation. Exotic settings include tropical gardens, beach gazebos and the white sand beach.

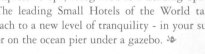
· **ROMANTIC FEATURES** ·

There are two private villas that will cater to every whim. The Rio Chico Estate sits on a 14-acre private estate and is surrounded by lush gardens, waterfalls and private cove beaches. While Villa Plantana offers a personal butler on call 24 hours and a personal chef that will cater to every unique taste. ෴

• at a glance
Location: Ocho Rios, Jamaica
Mailing Address: PO Box 51, Mamme Bay, Ocho Rios Jamaica, WI
Reservations: 1-866-SANDALS
Fax: 305-668-2775
Web Site: www.sandals.com
Size of Property: 25 acres
Meeting Space: 1,596 square feet
Accommodations: 250 rooms and suites
Range of Rates: $295 - $675

about the area
Currency: U.S. Dollars
Weather: Tropical
Languages: English
Nearest Airport: Sangster International

• nearby attractions

Dunn's River Falls, Coyaba River Garden & Museum, Port Antonio, Blue Mountain, Bicycle Tour Blue Mountain Trek 52', Catamaran Cruise, Sunset Cruise, Prospect Plantation, Shopping Tour, Deep Sea Fishing, Horseback Riding, Martha Brae River Rafting.

Sandals Dunn's River Golf Resort & Spa

OCHO RIOS, JAMAICA

Inspired by the great Italian Renaissance period and named after the world-famous waterfall located minutes away...This breathtaking all-inclusive resort combines Mediterranean elegance with Jamaican charm, creating Caribbean luxury on a grand scale.

Take up the opulent lobby with an ornate staircase reminiscent of an Italian palazzo. Be dazzled by the resort's majestic entrance lined with Royal Palms, bordered by lush fairways revealing its true nature, all which define classic elegance. Land enthusiasts can pitch and putt on property or head over to the nearby Sandals Golf & Country Club where a drive on the 18 hole golf course is surrounded by picturesque fairways. Make all sorts of waves with windsurfing, waterskiing and scuba or resort to the ultimate indulgence of a full service European Spa.*

With a choice of four gourmet restaurants and five bars including the exotic Tree bar, there's something for everyone's appetite. For those who want to dine in, Concierge level guests may enjoy the privilege of room service 24 hours a day. As part of the "Stay at one, Play at others" program, guests enjoy full exchange privileges and complimentary transfers to Sandals Grande Ocho Rios Beach and Villa Resort. Extended amenities include a private beach club, the largest rock climbing wall and an additional 9 restaurants to choose from. ❧

· ROMANTIC FEATURES ·

When you want a romantic bath drawn for two, only at Sandals can you say "The Butler did it." Stay in a suite with Butler service and you'll receive a level of luxury that is exclusive to Sandals guests. Trained by the elite *Guild of Professional English Butlers*, these Butlers will pamper you in extraordinary ways from a gourmet meal in-suite prepared expressly for you to unpacking or packing your clothes. There's no limit to the way that a Sandals suite with Butler service will ensure every moment of your stay is perfect. ❧

Certain spa services additional.

• onsite facilities

2 impressive freshwater pools with swim-up bars, sailing, snorkeling, scuba, windsurfing, pitch & putt course on property, challenging 18-hole course at nearby Sandals Golf and Country Club, tennis, fitness center, European spa*. Butler service for selected suites.

• wedding services

Free Wedding with minimum 5 nights. Package includes: document preparation, certified copies of marriage license, wedding reception with champagne and hors d'oeurves for four, wedding cake, honeymoon candlelight dinner, bouquet, and boutonniere.

• at a glance
Location: Negril, Jamaica
Mailing Address: P.O. Box 12 Negril,
Jamaica, W.I.
Reservations: 1-866-SANDALS
Fax: 305-668-2775
Web Site: www.sandals.com
Size of Property: 21 acres
Meeting Space: Capacity: 20 persons
Accommodation: 223 rooms and suites
Range of Rates: $325 - $650

about the area
Currency: U.S. Dollars
Weather: Tropical
Languages: English
Nearest Airport: Sangster
International

• nearby attractions

Dunn's River Falls, Ricks' Cafe, Horseback
Riding, Deep Sea Fishing, Negril Hi-Lite
Tour, Montego Bay Hi-Lite Tour, Wild Thing
Cruise, Rafting Negril, Lighthouse Anancy
Park.

Sandals Negril
Beach Resort & Spa

NEGRIL, JAMAICA

Amidst a pristine tropical setting, this all-inclusive world-class

resort combines a laid-back atmosphere with refined elegance. Spanning the longest and best stretch of Jamaica's famous seven-mile beach, this hotel won the coveted Green Globe Award and the CHA Green Hotel of the year, emblematic of its environmentally friendly ambiance.

Where even the architecture has been designed to be lower than the highest palm trees.

As a recipient of the Five Star Diamond Award, Sandals Negril epitomizes everything a Caribbean beach resort should be. Steps away from the sea are four specialty restaurants and five bars fulfilling every foodies dreams. You can kick back and surrender to the crystal blue water, or jump into one of the many activities available at the sports complex. ❧

• ROMANTIC FEATURES •

There are 223 of the Caribbean's finest rooms and suites in eight categories. Unparalleled luxury is evident in the lavishly appointed beachfront rooms, stunning honeymoon rooms and honeymoon suites, as well as the two story loft suites showcasing spiral stairs that lead to panoramic ocean views.

Trained by the elite *Guild of Professional English Butlers*, these Butlers will pamper you in extraordinary ways from a romantic bath drawn for the two of you, to unpacking or packing your clothes. There's no limit to the way that a Sandals suite with Butler service will ensure every moment of your stay is perfect. ❧

• onsite facilities

Sports Complex: racquetball, squash, tennis, basketball, fitness center, European Spa*, Watersports: waterskiing, scuba, snorkeling, sailing, windsurfing, kayaks, paddleboats, hobie cats. Butler service for select suites. *Certain spa services additional.*

• wedding services

Free Wedding with minimum 5 nights. Package includes: document preparation, certified copies of marriage license, wedding reception with champagne and hors d'oeurves for four, wedding cake, honeymoon candlelight dinner, bouquet, and boutonniere.

• at a glance

Location: Gros Islet, St. Lucia
Mailing Address: .P.O. Box G.I. 2247
Gros-Islet, St. Lucia, W.I.
Reservations: 1-866-SANDALS
Fax: 305-668-2775
Web Site: www.sandals.com
Size of Property: 17 acres
Meeting Space: 20,000 square feet
Accommodations: 284 rooms and suites
Range of Rates: $375 - $825

about the area
Currency: U.S. Dollars
Weather: Tropical
Languages: English
Nearest Airport: Vigie Airport

• nearby attractions

Soufrière Day Sail, Soufrière by Land & Sea, Deep Sea Fishing, Dolphin & Whale Watching, Jeep Rainforest Safari, Maria Island, The Jungle Trail, Marquis Plantation, Horseback Riding, Shopping Shuttle, Waterfall Bike Ride.

• onsite facilities

European Spa, Golf, 5 pools, 4 whirlpools, lawn chess, tennis, volleyball, fitness center, basketball, scuba, snorkeling, sailing, waterskiing, windsurfing, paddle boats. Butler service for select suites.

• wedding services

Free Wedding with minimum 5-night stay. Package includes: document preparation, certified copies of marriage license, wedding reception with champagne and hors d'oeurves for four, wedding cake, honeymoon candlelight dinner, bouquet, and boutonniere.

Sandals Grande St. Lucian
Spa & Beach Resort

GROS ISLET, ST. LUCIA

O n an island so "simply beautiful" the French and British fought over it for over 150 years, lies a Five Diamond resort considered impressive in every way. Set on its own spectacular peninsula surrounded by the sea on both sides, the resort offers breathtaking vistas of the bay and the mountains on one side and the island of Martinique's distant shores on the other. The all-inclusive amenities ensure a truly carefree stay. You can feast at five extraordinary restaurants including an authentic British Pub, spend time soaking up the sun at one of five freshwater pools, or enjoy endless land and water sports including golf, scuba, and water skiing.

All luxurious rooms and suites are custom appointed with king size beds, large private verandas, designer baths, and all with mesmerizing water views. For guests in search of some-

thing truly unique, there are 24 spectacular Lagoon Pool Rooms that allow you to swim right up to your patio.

For extra indulgence, spa services include the latest European treatments with a soothing Caribbean touch. For additional Sandals-style hospitality, you can hop over to Sandals Halcyon Beach or Sandals Regency St. Lucia through the exclusive "Stay at One, Play at Three" program. Your adventure extends to 14 restaurants and 2 spas to choose from and golf. Sandals Grande St. Lucian is truly a resort of grandeur. ✤

ROMANTIC FEATURES

When you want a romantic bath drawn for two, only at Sandals can you say "The Butler did it." Stay in a suite with Butler service and you'll receive a level of luxury that is exclusive to Sandals guests. Trained by the elite *Guild of Professional English Butlers*, these Butlers will pamper you in extraordinary ways from a gourmet meal in-suite prepared expressly for you to unpacking or packing your clothes. There's no limit to the way that a Sandals suite with Butler service will ensure every moment of your stay is perfect. ✤

Sandals Regency St. Lucia Golf Resort & Spa at La Toc

CASTRIES, ST. LUCIA

Set along a half-mile crescent-shaped beach, this 210 acre

Five Star Diamond resort takes you to the height of glamour. Where the service is rendered by a staff who is genuinely pleased to have you as their guest. No detail has been spared to bring you an infinitely romantic gateway on an exotic island that boasts the world's only drive through a volcano. All-inclusive amenities such as the largest freshwater pool in the Eastern Caribbean, a nine-hole golf course on property, and the magnificent Villa Suites on Sunset Bluff bring Sandals Regency St. Lucia to the pinnacle of perfection.

Every personalized comfort is provided in 327 rooms and suites in 13 different accommodation categories. For couples that wish for regal seclusions, the Sunset Bluff is its own spectacular sanctuary with a separate pool, restaurants, bars, fitness center and beautiful hillside villa suites with stunning ocean views and 24-hour room service.

All guests can indulge at six exquisite restaurants, nine bars, a range of land and water sports including scuba, and the option of a full service European Spa*. Full exchange privileges at two other all-inclusive resorts nearby gives you an additional eight restaurants. Sandals Regency St. Lucia achieves the true height of regal pampering. ✥

· ROMANTIC FEATURES ·

From beachfront rooms... to expansive honeymoon suites with a private plunge pool... to water's edge suites with split-level living rooms, Sandals Regency St. Lucia is the lover's retreat of a lifetime. When you want a romantic bath drawn for two, only at Sandals can you say "The Butler did it." Stay in a suite with Butler service and you'll receive a level of luxury that is exclusive to Sandals guests. Trained by the elite *Guild of Professional English Butlers*, these Butlers will pamper you in extraordinary ways from a gourmet meal in-suite prepared expressly for you to unpacking or packing your clothes. There's no limit to the way that a Sandals suite with Butler service will ensure every moment of your stay is perfect. ✥

Certain spa services additional.

· nearby attractions

Soufrière Day Sail, Soufrière by Land & Sea, Deep Sea Fishing, Dolphin & Whale Watching, Jeep Rainforest Safari, Maria Island, The Jungle Trail, Marquis Plantation, Horseback Riding, Shopping Shuttle, Waterfall Bike Ride.

· onsite facilities

2 fitness centers, European Spa*, 3 freshwater pools plus scuba pool, 4 whirlpools, 9 hole golf course on property, basketball, volleyball, lawn chess, tennis, scuba, snorkeling, waterskiing, hobie cats, canoes, kayaks, sailing. Butler service for select suites.

· wedding services

Free Wedding with minimum 5 nights. Package includes: document preparation, certified copies of marriage license, wedding reception with champagne and hors d'oeurves, wedding cake, honeymoon candlelight dinner, bouquet, and boutonniere.

St. James's Club

GROS ISLET, ST. LUCIA

• at a glance

Location: Gros Islet, St. Lucia
Mailing Address: P.O. Box 2167 Choc Bay Gros Islet, St. Lucia West Indies
Reservations: 954-481-8787 or 1-800-858-4618
Fax: 954-481-1661
Web Site: www.eliteislandresorts.com
Size of Property: 22 acres
Accommodations: 238 rooms
Range of Rates: $350 - $600

about the area

Currency: EC (Eastern Caribbean)
Weather: Tropical
Languages: English
Nearest Airport: George Charles (SLU)

• nearby attractions

An 18-hole golf course at nearby St. Lucia Golf & Country Club, duty-free shopping at Castries, Rodney Bay, Marigot Bay. Go on a sightseeing excursion into the rainforest, the drive-in volcano and the Pitons in the south of the island.

• onsite facilities

3 Restaurants, 4 Bars, Spa & Beauty Salon, Lighted Tennis Complex, Family Swimming Pool, "Bon View" Adult Swimming Pool & Bar, Fitness Center & Sauna, Gift Shop, Local Island Craft & Souvenir Hut, car rental, tour desk and guest services.

• wedding services

Experience Love In Tropical Elegance at St. James's Club, Morgan Bay where you will create loving memories to last a lifetime. Get married in style and enjoy a wonderful, romantic, worry-free day as all details are expertly handled by us.

Caribbean Splendor at its most sensual. You can escape from the ordinary to our surroundings that offer 22 acres of breeze-filled palms, bordered by a private white-sand beach and secluded privacy for your romantic getaway. Fabulous cuisine, themed buffets, unlimited refreshments, live entertainment, dancing, and exciting activities pamper from early morning into the late evening. Our Caribbean-club-style, 238 guest rooms feature a terrace or balcony with spectacular ocean or garden views. Enjoy poolside cocktails, water sports, or a life-size game of chess. Peer into a drive-in volcano, go scuba diving, discover deep sea fishing, or simply relax in the natural beauty of the renowned Pitons that is St. Lucia. Let your body, mind and soul feel the deep soothing effects of a day at our luxurious spa. Share in a "Couples Instructional Massage" and experience a sense of togetherness with your loved one. And trust us to help you experience the marvelous treasure that is this Caribbean isle. ✍

• ROMANTIC FEATURES •

Live for a while amid gently swaying trees, dazzling sunshine and the soothing sound of the ocean. With breathtaking views of the island's lush, hilly interiors and clear turquoise waters, you can express your feelings for your significant other in a place teaming with wonder and delight. Spend every moment in each other arms while flourishing on our private, sandy, palm-fringed beach or in the privacy of your luxuriously equipped room. The charm that is typically of a Caribbean nature will seep itself into your very soul. At nights you can dance to the beat of drums or stroll hand in hand under the spell of a starry sky. Fulfill your deep-seated desires on our shores and live your dream come true. ✍

Windjammer Landing

CASTRIES, ST. LUCIA

• at a glance

Location: Castries, St. Lucia
Mailing Address: Labrelotte Bay, P.O.Box 1504, Castries, St. Lucia West Indies
Reservations: 954-481-8787 or 1-800-858-4618
Fax: 954-481-1661
Web Site: www.eliteislandresorts.com
Size of Property: 60 acres
Accommodations: 290 rooms & 26 villas
Range of Rates: $365 - $590

about the area

Currency: EC (Eastern Caribbean)
Weather: Tropical
Languages: English
Nearest Airport: George Charles (SLU)

• nearby attractions

Windjammer is located 5 miles/15 minutes from St. Lucia's capital city, Castries. Rodney Bay Marina, St. Lucia Golf & Country Club, Horseback riding, Bounty Rum Factory, and Piton Flore Nature Trail are all places to go and things to see.

• onsite facilities

4 restaurants, 1 bar, 1 cafe, car rental company, fitness club, 2 tennis courts, 2 main pools, Serenity Health Spa, room & laundry services, 2 Souvenir Boutiques, and a Mini Mart are all located at the resort with your convenience in mind.

• wedding services

Experience Love In Tropical Elegance. At Windjammer we have a number of services that are available to make your special day complete. Our experience and skills will ensure that this occasion is one that you will remember for a lifetime!

W indjammer Landing is unique and unlike any other Caribbean resort. It was conceived, designed and built as a village. Brick paths meander through more than 60 acres of lush landscaping, scented gardens, sparkling pools and waterfalls, covered walkways, pickled wood, and hand-painted tiles. Stroll or take the continuous shuttle service to the heart of the village where you will find a full-service resort. Windjammer offers a playground of sports and recreation. From our beautiful 1,000 feet crescent-shaped white sandy beach where your every step leaves footprints that last a while and make memories that last forever to a wide choice of water sports and land activities. Our amazing room and villa accommodations offer a bevy of amenities all with your personal pleasure in mind from private terraces & sun decks, air conditioning, mini-refrigerator, cable TV, coffee maker, hair dryers to private plunge pools. Never leaving the resort with all its conveniences is a definite possibility.

· **ROMANTIC FEATURES** ·

This villa by the sea, soaked in charm and elegance, is one of the most romantic spots on earth. Patterned after the picturesque villages of the Mediterranean, Windjammer Landing villas are uniquely designed and secluded from neighbors by magnificent trees and flowering bushes. With its panoramic ocean view this exclusive resort guarantees a romantic stay, whether you're making your vows on the beach, dining in an alfresco restaurant for relaxing in the private plunge pool of your villa. Romance is at the heart of every wedding and/or honeymoon. And at Windjammer our villas and deluxe rooms provide the perfect setting to awaken your spirits and magnify your love for each other.

Beaches Turks & Caicos Resort & Spa

PROVIDENCIALES, TURKS & CAICOS

• at a glance
Location: Providenciales, Turks & Caicos
Mailing Address: P.O. Box 186 Lower
Bight Road, Providenciales, Turks &
Caicos Islands, B.W.I.
Reservations: 1-866-BEACHES
Fax: 305-668-2775
Web Site: www.beaches.com
Size of Property: 125 acres
Meeting Space: 2,500 square feet
Accommodations: 453 rooms & suites
Range of Rates: $340 - $1,625

about the area
Currency: U.S. Dollars
Weather: Tropical
Languages: English
Nearest Airport: Turks & Caicos
International

• **nearby attractions**

Sunset Sail Island Getaway, Half-Day
Cruise, Glass Bottom Boat, French Cay,
Deep Sea Fishing, Middle Caicos Caves,
and a Conch Cruise.

• **onsite facilities**

6 freshwater pools, 4 with swim ups, scuba
pool, kids pool, 3 whirlpool, European
Spa*, waterslides, state of the art video
game center, fitness center, volleyball, tennis, basketball, scuba, snorkeling, windsurfing, kayaks. Butler service for select
suites.

• **wedding services**

Free Wedding with minimum 5 nights.
Package includes: document preparation,
certified copies of marriage license, wedding reception with champagne and hors
d'oeurves for four, wedding cake, honeymoon candlelight dinner, bouquet, and
boutonniere.

Anyone looking for the rare and exotic will find this destination the crystal clear choice. Set on 12 miles of unspoiled white sand beach, Beaches Turks and Caicos is the ultimate vacation for families. The all-inclusive resort provides super-vised kids programs, endless adventures such as action packed Pirates Island Themed Water Park, Xbox Game Oasis Center, and the Caribbean Adventure with Sesame Street featuring themed activities with Elmo and friends. Adults have a vacation of their own with the sophisticated pleasures of the French Village's formal gardens reminiscent of Versailles, the world's best scuba diving, and the option of a full service European Spa.* 🌺

ROMANTIC FEATURES

When you want your bags unpacked, only at Beaches can you say, "The Butler Did It." Stay in a suite with Butler service and you'll receive a level of luxury that is exclusive to Beaches' guests. Trained by the elite *Guild of Professional English Butlers*, these Butlers will pamper you in extraordinary ways from a gourmet meal in-suite prepared expressly for your family to organizing personal shopping and island tours. There's no limit to the way that a Beaches suite with Butler service will ensure every moment of your family's stay is perfect.

Ask about our FamilyMoons package where your family and friends can share in your wedding & honeymoon. 🌺

Certain spa services additional.

Estancia La Jolla Hotel & Spa

LA JOLLA, CALIFORNIA, USA

Luxurious amenities, exquisite surroundings and impeccable service define the essence of Estancia La Jolla Hotel & Spa. Whether you are searching for a quiet spa weekend, or the excitement of ocean water sports, we offer glorious vacation and get-away experiences you are sure to treasure.

A romantic California coastal retreat where time stands still, Estancia La Jolla features wrought iron railings, arched doorways, and picturesque clay tile roofs among lushly landscaped gardens. From the moment you arrive, the open-air arcades and garden courtyards create a tranquil setting that provides a sense of intimacy. Built on the former Black Family Equestrian Estate, our location in La Jolla provides the perfect climate for our world class spa, featuring tranquil indoor and outdoor treatment rooms.

Estancia La Jolla is located just minutes from the beautiful beaches of La Jolla and Del Mar, and only 14 miles from San Diego International Airport. ❧

· ROMANTIC FEATURES ·

Stroll hand in hand through Estancia La Jolla's beautifully landscaped courtyards and gardens, including our signature Rose Garden.

Experience a sensational California sunset on one of our outdoor patios. Enjoy a margarita or glass of wine next to one of two outdoor fireplaces or in the Library, an intimate, gracious room adjacent to the Bodega Wine Bar.

Indoor and outdoor dining rooms will showcase local flavors and provide a variety of culinary delights as our Chef presents some of San Diego's finest culinary tastes, in an atmosphere of warm sophistication.

Couples can spend a relaxing and memorable day together at The Spa with "His & Hers" massage or body treatments. ❧

• at a glance

Location: La Jolla, California USA
Mailing Address: 9700 North Torrey Pines Road, La Jolla, CA 92037
Reservations: 858-550-1000
Fax: 858-550-1001
Web Site: www.estancialajolla.com
Size of Property: 9.5 acres
Meeting Space: 29,681 square feet
Accommodations: 199 rooms and 11 suites
Range of Rates: $229 - $750

about the area
Currency: U.S. Dollars
Weather: Temperate
Languages: English
Nearest Airport: San Diego Lindbergh Field

• nearby attractions

Walk to beautiful Black's beach and Torrey Pines State Park. The beaches of Del Mar and La Jolla, famous Torrey Pines Golf Course and the shops of La Jolla Village are just 5 minutes away. Close to Del Mar Race Track and San Diego attractions.

• onsite facilities

Enjoy a cabana by the pool, a massage in our full-service spa, or relax in one of our three jacuzzis. Indoor & outdoor seating at both restaurants. Bodega Wine Bar features wines from California's eclectic vineyards. 24-hour in-room dining.

• wedding services

From small intimate occasions to the most lavish affair, our full service wedding planning is provided by one of our catering professionals. Custom menu selections and elegant decor assure that your celebration will be one of a kind.

Bellagio

LAS VEGAS, NEVADA, USA

Inspired by the idyllic villages and towns of Europe, AAA Five Diamond Bellagio overlooks a Mediterranean-blue eight-acre lake featuring a magnificent ballet of dancing fountains. Choreographed to music and lights, the fountains are a prelude to the remarkable sights awaiting guests. From unrivaled accommodations, award-winning dining and a gallery of fine art to designer shopping and Cirque du Soleil's stunning "O," Bellagio offers an unforgettable experience.

Bellagio builds on its unrivaled reputation for luxury and service with the opening of its $375 million Spa Tower in December. An additional 928 rooms and suites, the 65,000-square-foot Spa & Salon Bellagio offers an international array of innovative treatments, 60,000 square feet of meeting and convention space including an exhibition kitchen. The casually elegant restaurant Sensi and Jean Philippe Pâtisserie, a French pastry shop unlike anything else in the world, are just some of the new features.

ROMANTIC FEATURES

The Wedding Chapels and Terrace of Dreams were created in an effort to provide couples with elegant surroundings in which to share their wedding with family and friends. Both chapels are beautifully inspired by timeless European design with colorful stained glass windows that adorn the wall behind each altar.

Terrazza di Sogno (Terrace of Dreams), an Italian balcony with toasted marble flooring and walls tinted a warm golden patina, is available for couples wanting the perfect outdoor wedding. Couples overlook stunning views of a Tuscan landscape and a Mediterranean-blue lake with the Fountains of Bellagio soaring to the sky at the moment of the long-awaited first kiss.

• at a glance

Location: Las Vegas, Nevada USA
Mailing Address: 3600 S. Las Vegas Blvd. Las Vegas, Nevada 89109 USA
Reservations: 888-987-6667
Fax: 702-693-8559
Web Site: www.bellagio.com
Meeting Space: 200,000 sq. ft
Accommodations: 3,421 rooms and 512 suites
Range of Rates: $159 - $6,000

about the area

Currency: U.S. Dollars
Weather: Desert
Languages: English
Nearest Airport: McCarran Int'l (LAS)

• nearby attractions

Just beyond Bellagio's gracious lobby lies the Conservatory & Botanical Gardens, a kaleidoscope for your senses. You will want to take a moment to appreciate the intricate detail blooming before your very eyes.

• onsite facilities

Spa Bellagio offers a full complement of therapeutic and rejuvenating body care treatments. Guests can choose among a variety of treatments including Aromatherapy, Combination Massage and Swedish Massage, facials, and body treatments.

• wedding services

An attentive staff specializing in personalized service enhances the exquisite atmosphere of the chapels and the terrace. A wedding coordinator is appointed to each couple and can assist the couple in making necessary arrangements.

Aventura Spa Palace

CANCÚN, MÉXICO

• at a glance

Location: Riviera Maya, México
Mailing Address: KM. 72 Carretera Cancún - Tulum, Riviera Maya, Q.Roo 77710
Reservations: 011-52-984-875-1100
Fax: 011-52-984-875-1101
Web Site: www.palaceresorts.com
Size of Property: 85 acres
Accommodations: 1,266 rooms and suites
Rage of Rates: Contact Hotel for Rates

about the area
Currency: MXN - Mexican Pesos
Weather: Tropical
Languages: Spanish & English
Nearest Airport: Cancún Airport

• nearby attractions

Discover the unique archaeological site of Ek-Balam, known as the City of the "Black Jaguar," or take a first class boat ride to the private beach club of Isla Mujeres.

Take your body, mind, and spirit on a journey that will at once purify, restore, and revitalize the senses. Ideally positioned in the heart of the Riviera Maya, where the tropical sun meets the turquoise waters of the Caribbean Sea, the ultimate pampering experience of Aventura Spa Palace awaits you. This adults only resort is set within 85-acres of exuberant virgin jungle with wide and spacious lawns and gardens.

The focus of well-being extends to Aventura Spa Palace's six restaurants. Begin the day poolside with a delicious breakfast or take advantage of our room service menu and savor a romantic dinner for two in the privacy of your suite.

Aventura offers a wealth of fitness activities including spinning, step, yoga, meditation and exceptional therapeutic pools. Our cross-current marine pool refreshes with cascading waterfalls. Our lap pool energizes. Our sound pool soothes. And our outdoor pools encourage traditional lounging. ॐ

• ROMANTIC FEATURES •

Begin your lives in a breathtaking beachfront setting where every detail will be perfectly planned by our experienced wedding coordinators.

The Aventura Spa Palace offers a beautiful fairy tale wedding, where the bride arrives on a horse-drawn carriage. The Palace brings seclusion and romance where the ceremony is held in a gazebo overlooking the ocean.

From the Aventura Spa Palace's central patio with its colonial fountain, through the romantic archways, down to the natural tile floor, to the carefully handcrafted furniture, it all combines to create a magical setting for your special wedding or honeymoon getaway. ॐ

• onsite facilities

Non-motorized water sports, dive tank, scuba lessons, therapeutic pools, fitness centers, outdoor free-weight gym, spinning room, aerobic room, yoga hut, and one pathway labyrinth. Spa facilities with resting lounge, Zen garden, & saunas.

• wedding services

A beautiful fairytale wedding, where every detail will be planned by our experienced wedding coordinators. Our three wedding packages, Free, Superior, and Deluxe, offer a variety of amenities and services to complement your special day.

Moon Palace Golf Resort

CANCÚN, MÉXICO

Location: Cancún, México
Mailing Address: Carretera Cancún-Chetumal KM. 340 Cancún, Q.Roo 77500, México
Reservations: 1-800-635-1836
Fax: 011-52-998-881-6001
Web Site: www.palaceresorts.com
Size of Property: 123 acres
Meeting Space: Over 80,000 square feet
Accommodations: 2,031 rooms and suites
Range of Rates: Contact Hotel for Rates

about the area
Currency: MXN - Mexican Pesos
Weather: Tropical
Languages: English, Spanish
Nearest Airport: Cancún Airport

• nearby attractions

Sail aboard a first class boat to our exclusive beach club set in a quiet area of Isla Mujeres, or discover the unique archaeological site of Ek-Balam, known as the City of the "Black Jaguar." Plus many other exciting tours to choose from.

• onsite facilities

Includes a championship golf course, sauna/steam bath, 4 pools, 10 restaurants, 6 tennis courts, 7 bars including swim up bars, 2 fitness centers, discoteque, basketball courts, miniature golf, massage, beauty salons & daily activity programs.

• wedding services

A beautiful fairytale wedding, where every detail will be planned by our experienced wedding coordinators. Our three wedding packages, Free, Superior, and Deluxe offer a variety of amenities and services to compliment your special day.

Nestled between pristine white sand beach and acres

of tropical, foliage the magnificent Moon Palace Golf Resort awaits you. This all-inclusive luxury resort offers an incredible 2,031 rooms in 3-story villas. Most with ocean views and all with a double Jacuzzi and private terraces.

Look no further than Moon Palace Golf Resort for fun and excitement. Our two outdoor pools are among the the largest lagoon-style pools in all of México. Each winds its way along the beach with Jacuzzis, swim-up bars, and children's areas.

In addition, our new Jack Nicklaus Signature course offers golfers championship greens on par with some of México's top courses. The resort features 10 exceptional restaurants so you can dine at a different spot every night of the week & sample some of México's best cuisine.

With the largest function space in Cancún and a grand ballroom that seats up to 3,000 guests, Moon Palace Golf Resort offers an inspired setting for your wedding or special event. ॐ

· ROMANTIC FEATURES ·

Imagine your wedding day amid palm trees and a warm ocean breeze where the bride arrives on a horse-drawn carriage. These are only some of the things that you can expect at Moon Palace Golf Resort.

With flexible indoor banquet facilities and expansive poolside terraces, we have the ideal location you desire. Themed events bring the flavor of Cancún to life and may be customized for your wedding event. Whether transforming our ballroom to a tropical paradise or setting up for a night under the stars, Moon Palace Resort's events and catering staff exceed your expectations and ensure guests an affair to remember. ॐ

• at a glance

Location: Riviera Maya, México
Mailing Address: 6KM 265 Carretera
Chetumal Puerto-Juarez Riviera Maya,
México 77710
Reservations: 011-52-984-875-1010
Fax: 011-52-984-875-1012
Web Site: www.palaceresorts.com
Accommodations: 464 rooms & suites
Range of Rates: Contact hotel for rates

about the area
Currency: MXN - Mexican Pesos
Weather: Tropical
Languages: English, Spanish
Nearest Airport: Cancún Airport

Xpu-Ha Palace

RIVIERA MAYA, MÉXICO

• nearby attractions

Xpu-Ha Palace provides transportation to
Playa Del Carmen, Moon Palace Golf
Resort, Beach Palace and the Cancún
shopping area. Take a first class boat ride
to the quiet areas of Isla Mujeres or visit
unique archaeological sites near by.

Located in the Riviera Maya within wild tropical gardens
overlooking a white sandy beach is the magnificent Xpu-Ha Palace, the ultimate all-inclusive adventure for ecological and nature lovers.

Bungalow-style accommodations complement the resort's natural setting but don't be deceived. Under the thatched roofs you'll find plush beds, a double Jacuzzi and a large private terrace complete with hammock. Room service lets you enjoy a romantic meal on your terrace 24-hours a day.

With the Caribbean Sea in your backyard and an ecological park surrounding you, Xpu-Ha Palace offers more than just another day at the beach. Clear Caribbean waters guarantee excellent diving and snorkeling conditions and make for wonderful kayak excursions. Of course, those who prefer can also enjoy our private white sands and pools.

• onsite facilities

All-inclusive consist of non-motorized
water sports, 24-hour room service, pools,
private white sands, fitness center, scuba
demonstration, kayaking & nightly dinner
shows. Guests can also enjoy all of the
amenities of the other Palace Resorts.

• ROMANTIC FEATURES •

The natural surroundings at Xpu-Ha Palace will delight you with a spectacular lagoon view for your ideal wedding location. Imagine your wedding day amid palm trees, a warm ocean breeze and the beauty of México. These are only some of the things that you can expect from Xpu-Ha Palace.

Our wedding packages have been designed to meet our clients' expectations and make this special day a memorable one. Our Free, Superior, and Deluxe packages offer a variety of amenities and services to complement your special day. Our free wedding package includes a wedding gazebo, documents and legal fees, white decorations, red carpet walkway, wedding coordinator, and much more.

• wedding services

A wedding set in spectacular surroundings
where every detail is planned by our experienced event coordinators. Our three wedding packages free, Superior, & Deluxe
offer a variety of amenities and services to
compliment your special day.

· at a glance

Location: Canary Islands, Spain
Mailing Address: 38660 Costa Adeje -
Tenerife Sur Canary Islands, Spain
Reservations: 34-922-74-69-00
Fax: 34-922-74-69-16
Web Site: www.bahia-duque.com
Meeting Space: 53819 square feet
Accommodations: 482 rooms and suites
Range of Rates: $340 - $6,540

about the area
Currency: Euro
Weather: Mild
Languages: Spanish, English
Nearest Airport: Tenerife South
Airport

Gran Hotel Bahia del Duque

CANARY ISLANDS, SPAIN

The Gran Hotel Bahía del Duque Resort is located on the shoreline of the fashionable Costa Adeje in southern Tenerife. Washed by a 900 meter long sandy beach, the outline of La Gomera Island can be made out in the distance.

The hotel is a perfect setting for a family holiday. You can relax on the beach or be as active as you choose, with an array of fine sports facilities, both land and water based. The latter comprise 8 swimming pools, including 2 children's pools, 1 salt water pool and 2 heated pools, a beach club, watersports including waterskiing and parascending, 3 floodlit tennis courts, 2 squash courts, fitness centre, jogging circuits, 5 golf nearby courses, games room, beauty salon, boutiques, gift and tobacco shops.

· nearby attractions

The Gran Hotel Bahía del Duque Resort has 56,000sq meters of exuberant tropical and sub-tropical vegetation, which has created a particular microclimate, with all kinds of trees, cacti and different European plants.

· onsite facilities

The rooms have been decorated in a style that is equally baroque and simple with moroccan influences, with the light and freshness provided by their ochre and sienna-colored tones.

· ROMANTIC FEATURES ·

The hotel retains a peaceful and private atmosphere as the rooms are spread across twenty houses, all reflecting traditional Canarian architecture, with Victorian and Venetian turn-of-the-century influences and set amongst luxuriant gardens sloping down to the beach.   The philosophy of the hotel can be clearly perceived as soon as you see the building from a distance. "Live the difference" is what is offered to all who stay here, from the first moment guests arrive until they leave. Just outside the entrance area is the beginning of a lake that is formed by several swimming pools that are connected by waterfalls. Amongst the gardens is an impressive selection of 11 fine restaurants, 10 bars and cafés to choose from. Cuisines range from Spanish, French, and Italian to typical Canarian, Latin American and Gourmet.

· wedding services

From the moment of your first contact with the Gran Hotel Bahía del Duque Resort you will be attended to by highly qualified personnel who speak several languages so that you may use your native language at all times.

Bora Bora Lagoon Resort

MOTU TOOPUA, BORA BORA, TAHITI

• at a glance

Location: Motu Toopua, Bora Bora, Tahiti
Mailing Address: B.P. 175, Vaitape Bora Bora French Polynesia
Reservations: 011-689-604002
Fax: 011-689-604003
Web Site: www.boraboralagoonresort.orient-express.com
Size of Property: 13 acres
Meeting Space: Approx. 1,000 square feet
Accommodations: 80 rooms and suites
Range of Rates: $450 - $1800

about the area
Currency: XPF - French Pacific Franc, Euros
Weather: Tropical
Languages: French, English, Tahitian
Nearest Airport: Bora Bora

From its ideal location on its own lush motu (islet) in the center of Bora Bora's spectacular lagoon, Orient Express Hotels' award winning Bora Bora Lagoon Resort features 80 luxurious bungalows in overwater, beach and garden settings and serves as Tahiti's most authentic luxury resort. Each air-conditioned bungalow offers a private terrace, television with DVD, telephone, mini-bar, coffee/tea maker and personal safe; overwater bungalows feature glass-topped coffee tables for unique views of Bora Bora's abundant marine life. Guests dine on the finest cuisine in the islands in two superb restaurants. Activities offered daily include swimming pool, tennis courts, state of the art fitness center, a full array of water activities, and boat shuttle service to Vaitape, just five minutes across the lagoon. Bora Bora Lagoon Resort embodies the ideal South Seas hideaway - the seclusion of a private island setting, yet within easy reach of the main attractions of Bora Bora island. ❧

• nearby attractions

Bora Bora Lagoon Resort is surrounded by the most beautiful lagoon in the world. Most activities take place in, on and under the lagoon - snorkeling, scuba diving, shark feeding. The main village of Vaitape is just 5 minutes away.

• onsite facilities

Resort features two restaurants; two bars; swimming pool; fitness center; two tennis courts; Game room; wide selection of water sports; beaches and snorkeling and, new for 2004, a beachfront, tree-house style Spa.

· ROMANTIC FEATURES ·

Voted #1 Honeymoon Suite/Overwater Bungalows and #1 Most Secluded Resort three years in a row by the readers of Modern Bride Magazine, the Bora Bora Lagoon Resort is the ideal South Seas Island honeymoon resort. The resort's white sand beaches, swaying palms, lush gardens, beautiful scented flowers, crystal blue waters teaming with bright, colorful fish, magical sunsets and romantic, starry nights create the perfect setting for a celebration of love. At Bora Bora we offer a range of romantic packages and an exclusive Tahitian wedding ceremony, which takes place on the main beach and is carried out in traditional Tahitian style. ❧

• wedding services

Whether renewing vows or celebrating a new beginning, two Tahitian style blessing ceremonies are available. One takes place at the hotel, the other on a private motu. Both include the blessing, flowers, entertainment and a romantic dinner.

• at a glance

Location: Bora Bora, French Polynesia
Mailing Address: BP 190 Vaitape Bora
Bora Polynésie Française
Reservations: 00-689-47-07-29
Fax: 00-689-47-07-28
Web Site: www.lemeridien.com
Size of Property: 5 acres
Accommodations: 100 bungalows
Range of Rates: Beach Bungalows $650

about the area
Currency: XPF- French Pacific Franc
Weather: Tropical
Languages: French, Tahitian
Nearest Airport: Bora Bora Airport

• nearby attractions

Le Méridien Bora Bora is located on a 10 km long "motu" islet within the most beautiful lagoon in the world. Water sports and idle pleasure will be the key words of your stay! You will enjoy our private lagoon and the turtle's care centre.

• onsite facilities

Le Méridien offers 15 beach bungalows and 85 overwater bungalows with a windowed surface in the floor to observe the underwater world. The hotel's restaurants combine the delights of authentic local dishes and international cuisine. You will enjoy the spa with a wide selection of massages and treatments.

• wedding services

Le Méridien Bora Bora provides tailor-made wedding ceremonies with flowers, dinner, dancing, and more! You can also experience a Polynesian wedding and enjoy the church located on the motu (note: the Polynesian wedding has no legal value)

Le Méridien Bora Bora

BORA BORA, FRENCH POLYNESIA

Le Méridien Bora Bora is located in the Southern tip of a motu, facing the island of Bora Bora, with an open view on the famous Mountain Otemanu.

The hotel is only 20 minutes from the airport by private boat, and 5 minutes from the main island, and just some knocks of palms from the "Lagoonarium."

Stay in one of our 65 overwater bungalows, 16 premium bungalows, or one of our 18 beach bungalows with private beach.

The bungalows provide an exceptionally warm welcome with their burnished hardwoods, louvred windows, thatched ceilings and earth-toned fabrics. Each bungalow includes a main room and a terrace, and a wide glass window integrated into the floor allows guests to admire the submarine life in the lagoon.

All rooms and bungalows include air-conditioning, a dressing-room, tea and coffee facilities, mini-bar, cable television, safe, direct telephone, and a separate shower and bath. The two restaurants in the hotel offer a variety of local and european specialities.

ROMANTIC FEATURES

With an enchanting setting and beautiful sunsets, Le Méridien offers you a traditional Polynesian wedding ceremony with costumes, Polynesian dances, and a priest sermon.

In their bungalow, the bride and groom are dressed by the "Mamas." The groom travels to the ceremony location on board a Polynesian pirogue. A Tahitian dancer and a second pirogue accompany the groom as he crosses the lagoon. The bride and bridesmaids travel to the ceremony site sitting in a "Pomare" chair carried by a Maohi warrior, in accordance with the tradition. At the end of the ceremony, the bride and groom board a boat where they will enjoy the sunset on the mountain...

Hilton Maldives Resort & Spa

THE MALDIVES

• at a glance

Location: The Maldives
Mailing Address: PO Box 2034, South Ari Atoll, Republic of the Maldives
Reservations: 960-450-629
Fax: 960-450-691
Web Site: www.hilton.com/worldwideresorts
Size of Property: Two islands
Accommodations: 150 bungalows
Range of Rates: $250 - $5,000

about the area
Currency: U.S. Dollars
Weather: Tropical
Languages: English, German, Japanese
Nearest Airport: Male

• nearby attractions

The Maldives is a stunning archipelago of over 1000 islands, set in the jewel-blue waters of the Indian Ocean. Nearby attractions include coral reefs and fishing. The capital city of Male, 100km away by local dhoni boat, is of interest.

• onsite facilities

The resort offers some of the most luxurious Water Villas in the Indian Ocean, first class dining in 5 outlets, the only in-house sommelier in the Maldives, its own reef, water sports, dive centre, tennis court & a stunning over-water spa.

• wedding services

As one of the most idyllic settings in the world, couples can chose from 3 ceremonies, each including a wedding cake, Champagne, bouquet, photography, complimentary 'pre-wedding' Spa treatments, sunset cruise on a yacht, and dinner.

Reached by seaplane, the Hilton Maldives Resort & Spa on Rangali Island has become one of the Maldives' premier resorts and lies in one of the most beautiful areas in the world. Complemented by two uninhabited islands and a deep blue lagoon surrounded by a dramatic reef, the resort fulfills the ideal dream of a tropical paradise.

Rangali Island is home to 40 Water Villas and eight Deluxe Water Villas, all built over the crystal-clear Indian Ocean. Completely self-contained and air-conditioned, their wooden interiors evoke the best of the tropics. Surrounded by a natural lagoon, all Water Villas boast ocean view baths and sun terraces with lagoon access. Two secluded Sunset Water Villas are also available. These unrivaled, private villas boast an array of luxurious amenities including personal butler service, a jet boat shuttle and a divine circular bed which rotates 180 degrees to follow the sunset.

The hotel is proud of its fresh and innovative cuisine, available to guests in each of its restaurants. An eclectic mix of East meets West and a cross-section of ingredients and flavors combine to produce a totally new eating experience. First-class dining includes the sand-floored, buffet style Atoll Restaurant; the beautifully located Sunset Grill standing 50 meters out to sea; a la carte dining at the Vilu Restaurant; and Japanese style Teppan Yaki at the Koko Grill. The two underground wine cellars are home to over 10,000 bottles of wines selected by the resort's Wine Master. Its dedication to providing exquisite cuisine and delectable wines, topped with warm and friendly service, has put the hotel on the map as being one of the most unique fine dining experiences in Asia Pacific.

Five-star treatment continues at the overwater Spa, designed to let the mind and body unwind in harmony with the beauty of the natural environment. The ultimate relaxation therapies have been effortlessly combined to provide all guests with a chance to experience the best massage and 'wellness' treatments in the world. An extensive selection of treatments is offered by a team of professional therapists who pamper to guests wishing not only to have a relaxing vacation but also a revitalizing or healthy break in paradise. A full glass floor gives guests stunning views of the beautiful marine life whilst being pampered by expert therapists. Reached by a 40m bridge, the four treatment rooms are all well planned with cool, nautical interiors. Three have spectacular glass floors providing unbeatable views of the colorful marine life below whilst guests enjoy the wonderful selection of treatments. Guests can also relax in the open air Jacuzzi in the tranquil relaxation area looking out onto the Indian Ocean. Couples wishing to have the most romantic 'honeymooners' experience ever can enjoy joint massages and treatments in a double treatment room. The Spa treatments range from traditional Thai and Swedish massages, E'Spa facials, holistic and phytomer skin care programs, cleansing and detoxifying treatments and soothing body masks of seaweed and mineral extracts. All therapy sessions can be reserved ahead of time and individual Spa programs can be tailored to suit each guest.

Leisure facilities are equally outstanding with an on-site dive centre, fishing, watersports, tennis and numerous excursions available each day. A stunning coral reef is within paddling distance of the hotel's sandy white beaches.

For the more energetic guest, there is a host of recreational activities available. Excursions to neighboring islands, snorkeling safaris, windsurfing, big-game fishing, jet skiing, catamaran sailing and cruising aboard the resort's luxury yacht 'Goma' are always popular. Fitness fanatics also enjoy the gymnasium, the tennis court and beach volleyball. The Maldives is a popular destination for SCUBA divers and the resort's dive centre, managed by Sub Aqua, offers PADI courses and guided dives for certified divers daily so that guests can explore the wonderful underwater world nearby.

• **over-water spa**

Indulge yourself with the best treatments in the world set in stunning rooms with underwater views. Choose from relaxing massages or pampering E'Spa treatments.

· ROMANTIC FEATURES ·

The Hilton Maldives Resort & Spa is extremely popular with couples wishing to have the ultimate romantic wedding ceremony. Couples can choose from three 'Renewal of Love' packages, each containing all the symbolic activities that nuptial ceremonies do, but taking place in paradise! All three ceremonies include a beautiful wedding cake, Champagne, bouquet, photography and complimentary 'pre-wedding' Spa treatments for him and her. Following the ceremony, the newly-weds sail into the sunset aboard the resort's yacht before returning for a gourmet, Champagne wedding dinner at the Sunset Grill Restaurant set 50m out to sea over a coral reef. The evening ends in a specially decorated wedding bed in their villa . . .

• **wedding services**

50 of the world's finest water villas await you, each offering stunning views of the ocean, Bose surround sound system, spacious bathrooms, and personal butler.

PURCHASE THIS BOOK & RECEIVE

A BRIDAL PACKAGE VALUED OVER $350

courtesy of WEDDINGSOLUTIONS.COM
FOR ALL YOUR WEDDING NEEDS

INCLUDES FOUR FABULOUS OFFERS

• Offer #1

Up To
$200 off
Wedding
INVITATIONS

Choose from one of the largest selections of INVITATIONS & STATIONERY available online. Receive 20% off and save up to $200 on your invitation order at WeddingSolutions.com. Cannot be combined with any other offer. For details or to redeem this offer, logon to www.WeddingSolutions.com/bookoffer369* (Minimum purchase required.)

• Offer #2

Up To
$100 off
Wedding
ACCESSORIES

Receive a 10% discount and save up to $100 on over 2,000 wedding accessories, favors, gifts, jewelry, unique items and more. Cannot be combined with any other offer. For details or to redeem this offer, logon to www.WeddingSolutions.com/bookoffer369*

• Offer #3

Free
$19.95
Wedding Planning UPGRADE

Receive a free WEDDING PLANNING UPGRADE on WeddingSolutions.com, valued at $19.95. Includes: Wedding Details, Checklist, Budget Analysis, Guest List, Service Providers, Stationery Items, Wedding Accessories. The UPGRADE will also allow you to create detailed timelines, create seating charts for the ceremony, reception and other events, and even print envelopes and labels. For details or to redeem this offer, logon to www.WeddingSolutions.com/bookoffer369*

* Logon to www.WeddingSolutions.com/bookoffer369* for more information.

PURCHASE THIS BOOK & RECEIVE

A BRIDAL PACKAGE VALUED OVER $350

• Offer #4

$50 off a Wedding WEBSITE

Create your very own 19-page

PERSONAL WEDDING WEBSITE

The perfect way to share your wedding and honeymoon with friends & family!

ANYBODY CAN DO IT!

YOUR WEBSITE INCLUDES:

- HOME PAGE
- OUR STORY
  - BRIDE'S SIDE
  - GROOM'S SIDE
- PHOTO GALLERY
- EVENTS
- WEDDING PARTY
- REGISTRY
- GUEST BOOK
- R.S.V.P.

- LOCAL INFO
  - CITY GUIDE
  - ACCOMODATIONS
  - THINGS TO DO
  - RESTAURANTS
- JOURNAL
- HONEYMOON
- MISCELLANEOUS
- CONTACT US

REGULAR PRICE $99. With the purchase of this book, you pay only $49.95 (plus $14.95 one-year hosting fee). For details or to redeem this offer, logon to www.WeddingSolutions.com/bookoffer369*

WEDDING PARTY

DETAILS OF EVENTS

WEDDING JOURNAL

REGISTRIES & MORE

* Logon to www.WeddingSolutions.com/bookoffer369 for more information.

Easy

Wedding Planning

Plus

The Most Comprehensive
and Informative Wedding Planner
Available Today!

Concise and Easy to Read

BY
ELIZABETH & ALEX LLUCH
Professional Wedding Consultants

Written by
Elizabeth & Alex Lluch; Professional Wedding Consultants

Published by Wedding Solutions Publishing, Inc.
' Copyright 1993, 1996, 1998, 2000, 2002, 2004

Reviewed & Approved by:
Wilda Hyer, California State Coordinator for the Association of Bridal Consultants
Owner of *Events Plus*, Ceres, California
&
Gayle Labenow, New York Metro Coordinator for the Association of Bridal Consultants
Owner of *You Are Cordially Invited*, Babylon, New York

Floral Descriptions Written and Researched by:
Joan Hahn Perilla, Partner, Public Relations Marketing, Inc.
Marketing Consultant to the Flower Council of Holland

A SPECIAL THANKS TO OUR CONTRIBUTING PHOTOGRAPHERS:

Jon Barber
Barber Photography
34085 Pacific Coast Highway #117
Dana Point, CA 92629
(800) 600-1061
E-mail: info@barberphoto.com
www. barberphotography.com

Paul Barnett
Barnett Photographics
4051 Adams Avenue
San Diego, CA 92116
(619) 285-1207
E-mail: paul1@barnettphoto.com
www.barnettphoto.com

Tina Carlone
Tina Carlone Photography
Los Angeles, CA
(323) 669-8455
E-mail: tina@tinacarlone.com
www.tinacarlone.com

John Corbett
John Corbett Photography
928 West Main Road
Middletown, RI 02842
(401) 846-4861
E-mail: johnc@corbettphotography.net
www.corbettphotography.net

Miguel and Jennifer Fairbanks
Fairbanks and Fairbanks
Wedding Photography
P.O. Box 903
Summerland, CA 93067
(805) 565-9119
E-mail: miguelfairbanks@aol.com
www.fairbanksandfairbanks.com

Tony Florez
Tony Florez Photography
2852 East Coast Hwy
Corona Del Mar, CA 92625
(866) 866-4862
E-mail: tonyflorez@tonyflorez.com
www.tonyflorez.com

Larry Monet
Photography by Monet
3708 Sixth Avenue
San Diego, CA 92103
(888) 827-7725
E-mail: info@photographybymonet.com
www.photographybymonet.com

Karen French
Karen French Photography
8351 Elmcrest Lane
Huntington Beach, CA 92646
(800) 734-6219
E-mail: info@karenfrenchphotography.com
www.karenfrenchphotography.com

Andy Marcus
Fred Marcus Photography
245 West 72nd Street
New York, NY 10023
(212) 873-5588
E-mail: info@fredmarcus.com
www.fredmarcus.com

Tim Otto
Tim Otto Photography
San Diego, CA
(858) 273-5889
E-mail: timotto@ix.netcom.com
www.timottophotography.com

Ryan and Carrie Phillips
Ryan Phillips Photography
P.O. Box 1636
Thousand Oaks, CA 91358
(805) 405-2131
E-mail: carrie@ryanphillipsphotography.com
www.ryanphillips.com

SOTA Weddings
SOTA Dzine INC.
2724 Dorr Ave. Bay #3
Fairfax, VA 22031
(703) 645-0900
E-mail: info@sotaphotography.com
www.sotaweddings.com

UVP- Ultimate Video Productions
1283 East Main Street
El Cajon, CA 92021
(866) 929-2200
E-mail: UVP1@sbcglobal.net
www.ultimatevideoproductions.com

ADDITIONAL PHOTO CREDITS:

COVER: Karen French

DIVIDERS & POCKETS: Photo credit appears next to each photograph.

DESIGN BY: Sarah Jang, Wedding Solutions Publishing Inc.

There is only one happiness in life, to love and to be loved -George Sand

Printed in Korea and China
ISBN 1-887169-36-9
5th Edition

The Wedding of

Wanda Michelle Shank

&

Troy Robert Harris

Who will be married on

July 12, 2008

At

Boeing Union Hall

DEDICATED TO:

All brides and grooms.
May their wedding day be the
happiest day of their life!

$\mathscr{C}$ONTENTS

*I*NTRODUCTION

*D*ear Bride and Groom:

Congratulations on your engagement! You must be very excited for having found that special person to share the rest of your life with. And you must be looking forward to what will be the happiest day of your life -- your wedding! Planning your wedding can be fun and exciting. But it can also be very stressful. That is why Wedding Solutions, a professional wedding planning company, created *Easy Wedding Planning Plus*.

Easy Wedding Planning Plus contains all the information in the best seller, *Easy Wedding Planning,* as well as over 100 worksheets to keep you organized and on top of your plans. New to this edition are full color dividers with inspirational wedding photos at the beginning of each section to make finding information quick and easy. *Easy Wedding Planning Plus* also has descriptions and 90 color photographs of the most popular wedding flowers. We hope this helps you make the appropriate flower selection and coordinate your overall color scheme.

Easy Wedding Planning Plus begins with a very detailed wedding planning checklist containing everything you need to do or consider when planning your wedding and the best time frame in which to accomplish each activity. Many of the items in the checklist are followed by the page number(s) where that item is explained within the book.

The checklist is followed by a comprehensive and detailed budget analysis, listing all the expenses that are typically incurred in a wedding as well as the percentage of the total budget that is typically spent in each category. Each expense item in the budget is followed by the page number(s) where that item is explained within the book. This makes it very easy to find detailed information on each item.

The budget analysis is followed by a detailed description of each item in the budget including: Options, Things To Consider, Questions To Ask, Things To Beware Of, Tips To Save Money, and Price Ranges. Our clients find this format to be both informative and easy to use, and we know you will too!

Included in this section is an informative chapter on the most popular flowers for weddings as well as 90 beautiful color photographs to help you make this important selection.

Following the detailed description of each item in the budget are wedding timelines for your bridal party as well as your service providers. Use these timelines to keep everyone on schedule.

Next is a short chapter on wedding traditions, explaining the symbolic meaning and historical purpose of some of the more common wedding traditions, and a list of "Do's" and "Don'ts" when planning your wedding.

We have also included a list of responsibilities for each member of your wedding party, a breakdown of who pays for what as well as the traditional formations for the ceremony, processional, recessional and receiving line for both Jewish and Christian weddings as well as the traditional seating arrangements at the reception.

Lastly, we have included a new section to help you prepare for your honeymoon. This planner will help you choose your ideal destination and develop a comprehensive budget as you plan for the vacation of your dreams. Also included are detailed packing lists, information on international travel, lists of useful resources, and more.

We are confident that you will enjoy planning your wedding with the help of *Easy Wedding Planning Plus*. So come join the many couples who have used this book to plan a stress-free wedding. Also, if you know other options, things to consider, tips to save money, or anything else that you would like to see included in this book, please write to us at: Wedding Solutions Publishing, Inc.; 6347 Caminito Tenedor; San Diego, CA 92120. We will include your ideas and suggestions in our next printing. We listen to brides and grooms like you -- that is why *Easy Wedding Planning Plus* has become the best wedding planner available today!

Sincerely,

Elizabeth H. Lluch

*S*WEET *M*EMORIES

*T*HE *P*ROPOSAL

Date: March 13, 2007   Time: 9:00pm

Location: Troy's Apartment   Proposed by: Troy R. Harris

He/She Said/Did: Wanda, would you marry me. I said, yes while laying back on the bed. He asked to see my class ring & said the guy out Cowtown cleaned it nice. He then slipped the engagedment ring on my finger. When I got up, he said, what are you gonna do with your class ring. I said put it back on & S-u-R-P-R-I-S-E There was my "huge" diamond ring on my finger.

You Said/Did: S-C-R-E-A-M & cried.

Then We Did/Went To: Kissed, cried together and called my niece Barbara and his sister Tee-Tee to come over & see the ring. The next day we showed it and each other off to family & friends until we said, I do!!

BREAKING THE NEWS

My Parents' Reaction was: Not embrassing of us.

Wanda.

His/Her Parents' Reaction was: His mother was happy and excited for the both of us. His father was smiling down from heaven.

Tray

My Best Friend's Reaction was: Didn't tell her first.

Wanda

His/Her Best Friend's Reaction was: Excited and happy for us both, they all can't wait to see us married.

Tray

Wedding Events At A Glance

Engagement Party Date: _____   Engagement Party Time:_____

Engagement Party Location: _____

Hostess: _____   Telephone Number: _____

Bridal Shower Date: _____   Bridal Shower Time: _____

Bridal Shower Location: _____

Hostess: _____   Telephone Number: _____

Bachelor Party Date: _____   Bachelor Party Time: _____

Bachelor Party Location: _____

Hostess: _____   Telephone Number: _____

Ceremony Rehearsal Date: _____   Ceremony Rehearsal Time: _____

Ceremony Rehearsal Location: _____

Contact Person: _____   Telephone Number: _____

Rehearsal Dinner Date: _____   Rehearsal Dinner Time: _____

Rehearsal Dinner Location: _____

Contact Person: _____   Telephone Number: _____

Ceremony Date: _____   Ceremony Time: _____

Ceremony Location: _____

Contact Person: _____   Telephone Number: _____

Reception Date: _____   Reception Time: _____

Reception Location: _____

Contact Person: _____   Telephone Number: _____

Information At A Glance

	Name	Contact Person	Telephone Number
Wedding Consultant			
Ceremony Site			
Officiant			
Reception Site			
Caterer			
Liquor Services			
Wedding Gown			
Tuxedo Rental			
Photographer			
Videographer			
Stationer			
Calligrapher			
Music (Ceremony)			
Music (Reception)			
Florist			
Bakery			
Decorations			
Ice Sculpture			
Party Favors			
Balloonist			
Transportation			
Rental & Supplies			
Gift Suppliers			
Valet Services			
Gift Attendant			
Rehearsal Dinner			

WEDDING PLANNING CHECKLIST

The following Wedding Planning Checklist itemizes everything you need to do or consider when planning your wedding, and the best time frame in which to accomplish each activity.

As you can see, many of the items are followed by the page number(s) where those items are explained in more detail within the book. This will help you find the information you need, when you need it.

This checklist assumes that you have nine months or more to plan your wedding. If your wedding is in less than nine months, just start at the beginning of the list and try to catch up as quickly as you can!

Use the boxes to the left of the items to check-off the activities as you accomplish them. This will enable you to see your progress and help you determine what has been done and what still needs to be done.

Nine Months and Earlier	Page
❑ Announce your engagement.	
☑ Select a date for your wedding.	
❑ Hire a professional wedding consultant.	210
☑ Determine the type of wedding you want: location, formality, time of day, number of guests, etc.	31
❑ Determine budget and how expenses will be shared.	21, 24
❑ Develop a record-keeping system for payments made.	30
❑ Consolidate all guest lists: bride's, groom's, bride's family, groom's family, and organize as follows:	79
1) those who must be invited	
2) those who should be invited	
3) those who would be nice to invite	
❑ Decide if you want to include children among guests.	79
❑ Select and reserve ceremony site.	31, 34
❑ Select and reserve your officiant.	31
❑ Select and reserve reception site.	103
❑ Select and order your bridal gown and headpiece.	45, 47
❑ Determine your color scheme.	
❑ Send engagement notice with a photograph to your local newspaper.	63
❑ Buy a calendar and note all important activities: showers, luncheons, parties, get-togethers, etc.	11, 205
❑ If ceremony or reception is at home, arrange for home or garden improvements as needed.	
❑ Order passport, visa or birth certificate, if needed for your honeymoon or marriage license.	207
❑ Select and book photographer.	59
❑ Select maid of honor, best man, bridesmaids and ushers (approx. one usher per 50 guests).	237

Six to Nine Months Before Wedding	*Page*
☐ Select flower girl and ring bearer.	241
☐ Give the *Wedding Party Responsibility Cards* to your wedding party.	237
☐ Reserve wedding night bridal suite.	
☐ Select attendants' dresses, shoes and accessories.	57
☐ Select flower girl's dress, shoes and accessories.	
☐ Select and book caterer, if needed.	104
☐ Select and book ceremony musicians.	125
☐ Select and book reception musicians or DJ.	126
☐ Schedule fittings and delivery dates for yourself, attendants, flower girl and ring bearer.	56
☐ Select and book videographer.	73
☐ Select and book florist.	139

Four to Six Months Before Wedding	*Page*
☐ Start shopping for each other's wedding gifts.	203
☐ Reserve rental items needed for ceremony & reception.	193
☐ Finalize guest list.	98
☐ Select and order wedding invitations, announcements and other stationery such as thank-you notes, wedding programs, and seating cards.	79
☐ Address invitations or hire a calligrapher.	89, 101
☐ Set date, time and location for your rehearsal dinner.	205
☐ Arrange accommodations for out-of-town guests.	100
☐ Start planning your honeymoon.	255
☐ Select and book all miscellaneous services, i.e. gift attendant, valet parking, etc. Register for gifts.	111
☐ Purchase shoes & accessories.	49
☐ Begin to break-in your shoes.	49

Two to Four Months Before Wedding	*Page*
☐ Select bakery and order wedding cake.	133
☐ Order party favors.	109
☐ Select and order room decorations.	187
☐ Purchase honeymoon attire & luggage.	290
☐ Select and book transportation for wedding day.	189
☐ Check blood test and marriage license requirements.	207
☐ Shop for wedding rings and engrave them.	
☐ Consider having your teeth cleaned or bleached.	
☐ Consider writing a will and/or prenuptial agreement.	208
☐ Plan activities for your out-of-town guests both before and after the wedding.	
☐ Purchase gifts for wedding attendants.	204

Six to Eight Weeks Before Wedding	*Page*
☐ Mail invitations. Include accommodation choices and a map to assist guests in finding the ceremony and reception sites.	79, 87
☐ Maintain a record of RSVPs and all gifts received. Send thank-you notes upon receipt of gifts.	89, 98
☐ Determine hair style and makeup.	49, 50
☐ Schedule to have your hair, makeup and nails done the day of the wedding.	49, 50
☐ Finalize shopping for wedding day accessories such as toasting glasses, ring pillow, guest book, etc.	32, 33, 135
☐ Set up an area or a table in your home to display gifts as you receive them.	
☐ Check with your local newspapers for wedding announcement requirements.	207
☐ Have your formal wedding portrait taken.	63

Six to Eight Weeks Before Wedding (Cont.)	*Page*
☐ Send wedding announcement & photograph to your local newspapers.	207
☐ Change name & address on drivers license, social security card, insurance policies, subscriptions, bank accounts, memberships, etc.	215, 216, 217
☐ Select and reserve wedding attire for groom, ushers, father of the bride and ring bearer.	51, 58
☐ Select a guest book attendant. Decide where and when to have guests sign in.	32
☐ Mail invitations to rehearsal dinner.	205
☐ Get blood test and health certificate.	207
☐ Obtain marriage license.	207
☐ Plan a luncheon or dinner with your bridesmaids. Give them their gifts at that time or at the rehearsal dinner.	205
☐ Find "something old, something new, something borrowed, something blue, and a six pence (or shiny penny) for your shoe."	230
☐ Finalize your menu, beverage and alcohol order.	104,106,107

Two to Six Weeks Before Wedding	*Page*
☐ Confirm ceremony details with your officiant.	31
☐ Arrange final fitting of bridesmaids' dresses.	57
☐ Have final fitting of your gown and headpiece.	47, 56
☐ Finalize rehearsal dinner plans; arrange seating and write names on place cards, if desired.	87, 205
☐ Make final floral selections.	139
☐ Make a detailed timeline for your wedding party.	220, 222
☐ Make a detailed timeline for your service providers.	224, 226
☐ Confirm details with all service providers, including attire. Give them a copy of your wedding timeline.	226

Two to Six Weeks Before Wedding (Cont.)	*Page*
☐ Start packing for your honeymoon.	290
☐ Finalize addressing and stamping announcements.	88
☐ Decide if you want to form a receiving line. If so, determine when and where to form the line.	250
☐ Contact guests who haven't responded.	
☐ Pick up rings and check for fit.	
☐ Meet with photographer and confirm special photos you want.	70
☐ Meet with videographer and confirm special events or people you want videotaped.	73
☐ Meet with musicians and confirm music to be played during special events such as first dance.	125, 132
☐ Continue writing thank-you notes as gifts arrive.	89
☐ Remind bridesmaids and ushers of when and where to pick up their wedding attire.	57, 58
☐ Purchase the lipstick, nail polish and any other accessories you want your bridesmaids to wear.	204
☐ Determine ceremony seating for special guests. Give a list to the ushers.	40
☐ Plan reception room layout and seating with your reception site manager or caterer. Write names on place cards for arranged seating.	87, 118

The Last Week	*Page*
☐ Pick up wedding attire and make sure everything fits.	56
☐ Do final guest count and notify your caterer or reception site manager.	104
☐ Gather everything you will need for the rehearsal and wedding day as listed in the *Wedding Party Responsibility Cards*.	251
☐ Arrange for someone to drive the getaway car.	238

*T*he Last Week (Cont.)	*P*age
❑ Review the schedule of events and last minute arrangements with your service providers.	226
❑ Confirm all honeymoon reservations and accommodations. Pick up tickets and travelers checks.	
❑ Finish packing your suitcases for the honeymoon.	290
❑ Familiarize yourself with guests' names. It will help during the receiving line and reception.	98
❑ Have the Post Office hold your mail while you are away on your honeymoon.	

*T*he Rehearsal Day	*P*age
❑ Review list of things to bring to the rehearsal as listed in the *Wedding Party Responsibility Cards*.	251
❑ Put suitcases in getaway car.	
❑ Give your bridesmaids the lipstick, nail polish and accessories you want them to wear for the wedding.	204
❑ Give best man the officiant's fee and any other checks for service providers. Instruct him to deliver these checks the day of the wedding.	238
❑ Arrange for someone to bring accessories such as flower basket, ring pillow, guest book & pen, toasting glasses, cake cutting knife and napkins to the ceremony and reception.	210
❑ Arrange for someone to mail announcements the day after the wedding.	88, 237
❑ Arrange for someone to return rental items such as tuxedos, slip and cake pillars after the wedding.	193, 237
❑ Provide each member of your wedding party with a detailed schedule of events for the wedding day.	222
❑ Review ceremony seating with ushers.	40

$\mathscr{T}$he Wedding Day	$\mathscr{P}$age
☐ Review list of things to bring to the ceremony as listed in the *Wedding Party Responsibility Cards*.	252
☐ Give the groom's ring to the maid of honor. Give the bride's ring to the best man.	237, 238
☐ Simply follow your detailed schedule of events.	222
☐ Relax and enjoy your wedding!	

This comprehensive Budget Analysis has been designed to provide you with all the expenses that can be incurred in any size wedding, including such hidden costs as taxes, gratuities and other "items" that can easily add up to thousands of dollars in a wedding. After you have completed this budget, you will have a much better idea of what your wedding will cost. You can then prioritize and allocate your expenses accordingly.

This budget is divided into fifteen categories: Ceremony, Wedding Attire, Photography, Videography, Stationery, Reception, Music, Bakery, Flowers, Decorations, Transportation, Rental Items, Gifts, Parties, and Miscellaneous.

At the beginning of each category is the percentage of your total wedding budget that is typically spent in that category, based on national averages. Multiply your intended wedding budget by this percentage and write that amount in the "typical" space provided.

To determine the total cost of your wedding, estimate the amount of money you will spend on each item in the budget analysis and write that amount in the "Budget" column after each item. Next to each expense item is the page number where you can find detailed information about that item. Items printed in italics are traditionally paid for by the groom or his family.

Add all the "Budget" amounts within each category and write the total amount in the "Budget Subtotal" space at the end of each category. Then add all the "Subtotal" figures to come up with your final wedding budget. The "Actual" column is for you to input your actual expenses as you purchase items or hire your service providers. Writing down the actual expenses will help you stay within your budget.

For example, if your total wedding budget is $60,000, write this amount at the top of page 24. To figure your typical ceremony expenses, multiply $60,000 x .05 (5%) = $3,000.00. Write this amount on the "Typical" line in the "Ceremony" category to serve as a guide for all your ceremony expenses.

If you find, after adding up all your "Budget Subtotals," that the total amount is more than what you had in mind to spend, simply decide which items are more important to you and adjust your expenses accordingly.

Checklist Of Budget Items

CEREMONY

- ☐ Ceremony Site Fee
- ☐ *Officiant's Fee*
- ☐ *Officiant's Gratuity*
- ☐ Guest Book, Pen
- ☐ Penholder
- ☐ Ring Bearer Pillow
- ☐ Flower Girl Basket

WEDDING ATTIRE

- ☐ Bridal Gown
- ☐ Alterations
- ☐ Headpiece & Veil
- ☐ Gloves
- ☐ Jewelry
- ☐ Stockings
- ☐ Garter
- ☐ Shoes
- ☐ Hairdresser
- ☐ Makeup Artist
- ☐ Manicure/Pedicure
- ☐ *Groom's Formal Wear*

PHOTOGRAPHY

- ☐ Bride & Groom's Album
- ☐ Parents' Album
- ☐ Extra Prints
- ☐ Proofs/Previews

PHOTOGRAPHY (Cont.)

- ☐ Negatives
- ☐ Engagement Photograph
- ☐ Formal Bridal Portrait

VIDEOGRAPHY

- ☐ Main Video
- ☐ Titles
- ☐ Extra Hours
- ☐ Photo Montage
- ☐ Extra Copies

STATIONERY

- ☐ Invitations
- ☐ Response Cards
- ☐ Reception Cards
- ☐ Ceremony Cards
- ☐ Pew Cards
- ☐ Seating/Place Cards
- ☐ Rain Cards/Maps
- ☐ Ceremony Programs
- ☐ Announcements
- ☐ Thank-You Notes
- ☐ Stamps
- ☐ Calligraphy
- ☐ Napkins/ Matchbooks

RECEPTION

- ☐ Reception Site Fee
- ☐ Hors D' Oeuvres
- ☐ Main Meal/Caterer
- ☐ Liquor/ Beverages
- ☐ Bartending Fee
- ☐ Bar Set-up Fee
- ☐ Corkage Fee
- ☐ Fee to Pour Coffee
- ☐ Service Providers' Meals
- ☐ Gratuity
- ☐ Party Favors
- ☐ Disposable Cameras
- ☐ Rose Petals/Rice
- ☐ Gift Attendant
- ☐ Parking Fee
- ☐ Valet Services

MUSIC

- ☐ Ceremony Music
- ☐ Reception Music

BAKERY

- ☐ Wedding Cake
- ☐ *Groom's Cake*
- ☐ Cake Delivery
- ☐ Set-up Fee
- ☐ Cake-Cutting Fee
- ☐ Cake Top
- ☐ Cake Knife/Toast Glasses

* Items in italics are traditionally paid for by the groom or his family

*C*HECKLIST *O*F *B*UDGET *I*TEMS (CONT).

FLOWERS

Bouquets

- ☐ *Bride's*
- ☐ Tossing
- ☐ Maid of Honor's
- ☐ Bridesmaids'

Floral Hairpiece

- ☐ Maid of Honor
- ☐ Bridesmaids'
- ☐ Flower Girl's

Corsages

- ☐ *Bride's Going Away*
- ☐ *Other Family Members'*

Boutonnieres
- ☐ *Groom's*
- ☐ *Ushers*
- ☐ *Other Family's*

Ceremony Site

- ☐ Main Altar
- ☐ Alter Candelabra
- ☐ Aisle Pews

FLOWERS (Cont.)

Reception Site

- ☐ Reception Site
- ☐ Head Table
- ☐ Guest Tables
- ☐ Buffet Table
- ☐ Punch Table
- ☐ Cake Table
- ☐ Cake
- ☐ Cake Knife
- ☐ Toasting Glasses
- ☐ Floral Delivery & Setup

DECORATIONS

- ☐ Table Centerpieces
- ☐ Balloons

TRANSPORTATION

- ☐ Transportation

RENTAL ITEMS

- ☐ Bridal Slip
- ☐ Ceremony Accessories
- ☐ Tent/Canopy

RENTAL ITEMS (Cont.)

- ☐ Dance Floor
- ☐ Tables/Chairs
- ☐ Linen/Tableware
- ☐ Heaters
- ☐ Lanterns

GIFTS

- ☐ *Bride's Gift*
- ☐ Groom's Gift
- ☐ Bridesmaids' Gifts
- ☐ *Ushers' Gifts*

PARTIES

- ☐ Bridesmaids' Luncheon
- ☐ *Rehearsal Dinner*

MISCELLANEOUS

- ☐ Newspaper Announ.
- ☐ *Marriage License*
- ☐ *Prenuptial Agreement*
- ☐ Bridal Gown/Bouquet
- ☐ Preservation
- ☐ Wedding Consultant
- ☐ Wedding Software
- ☐ Taxes

* Items in italics are traditionally paid for by the groom or his family

Budget Analysis

	BUDGET	ACTUAL	PAGE
Your Total Wedding Budget	$	$	
CEREMONY (Typical = 5% of Budget)			
Ceremony Site Fee	$	$	31
Officiant's Fee	$	$	31
Officiant's Gratuity	$	$	32
Guest Book, Pen, Penholder	$	$	32
Ring Bearer Pillow	$	$	33
Flower Girl Basket	$	$	33
Subtotal 1	$	$	
WEDDING ATTIRE (Typical = 10% of Budget)			
Bridal Gown	$	$	45
Alterations	$	$	47
Headpiece & Veil	$	$	47
Gloves	$	$	48
Jewelry	$	$	48
Stockings	$	$	48
Garter	$	$	49
Shoes	$	$	49
Hairdresser	$	$	49
Makeup Artist	$	$	50
Manicure/Pedicure	$	$	50
Groom's Formal Wear	$	$	51
Subtotal 2	$	$	

* Items in italics are traditionally paid for by the groom or his family

	BUDGET	ACTUAL	PAGE
PHOTOGRAPHY (Typical = 9% of Budget)			
Bride & Groom's Album	$	$	59
Parents' Album	$	$	61
Extra Prints	$	$	61
Proofs/Previews	$	$	61
Negatives	$	$	62
Engagement Photograph	$	$	63
Formal Bridal Portrait	$	$	63
Subtotal 3	$	$	
VIDEOGRAPHY (Typical = 5% of Budget)			
Main Video	$	$	73
Titles	$	$	74
Extra Hours	$	$	74
Photo Montage	$	$	75
Extra Copies	$	$	75
Subtotal 4	$	$	
STATIONERY (Typical = 4% of Budget)			
Invitations	$	$	79
Response Cards	$	$	84
Reception Cards	$	$	85
Ceremony Cards	$	$	86
Pew Cards	$	$	86
Seating/Place Cards	$	$	87
Rain Cards/Maps	$	$	87
Ceremony Programs	$	$	88
Announcements	$	$	88
Thank-You Notes	$	$	89
Stamps	$	$	89
Calligraphy	$	$	89

*   Items in italics are traditionally paid for by the groom or his family

	BUDGET	ACTUAL	PAGE
STATIONERY (CONT.)			
Napkins and Matchbooks	$	$	90
Subtotal 5	$	$	
RECEPTION (Typical = 35% of Budget)			
Reception Site Fee	$	$	103
Hors D' Oeuvres	$	$	104
Main Meal/Caterer	$	$	104
Liquor/ Beverages	$	$	106
Bartending/Bar Set-up Fee	$	$	107
Corkage Fee	$	$	108
Fee To Pour Coffee	$	$	108
Service Providers' Meals	$	$	108
Gratuity	$	$	109
Party Favors/Disposable Cameras	$	$	109
Rose Petals/Rice	$	$	110
Gift Attendant	$	$	111
Parking Fee/Valet Services	$	$	111
Subtotal 6	$	$	
MUSIC (Typical = 5% of Budget)			
Ceremony Music	$	$	125
Reception Music	$	$	126
Subtotal 7	$	$	
BAKERY (Typical = 2% of Budget)			
Wedding Cake	$	$	133
Groom's Cake	$	$	134
Cake Delivery & Set-up Fee	$	$	134
Cake-Cutting Fee	$	$	134
Cake Top, Cake Knife, Toasting Glasses	$	$	135

* Items in italics are traditionally paid for by the groom or his family

	BUDGET	ACTUAL	PAGE
BAKERY (CONT.)			
Subtotal 8	$	$	
FLOWERS (Typical = 6% of Budget)			
BOUQUETS			
Bride's	$	$	171
Tossing	$	$	172
Maid of Honor's	$	$	173
Bridesmaids'	$	$	173
FLORAL HAIRPIECES			
Maid of Honor/ Bridesmaids'	$	$	173
Flower Girl's	$	$	174
CORSAGES			
Bride's Going Away	$	$	174
Other Family Members'	$	$	174
BOUTONNIERES			
Groom's	$	$	175
Ushers and Other Family's	$	$	176
CEREMONY SITE FLOWERS			
Main Altar	$	$	176
Alter Candelabra	$	$	177
Aisle Pews	$	$	177
RECEPTION SITE FLOWERS			
Reception Site	$	$	178
Head Table	$	$	178
Guest Tables	$	$	178
Buffet Table	$	$	179
Punch Table	$	$	179
Cake Table	$	$	180

* Items in italics are traditionally paid for by the groom or his family

RECEPTION SITE FLOWERS (CONT.)			
Cake	$	$	148
Cake Knife	$	$	148
Toasting Glasses	$	$	148
Floral Delivery & Setup	$	$	149
Subtotal 9	$	$	
DECORATIONS (Typical = 3% of Budget)			
Table Centerpieces	$	$	187
Balloons	$	$	187
Subtotal 10	$	$	
TRANSPORTATION (Typical = 2% of Budget)			
Transportation	$	$	189
Subtotal 11	$	$	
RENTAL ITEMS (Typical = 3% of Budget)			
Bridal Slip	$	$	193
Ceremony Accessories	$	$	193
Tent/Canopy	$	$	194
Dance Floor	$	$	195
Tables/Chairs	$	$	195
Linen/Tableware	$	$	195
Heaters, Lanterns, Other	$	$	196
Subtotal 12	$	$	
GIFTS (Typical = 3% of Budget)			
*Bride's/*Groom's *Gift*	$	$	203
Bridesmaids'/ *Ushers' Gifts*	$	$	204
Subtotal 13	$	$	

*   Items in italics are traditionally paid for by the groom or his family

	BUDGET	ACTUAL	PAGE
PARTIES (Typical = 4% of Budget)			
Bridesmaids' Luncheon	$	$	205
Rehearsal Dinner	$	$	205
Subtotal 14	$	$	
MISCELLANEOUS (Typical = 4% of Budget)			
Newspaper Announcements	$	$	207
Marriage License	$	$	207
Prenuptial Agreement	$	$	208
Bridal Gown/Bouquet Preservation	$	$	209
Wedding Consultant	$	$	210
Wedding Planning Software	$	$	211
Taxes	$	$	211
Subtotal 15	$	$	
GRAND TOTAL (Add "Budget" & "Actual" Subtotals 1-15)	$	$	

*   Items in italics are traditionally paid for by the groom or his family

Vendor Payment Tracking Chart

	Business Name & Phone No.	Website & Email Address	Contract Date & Total Cost	Deposit & Date	Final Pay & Date
Wedding Consultant					
Ceremony Site					
Officiant					
Reception Site					
Caterer					
Liquor Services					
Wedding Gown					
Tuxedo Rental					
Photographer					
Videographer					
Stationer					
Calligrapher					
Music (Ceremony)					
Music (Reception)					
Florist					
Bakery					
Decorations					
Ice Sculpture					
Party Favors					
Balloonist					
Transportation					
Rental & Supplies					
Gift Suppliers					
Valet Services					
Gift Attendant					
Rehearsal Dinner					

IN DREAMS AND IN LOVE THERE ARE
NO IMPOSSIBILITIES
James Arany

C E R E M O N Y

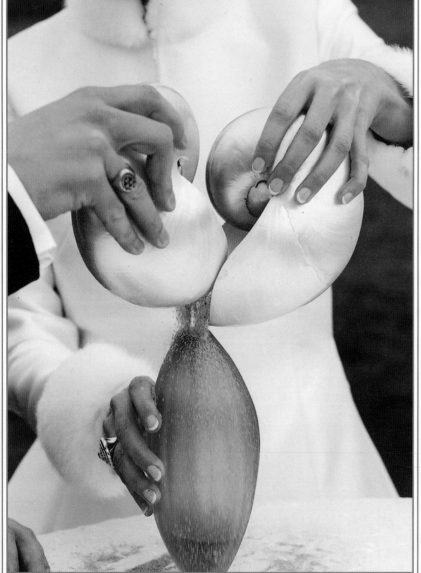

*C*EREMONY

*C*EREMONY SITE FEE

The ceremony site fee is the fee to rent a facility for your wedding. In churches, cathedrals, chapels, temples, or synagogues, this fee may include the organist, wedding coordinator, custodian, changing rooms for the bridal party, and miscellaneous items such as kneeling cushions, aisle runner, and candelabra. Be sure to ask what the site fee includes prior to booking a facility. Throughout this book, the word church will be used to refer to the site where the ceremony will take place.

Options: Churches, cathedrals, chapels, temples, synagogues, private homes, gardens, hotels, clubs, halls, parks, museums, yachts, wineries, beaches, and hot air balloons.

Things To Consider: Your selection of a ceremony site will be influenced by the formality of your wedding, the season of the year, the number of guests expected and your religious affiliation. Make sure you ask about restrictions or guidelines regarding photography, videography, music, decorations, candles, and rice or rose petal-tossing. Consider issues such as proximity of the ceremony site to the reception site, parking availability, handicapped accessibility, and time constraints.

Tips To Save Money: Have your ceremony at the same facility as your reception to save a second rental fee. Set a realistic guest list and stick to it. Hire an experienced wedding consultant. At a church or temple, ask if there is another wedding that day and share the cost of floral decorations with that bride. Membership in a church, temple or club can reduce rental fees. At a garden wedding, have guests stand and omit the cost of renting chairs.

Price Range: $100 - $1,000

*O*FFICIANT'S FEE

The officiant's fee is the fee paid to whomever performs your wedding ceremony.

Options: Priest, Clergyman, Minister, Pastor, Chaplain, Rabbi, Judge, or Justice of the Peace.

Discuss with your officiant the readings you would like incorporated into your ceremony. Some popular readings are:

Beatitudes	Corinthians 13:1-13	Ecclesiastes 3:1-9
Ephesians 3:14-19; 5:1-2	Genesis 1:26-28	Genesis 2:4-9, 15-24
Hosea 2:19-21	Isaiah 61:10I	John 4:7-16
John 15:9-12, 17:22-24	Mark 10:6-9	Proverbs 31:10-31
Romans 12:1-2, 9-18	Ruth 1:16-17	Tobit 8:56-58

Things To Consider: Some officiants may not accept a fee, depending on your relationship with him/her. If a fee is refused, send a donation to the officiant's church or synagogue.

Price Range: $100 - $500

*O*FFICIANT'S GRATUITY

The officiant's gratuity is a discretionary amount of money given to the officiant.

Things To Consider: This amount should depend on your relationship with the officiant and the amount of time s/he has spent with you prior to the ceremony. The groom puts this fee in a sealed envelope and gives it to his best man or wedding consultant, who gives it to the officiant either before or immediately after the ceremony.

Price Range: $50 - $250

*G*UEST BOOK / PEN / PENHOLDER

The guest book is a formal register where your guests sign-in as they arrive at the ceremony or reception. It serves as a memento of who attended your wedding. This book is often placed outside the ceremony or reception site, along with an elegant pen and penholder. A guest book attendant is responsible for inviting all guests to sign-in. A younger sibling or close friend who is not part of the wedding party may be well-suited for this position.

Options: There are many styles of guest books, pens and penholders to choose from. Some books have space for your guests to write a short note to the bride and groom.

Things To Consider: Make sure you have more than one pen in case one runs out of ink. If you are planning a large ceremony (over 300 guests), consider having more than one book and pen so that your guests don't have to wait in line to sign-in.

Price Range: $30 - $100

RING BEARER PILLOW

The ring bearer, usually a boy between the ages of four and eight, carries the bride and groom's rings or mock rings on a pillow. He follows the maid of honor and precedes the flower girl or bride in the processional.

Options: These pillows come in many styles and colors. You can find them at most gift shops and bridal boutiques.

Things To Consider: If the ring bearer is very young (less than 7 years), place mock rings on the pillow in place of the real rings to prevent losing them. If mock rings are used, instruct your ring bearer to put the pillow upside down during the recessional so your guests don't see the mock rings.

Tips To Save Money: Make your own ring bearer pillow by taking a small white pillow and attaching a pretty ribbon to it to hold the rings.

Price Range: $15 - $75

FLOWER GIRL BASKET

The flower girl, usually between the ages of four and eight, carries a basket filled with flowers, rose or paper rose petals to strew as she walks down the aisle. She follows the ring bearer or maid of honor and precedes the bride during the processional.

Options: Flower girl baskets come in many styles and colors. You can find them at most florists, gift shops, and bridal boutiques.

Things To Consider: Discuss any restrictions regarding rose petal, flower, or paper-tossing with your ceremony site. Select a basket which complements your guest book and ring bearer pillow. If the flower girl is very young (less than 7 years), consider giving her a small bouquet instead of a flower basket.

Tips To Save Money: Ask your florist if you can borrow a basket and attach a pretty white bow to it.

Price Range: $20 - $75

Ceremony Site Comparison Chart

QUESTIONS	POSSIBILITY 1	POSSIBILITY 2
What is the name of the ceremony site?		
What is the website & email address of the ceremony site?		
What is the address of the ceremony site?		
What is the name & phone number of my contact person?		
What dates & times are available?		
Do vows need to be approved?		
What is the ceremony site fee?		
What is the payment policy?		
What is the cancellation policy?		
Does the facility have liability insurance?		
What are the minimum & maximum number of guests		
What is the denomination, if any, of the facility?		
What restrictions are there with regards to denomination?		
Is an officiant available? At what cost?		
Are outside officiants allowed?		
Are any musical instruments available for our use?		
If so, what is the fee?		

CEREMONY SITE COMPARISON CHART

POSSIBILITY 3	POSSIBILITY 4	POSSIBILITY 5

CEREMONY SITE COMPARISON CHART (CONT.)

QUESTIONS	POSSIBILITY 1	POSSIBILITY 2
What music restrictions are there, if any?		
What photography restrictions are there, if any?		
What videography restrictions are there, if any?		
Are there are any restrictions for rice or rose petal-tossing?		
Are candlelight ceremonies allowed?		
What floral decorations are available/allowed?		
When is my rehearsal to be scheduled?		
Is there handicap accessibility and parking?		
How many parking spaces are available for my wedding party?		
Where are they located?		
How many parking spaces are available for my guests?		
What rental items are necessary?		

CEREMONY SITE COMPARISON CHART (CONT.)

POSSIBILITY 3	POSSIBILITY 4	POSSIBILITY 5

CEREMONY READING SELECTIONS

SOURCE	SELECTION	READ BY	WHEN

CEREMONY MUSIC SELECTIONS

WHEN	SELECTION	AUTHOR	PLAYED BY
Prelude			
Prelude			
Processional			
Bride's Processional			
Ceremony			
Ceremony			
Recessional			
Postlude			

PERSONALIZED VOWS

Bride's Vows

_____
_____
_____
_____
_____
_____
_____
_____

Groom's Vows

_____
_____
_____
_____
_____
_____
_____
_____
_____

PERSONALIZED RING CEREMONY

_____
_____
_____
_____
_____
_____
_____
_____
_____

Pew Seating Arrangements

(Complete this form only after finalizing your guest list)

BRIDE'S FAMILY SECTION

PEW 1	PEW 2	PEW 3
_____	_____	_____
_____	_____	_____
_____	_____	_____
_____	_____	_____
_____	_____	_____
_____	_____	_____
_____	_____	_____
_____	_____	_____

PEW 4	PEW 5	PEW 6
_____	_____	_____
_____	_____	_____
_____	_____	_____
_____	_____	_____
_____	_____	_____
_____	_____	_____
_____	_____	_____
_____	_____	_____

PEW 7	PEW 8	PEW 9
_____	_____	_____
_____	_____	_____
_____	_____	_____
_____	_____	_____
_____	_____	_____
_____	_____	_____
_____	_____	_____

*P*EW *S*EATING *A*RRANGEMENTS

(Complete this form only after finalizing your guest list)

GROOM'S FAMILY SECTION

PEW 1   PEW 2   PEW 3

_____   _____   _____
_____   _____   _____
_____   _____   _____
_____   _____   _____
_____   _____   _____
_____   _____   _____
_____   _____   _____
_____   _____   _____

PEW 4   PEW 5   PEW 6

_____   _____   _____
_____   _____   _____
_____   _____   _____
_____   _____   _____
_____   _____   _____
_____   _____   _____
_____   _____   _____
_____   _____   _____

PEW 7   PEW 8   PEW 9

_____   _____   _____
_____   _____   _____
_____   _____   _____
_____   _____   _____
_____   _____   _____
_____   _____   _____

Personal Notes

Unique Wedding Ideas

IDEAS TO PERSONALIZE YOUR CEREMONY

Regardless of your religious affiliation, there are numerous ways in which you can personalize your wedding ceremony to add a more creative touch. If you're planning a religious ceremony at a church or temple, be sure to discuss all ideas with your officiant.

The following list incorporates some ideas to personalize your wedding ceremony:

- Invite the bride's mother to be part of the processional. Have her walk down the aisle with you and your father. (This is the traditional Jewish processional).
- Invite the groom's parents to be part of the processional also.
- Ask friends and family members to perform special readings.
- Ask a friend or family member with musical talent to perform at the ceremony.
- Incorporate poetry and/or literature into your readings.
- Change places with the officiant and face your guests during the ceremony.
- Light a unity candle to symbolize your two lives joining together as one.
- Drink wine from a shared "loving" cup to symbolize bonding with each other.
- Hand a rose to each of your mothers as you pass by them during the recessional.
- Release white doves or balloons into the air after being pronounced "husband and wife."
- If the ceremony is held outside on a grassy area, have your guests toss grass or flower seeds over you instead of rice.
- Publicly express gratitude for all that your parents have done for you.
- Use a canopy to designate an altar for a non-church setting. Decorate it in ways that are symbolic or meaningful to you.
- Burn incense to give the ceremony an exotic feeling.

IDEAS TO PERSONALIZE YOUR MARRIAGE VOWS

Regardless of your religious affiliation and whether you're planning a church or outdoor ceremony, there are ways in which you can personalize your marriage vows to make them more meaningful for you. As with all your ceremony plans, be sure to discuss your ideas for marriage vows with your officiant.

The following list incorporates some ideas that you might want to consider when planning your marriage vows:

- You and your fiancé could write your own personal marriage vows and keep them secret from one another until the actual ceremony.

- Incorporate your guests and family members into your vows by acknowledging their presence at the ceremony.

- Describe what you most cherish about your partner and what you hope for in the future together.

- Describe your commitment to and love for one another.

- Discuss your feelings and beliefs about marriage.

- If either of you has children from a previous marriage, mention these children in your vows and discuss your mutual love for and commitment to them.

LOVE IS A GREAT
BEAUTIFIER
Louisa May Alcott

PHOTO: TONY FLOREZ

· A T T I R E ·

WEDDING ATTIRE

BRIDAL GOWN

Bridal gowns come in a wide variety of styles, materials, colors, lengths and prices. You should order your gown at least four to six months before your wedding if your gown has to be ordered and then fitted.

Options: Different gown styles can help create a shorter, taller, heavier, or thinner look. Here are some tips:

♦ **A short, heavy figure:** To look taller and slimmer, avoid knit fabrics. Use the princess or A-line style. Chiffon is the best fabric choice because it produces a floating effect and camouflages weight.

♦ **A short, thin figure:** A shirtwaist or natural waist style with bouffant skirt will produce a taller, more rounded figure. Chiffon, velvet, lace and Schiffli net are probably the best fabric choices.

♦ **A tall, heavy figure:** Princess or A-line are the best styles for slimming the figure; satin, chiffon and lace fabrics are recommended.

♦ **A tall, thin figure:** Tiers or flounces will help reduce the impression of height. A shirtwaist or natural waist style with a full skirt are ideal choices. Satin and lace are the best fabrics.

The guidelines below will help you select the most appropriate gown for your wedding:

Informal wedding:

Street-length gown or suit
Corsage or small bouquet
No veil or train

Semi-formal wedding:

Floor-length gown
Chapel train
Finger-tip veil
Small bouquet

Formal daytime wedding:	Floor-length gown
	Chapel or sweep train
	Fingertip veil or hat
	Gloves
	Medium-sized bouquet

| **Formal evening wedding:** | Same as formal daytime except longer veil |

Very formal wedding:	Floor-length gown
	Cathedral train
	Full-length veil
	Elaborate headpiece
	Long sleeves or long arm-covering gloves
	Cascading bouquet

Things To Consider: In selecting your bridal gown, keep in mind the time of year and formality of your wedding. It is a good idea to look at bridal magazines to compare the various styles and colors. If you see a gown you like, call boutiques in your area to see if they carry that line. Always try on the gown before ordering it.

When ordering a gown, make sure you order the correct size. If you are between sizes, order the larger one. You can always have your gown tailored down to fit, but it is not always possible to have it enlarged or to lose enough weight to fit into it! Don't forget to ask when your gown will arrive, and be sure to get this in writing. The gown should arrive at least six weeks before the wedding so you can have it tailored and select the appropriate accessories to complement it.

Beware: Some gown manufacturers suggest ordering a size larger than needed. This is a good idea but it requires more alterations which may mean extra charges. Also, gowns often fail to arrive on time, creating unnecessary stress for you. Be sure to order your gown with enough time to allow for delivery delays. And be sure to check the reputation of the boutique before buying.

Tips To Save Money: Consider renting a gown or buying one secondhand. Renting a gown usually costs about forty to sixty percent of its retail price. Consider this practical option if you are not planning to preserve the gown. The disadvantage of renting, however, is that your options are more limited. Also, a rented gown usually does not fit as well as a custom tailored gown.

Ask about discontinued styles and gowns. Watch for clearances and sales, or buy your gown "off the rack."

Restore or refurbish a family heirloom gown. If you have a friend, sister, or other family member who is planning a wedding, consider purchasing a gown that you could both wear. Change the veil and headpiece to personalize it

Price Range: $500 - $10,000

ALTERATIONS

Alterations may be necessary in order to make your gown fit perfectly and conform smoothly to your body.

Things To Consider: Alterations usually require several fittings. Allow four to six weeks for alterations to be completed. However, do not alter your gown months before the wedding. Your weight may fluctuate during the final weeks of planning and the gown might not fit properly. Alterations are usually not included in the cost of the gown.

You may also want to consider making some modifications to your gown such as shortening or lengthening the train, customizing the sleeves, beading and so forth. Ask your bridal boutique what they charge for the modifications you are considering.

Tips To Save Money: Consider hiring an independent tailor. Their fees are usually lower than bridal boutiques.

Price Range: $75 - $500

HEADPIECE & VEIL

The headpiece is the part of the bride's outfit to which the veil is attached.

Options for Headpieces: Banana Clip, Bow, Garden Hat, Headband, Juliet Cap, Mantilla, Pillbox, Pouf, Snood, Tiara.

Options for Veils: Ballet, Bird Cage, Blusher, Cathedral Length, Chapel Length, Fingertip, Flyaway.

Things To Consider: The headpiece should complement but not overshadow your gown. In addition to the headpiece, you might want a veil. Veils come in different styles and lengths.

Select a length which complements the length of your train. Consider the total look you're trying to achieve with your gown, headpiece, veil, and hairstyle.

Tips To Save Money: Some boutiques offer a free headpiece or veil with the purchase of a gown. Make sure you ask for this before purchasing your gown.

Price Range: $60 - $500

GLOVES

Gloves add a nice touch with either short-sleeved, three-quarter length, or sleeveless gowns.

Options: Gloves come in various styles and lengths. Depending on the length of your sleeves, select gloves that reach above your elbow, just below your elbow, halfway between your wrist and elbow, or only to your wrist. Fingerless mitts are another option that you may want to consider.

Things To Consider: You may want to consider fingerless mitts which allow the groom to place the wedding ring on your ring finger without having to remove your glove. You should not wear gloves if your gown has long sleeves, or if you're planning a small, at-home wedding.

Price Range: $15 - $100

JEWELRY

You will need to decide what jewelry to wear on your wedding day.

Options: Select pieces of jewelry that can be classified as "something old, something new, something borrowed, or something blue" (see page 230).

Things To Consider: Brides look best with just a few pieces of jewelry -- perhaps a string of pearls and earrings with a simple bracelet. Purchase complementary jewelry for your bridesmaids, to match the colors of their dresses. This will give your bridal party a coordinated look.

Price Range: $60 - $2,000

STOCKINGS

Stockings should be selected with care, especially if the groom will be removing a garter from your leg at the reception.

Things To Consider: Consider having your maid of honor carry an extra pair, just in case you get a run.

Price Range: $15 - $60

𝒢ARTER

It is customary for the bride to wear a garter just above or below the knee on her wedding day. After the bouquet tossing ceremony, the groom takes the garter off the bride's leg. All the single men gather on the dance floor. The groom then tosses the garter to them over his back. According to age-old tradition, whoever catches the garter is the next to be married!

Things To Consider: You will need to choose the proper music for this event. A popular and fun song to play during the garter removal ceremony is *The Stripper,* by David Rose.

Price Range: $15 - $60

𝒮HOES

Things To Consider: Make sure you select comfortable shoes that complement your gown; and don't forget to break them in well before your wedding day. Tight shoes can make you miserable and ruin your wedding day!

Price Range: $50 - $500

ℋAIRDRESSER

Many brides prefer to have their hair professionally arranged with their headpiece the day of the wedding rather than trying to do it themselves.

Things To Consider: Consider having your professional hairdresser experiment with your hair and headpiece before your wedding day so that there are no surprises. On your wedding day, you can go to the salon or have the stylist meet you at your home or dressing site. Consider having him/her arrange your mother's and your bridesmaids' hair for a consistent look.

Tips To Save Money: Negotiate having your hair arranged free of charge or at a discount in exchange for bringing your mother, your fiancé's mother and your wedding party to the salon.

Price Range: $50 - $200 per person

MAKEUP ARTIST

Many brides prefer to have their makeup professionally applied on their wedding day rather than trying to do it themselves.

Things To Consider: It's smart to go for a trial run before the day of the wedding so that there are no surprises. You can either go to the salon or have the makeup artist meet you at your home or dressing site. Consider having him/her apply makeup for your mother, your fiancé's mother and your bridesmaids for a consistent look. In selecting a makeup artist, make sure s/he has been trained in makeup for photography. It is very important to wear the proper amount of makeup for photographs.

Tips To Save Money: Try to negotiate having your makeup applied free of charge or at a discount in exchange for bringing your mother, your fiancé's mother and your wedding party to the salon.

Price Range: $30 - $150 per person

MANICURE / PEDICURE

As a final touch, it's nice to have a professional manicure and/or pedicure the day of your wedding.

Things To Consider: Don't forget to bring the appropriate color nail polish with you for your appointment. You can either go to the salon or have the manicurist meet you at your home or dressing site. Consider having him/her give your mother, your fiancé's mother and your brides-maids a manicure in the same color for a consistent look.

Tips To Save Money: Try to negotiate getting a manicure or pedicure free of charge or at a discount in exchange for bringing your mother, your fiancé's mother and your wedding party to the salon.

Price Range: $15 - $75 per person

GROOM'S FORMAL WEAR

The groom should select his formal wear based on the formality of the wedding. For a semi-formal or formal wedding, the groom will need a tuxedo. A tuxedo is the formal jacket worn by men on special or formal occasions. The most popular colors are black, white, and gray.

Options: Use the following guidelines to select customary attire for the groom:

Informal wedding:	Business suit White dress shirt and tie
Semi-formal daytime:	Formal suit White dress shirt Cummerbund or vest Four-in-hand or bow tie
Semi-formal evening:	Formal suit or dinner jacket Matching trousers White shirt Cummerbund or vest Black bow tie Cufflinks and studs
Formal daytime:	Cutaway or stroller jacket Waistcoat Striped trousers White wing-collared shirt Striped tie Studs and cufflinks
Formal evening:	Black dinner jacket Matching trousers Waistcoat White tuxedo shirt Bow tie Cummerbund or vest Cufflinks

Very formal daytime:	Cutaway coat
	Wing-collared shirt
	Ascot
	Striped trousers
	Cufflinks
	Gloves
Very formal evening:	Black tailcoat
	Matching striped trousers
	Bow tie
	White wing-collared shirt
	Waistcoat
	Patent leather shoes
	Studs and cufflinks
	Gloves

Things To Consider: In selecting your formal wear, keep in mind the formality of your wedding, the time of day, and the bride's gown. Consider darker colors for a fall or winter wedding and lighter colors for a spring or summer wedding. When selecting a place to rent your tuxedo, check the reputation of the shop. Make sure they have a wide variety of makes and styles to choose from.

Reserve tuxedos for yourself and your ushers several weeks before the wedding to insure a wide selection and to allow enough time for alterations. Plan to pick up the tuxedos a few days before the wedding to allow time for last minute alterations in case they don't fit properly. Out-of-town men in your wedding party can be sized at any tuxedo shop. They can send their measurements to you or directly to the shop where you are going to rent your tuxedos.

Ask about the store's return policy and be sure you delegate to the appropriate person (usually your best man) the responsibility of returning all tuxedos within the time allotted. Ushers customarily pay for their own tuxedos.

Tips To Save Money: Try to negotiate getting your tuxedo for free or at a discount in exchange for having your father, your fiancé's father and ushers rent their tuxedos at that shop.

Price Range: $60 - $200

Bride's Attire Checklist

ITEM	DESCRIPTION	SOURCE
Full Slip	_____	_____
Garter	_____	_____
Gloves	_____	_____
Gown	_____	_____
Handbag	_____	_____
Jewelry	_____	_____
Lingerie	_____	_____
Pantyhose	_____	_____
Petticoat or Slip	_____	_____
Shoes	_____	_____
Something Old	_____	_____
Something New	_____	_____
Something Borrowed	_____	_____
Something Blue	_____	_____
Stocking	_____	_____
Veil/Hat	_____	_____

Bridal Boutique Comparison Chart

QUESTIONS	POSSIBILITY 1	POSSIBILITY 2
What is the name of the bridal boutique?		
What is the website & email address of the bridal boutique?		
What is the address of the bridal boutique?		
What is the name & phone number of my contact person?		
What are your hours of operation? Are appointments needed?		
Do you offer any discounts or give-aways?		
What major bridal gown lines do you carry?		
Do you carry outfits for the mother of the bride?		
Do you carry bridesmaids gowns and/or tuxedos?		
Do you carry outfits for the flower girl and ring bearer?		
What is the cost of the desired bridal gown?		
What is the cost of the desired headpiece?		
Do you offer in-house alterations? If so, what are your fees?		
Do you carry bridal shoes? What is their price range?		
Do you dye shoes to match outfits		
Do you rent bridal slips? If so, what is the rental fee?		
What is the estimated date of delivery for my gown?		
What is your payment policy/cancellation policy?		

Bridal Boutique Comparison Chart

POSSIBILITY 3	POSSIBILITY 4	POSSIBILITY 5

Bridal Attire Information Sheet

BRIDAL ATTIRE

Bridal Boutique _____ Date Ordered _____

Salesperson _____ Phone No. _____

Website _____ Email Address _____

Address _____

	Manufacturer	Style	Size	Cost	Date Ready	Pick-up Date
Wedding Gown						
Headpiece						
Veil/Hat						
Shoes						

GOWN ALTERATIONS

Location _____ Cost _____

Tailor _____ Phone No. _____

Website _____ Email Address _____

Address _____

	Date	Time
First Alteration		
Second Alteration		
Third Alteration		
Final Alteration		

*B*RIDESMAIDS' *A*TTIRE

BRIDESMAIDS' ATTIRE

Bridal Boutique _____   Date Ordered _____

Salesperson _____   Phone No. _____

Website _____   Email Address _____

Address _____   Cost _____

Description of dress _____

Manufacturer _____   Date ready _____

BRIDESMAIDS' SIZES

Name	Dress	Head	Weight	Height	Waist	Gloves	Shoes	Hose
1 Donetta Statts								
2 Denise Delluciano								
3 Barbara Thomas								
4 Tacy Foster								
5 Maiesha Brabham								
6 MaKayla Lawton								

Groomsmen's Attire

GROOMSMEN'S ATTIRE

Store Name _____   Date Ordered _____

Sales Person _____   Phone No. _____

Website _____   Email Address _____

Address _____   Cost _____

Description of tuxedo _____

Manufacturer _____   Date ready _____

GROOMSMEN'S SIZES

Name	Height	Weight	Waist	Sleeve	Inseam	Jacket	Neck	Shoes

LOVE IS A MOMENT THAT
LASTS FOREVER
Anonymous

• P H O T O G R A P H Y •

PHOTO: SOTA PHOTOGRAPHY

KAREN FRENCH

TONY FLOREZ

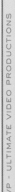

UVP – ULTIMATE VIDEO PRODUCTIONS

*P*HOTOGRAPHY

*B*RIDE & GROOM'S ALBUM

The bride and groom's photo album is the best way to preserve your special day. Chances are you and your fiancé will look at the photos many times during your lifetime. Therefore, hiring a good photographer is one of the most important tasks in planning your wedding.

Options: There are a large variety of wedding albums. They vary in size, color, material, construction and price. Find one that you like and will feel proud of showing to your friends and family. Some of the most popular manufacturers of wedding albums are Art Leather, Leather Craftsman and Renaissance.

Make sure you review the differences between these albums before selecting one. You will also need to select the finish process of your photos. Ask your photographer to show you samples of various finishes. Some of the most popular finishes are glossy, luster, semi-matte, pebble finish, spray texture and oil.

Things to Consider: Make sure you hire a photographer who specializes in weddings. Your photographer should be experienced in wedding procedures and familiar with your ceremony and reception sites. This will allow him/her to anticipate your next move and be in the proper place at the right time to capture all the special moments. Personal rapport is extremely important. The photographer may be an expert, but if you don't feel comfortable or at ease with him or her, your photography will reflect this. Comfort and compatibility with your photographer can make or break your wedding day and your photographs!

Look at his/her work. See if the photographer captured the excitement and emotion of the bridal couple. Also, remember that the wedding album should unfold like a storybook -- the story of your wedding. Be sure to discuss with your photographer the photos you want so that there is no misunderstanding. A good wedding photographer should have a list of suggested poses to choose from. Use the form on page 70 to select photos you must have. Give a copy of this form to your photographer. Look at albums ready to be delivered, or proofs of weddings recently photographed by your photographer. Notice the photographer's preferred style. Some photographers are known for formal poses, while others specialize in more candid, creative shots. Some can do both.

When asked to provide references, many photographers will give you the names of people they know are happy with their work. Some may even give you names from weddings they performed several years ago. This may not indicate the photographer's current ability or reputation. So when asking for references, be sure to ask for recent weddings the photographer has performed. This will give you a good idea of his/her current work. Be sure to ask if the photographer was prompt, cordial, properly dressed and whether s/he performed his/her duties as expected.

When comparing prices, consider the number, size and finish of the photographs and the type of album the photographer will use. Ask how many proofs you will get to choose from. The more proofs, the better the selection you will have. Some photographers do not work with proofs. Rather, they simply supply you with a finished album after the wedding. Doing this may reduce the cost of your album but will also reduce your selection of photographs.

Many photographers are switching to digital format cameras. This can be great, because it makes it easy to switch between black & white and color without having to replace rolls of films or use multiple cameras. You may also get a lot more images to choose from, as photographers using a digital camera can shoot far more pictures and take more chances than a photographer shooting with film.

Beware: Make sure the photographer you interview is the one who will actually photograph your wedding. There are many companies with more than one photographer. Often these companies use the work of the best photographer to sell their packages and then send a less experienced photographer to the wedding. Don't get caught in this trap! Be sure you meet with the photographer who will shoot your wedding. That way you can get an idea of his/her style and personality.

Also, some churches do not allow photographs to be shot during the ceremony. Make sure your photographer understands the rules and regulations of your church before planning the ceremony shots.

Tips to Save Money: Consider hiring a professional photographer for the formal shots of your ceremony only. You can then place disposable cameras on each table at the reception and let your guests take candid shots. This will save you a considerable amount of money in photography.

You can also lower the price of your album by paying for the photographs and then putting them into the album yourself. This is a very time-consuming task, so your photographer may reduce the price of his/her package if you opt to do this. To really save money, select a photographer who charges a flat fee to shoot the wedding and allows you to purchase the film. Compare at least 3 photographers for quality, value and price. Photographers who shoot weddings "on the side" are usually less expensive, but the quality of their photographs may not be as good.

Select less 8" x 10"s for your album and more 4" x 5"s, and choose a moderately priced album. Ask for specials and package deals.

Price Range: $900 - $9,000

$\mathscr{P}$ARENTS' ALBUM

The parents' album is a smaller version of the bride and groom's album. It usually contains about twenty 5" x 7" photographs. Photos should be carefully selected for each individual family. If given as a gift, the album can be personalized with the bride and groom's names and date of their wedding on the front cover.

Tips to Save Money: Try to negotiate at least one free parents' album with the purchase of the bride and groom's album.

Price Range: $100 - 600

$\mathscr{E}$XTRA PRINTS

Extra prints are photographs ordered in addition to the main album or parents' albums. These are usually purchased as gifts for the bridal party, close friends and family members.

Things to Consider: It is important to discuss the cost of extra prints with your photographer since prices vary considerably. Some photographers offer the main album at great bargains to get the job, but then charge a fortune on extra prints. Think about how many extra prints you would like to order and figure this into your budget before selecting a photographer.

Tips to Save Money: If you can wait, consider not ordering any reprints during the first few years after the wedding. A few years later, contact the photographer and ask if s/he will sell you the negatives. Most photographers will be glad to sell them at a bargain price at a later date. You can then make as many prints as you wish for a fraction of the cost.

Price Range: (5" x 7") = $3 - $15; (8" x 10") = $10 - $25; (11" x 14") = $25 - 125

$\mathscr{P}$ROOFS / PREVIEWS

Proofs/previews are the preliminary prints from which the bride and groom select photographs for their album and their parents' albums. They are normally 5" x 5" in size. With the advent of digital technology, many photographers who shoot with digital cameras make your proofs available online. You (and your guests) can browse the available photographs on the Internet and select the ones you'd like to receive prints of. You can often view your photographs within a few days of the wedding!

Things to Consider: When selecting a package, ask how many proofs the photographer will take. The more proofs, the wider the selection you will have to choose from. For a wide selection, the photographer must take at least 2 to 3 times the number of prints that will go into your album. Digital technology makes this much easier.

Ask the photographer how soon after the wedding you will get your proofs. Request this in writing. The proofs should be ready by the time you get back from your honeymoon. Also request to see your proofs before you make the final payment.

Tips to Save Money: Ask your photographer to use your proofs as part of your album package to save developing costs.

Price Range: $100 - $600

*N*EGATIVES

Negatives come in different sizes depending on the type of film and equipment used. The most popular camera for weddings is the medium format camera. When a medium format camera is used, the size of the negatives is 2 1/4" x 2 1/4." When a 35 mm camera is used, the negatives are only 1" x 1 1/2." The larger the negative, the higher the quality of the photograph, especially when enlarged. Don't let a photographer convince you that there is no difference in quality between a 35 mm camera and a medium format camera.

The quality of a digital camera's photograph depends on the resolution of the camera. The higher the resolutions, the better quality of the photograph will be, especially in larger sizes. Digital cameras do not produce negatives. You can see the proofs in the computer.

Things to Consider: Many photographers will not sell you the negatives or photo files since they hope to make a profit on selling extra prints after the wedding. Ask the photographers you interview how long they keep the negatives or files and whether they are included in your package. A professional photographer should keep the negatives or files at least five years. Make sure you get this in writing.

Tips to Save Money: If you can wait, consider contacting the photographer a few years later and ask if s/he will sell you the negatives or files at that time. Most photographers will be glad to sell them at a bargain price.

Price Range: $100 - $800

*E*NGAGEMENT PHOTOGRAPH

The engagement photograph is sent to your local newspapers, along with information announcing your engagement to the public. The bride's parents or her immediate family usually make this announcement.

Things to Consider: You will need to have this photograph taken well in advance of your wedding. Try not to make any drastic changes in appearance (major haircuts) around that time, as you want to look like yourselves!

Tips to Save Money: Look at engagement photographs in your local newspaper. Then have a friend or family member take a photo of you and your fiancé in a pose and with a backdrop similar to the ones you have seen.

Price Range: $35 - $300

*F*ORMAL BRIDAL PORTRAIT

If you intend to announce your marriage in the newspaper the day after your wedding, you will need to have a formal bridal portrait taken several weeks before the wedding. This is a photograph of the bride taken before the wedding in the photographer's studio. This photograph, along with an announcement, must be sent to your local newspapers as soon as possible.

Things to Consider: Some fine bridal salons provide an attractive background where the bride may arrange to have her formal bridal photograph taken after the final fitting of her gown. This will save you the hassle of bringing your gown and headpiece to the photographer's studio and dressing up once again. Consider having your trial makeup and hair styling appointment the same day that your formal portrait is taken.

Tips to Save Money: If you don't mind announcing your marriage several weeks after the wedding, consider having your formal portrait taken the day of your wedding. This will save you the studio costs, the hassle of getting dressed for the photo, and the photograph will be more natural since the bridal bouquet will be the one you carry down the aisle. Also, brides are always most beautiful on their wedding day!

Price Range: $100 - $500

Photographers Comparison Chart

QUESTIONS	POSSIBILITY 1	POSSIBILITY 2
What is the name & phone number of the photographer?		
What is the website & email address of the photographer?		
What is the address of the photographer?		
How many years of experience do you have as a photographer?		
What percentage of your business is dedicated to weddings?		
Approximately how many weddings have you photographed?		
Are you the person who will photograph my wedding?		
Will you bring an assistant with you to my wedding?		
How do you typically dress for weddings?		
Do you have a professional studio?		
What type of equipment do you use?		
Do you bring backup equipment with you to weddings?		
Do you visit the ceremony and reception sites prior to the wedding?		
Do you have liability insurance?		
Are you skilled in diffused lighting & soft focus?		
Can you take studio portraits?		

PHOTOGRAPHERS COMPARISON CHART

POSSIBILITY 3	POSSIBILITY 4	POSSIBILITY 5

Photographers Comparison Chart (CONT.)

QUESTIONS	POSSIBILITY 1	POSSIBILITY 2
Can you retouch negatives?		
Can negatives be purchased? If so, what is the cost?		
What is the cost of the package I am interested in?		
What is your payment policy?		
What is your cancellation policy?		
Do you offer a money-back guarantee?		
Do you use proofs?		
How many proofs will I get?		
When will I get my proofs?		
When will I get my album?		
What is the cost of an engagement portrait? Formal bridal portrait?		
What is the cost of a parent album?		
What is the cost of a 5" x 7" reprint?		
What is the cost of an 8" x 10" reprint?		
What is the cost of an 11" x 14" reprint?		
What is the cost per additional hour of shooting at the wedding?		

PHOTOGRAPHERS COMPARISON CHART (CONT.)

POSSIBILITY 3	POSSIBILITY 4	POSSIBILITY 5

PHOTOGRAPHER'S INFORMATION

(Make a copy of this form and give it to your photographer as a reminder of your various events).

THE WEDDING OF:

_____ Tel. No.: _____

PHOTOGRAPHER'S COMPANY:

_____

Address: _____

Website: _____ Email Address: _____

Photographer's Name: _____ Tel. No.: _____

Assistant's Name: _____ Tel. No.: _____

ENGAGEMENT PORTRAIT

Date: _____ Time: _____

Location: _____

Address: _____

BRIDAL PORTRAIT

Date: _____ Time: _____

Location: _____

Address: _____

PHOTOGRAPHER'S INFORMATION (Cont.)

(Make a copy of this form and give it to your photographer as a reminder of your various events).

OTHER EVENTS

Date: _____   Time: _____

Location: _____

Address: _____

CEREMONY

Date: _____ Arrival Time: _____ Departure Time: _____

Location: _____

Address: _____

Ceremony Restrictions/Guidelines: _____

_____

RECEPTION

Date: _____ Arrival Time: _____ Departure Time: _____

Location: _____

Address: _____

Ceremony Restrictions/Guidelines: _____

_____

$\mathcal{W}$EDDING $\mathcal{P}$HOTOS

(Make a copy of this form and give it to your photographer).

Pre-Ceremony Photos:

☐　　Bride leaving her house
☐　　Wedding rings with the invitation
☐　　Bride getting dressed for the ceremony
☐　　Bride looking at her bridal bouquet
☐　　Maid of honor putting garter on bride's leg
☐　　Groom and best man before ceremony
☐　　Bride by herself
☐　　Bride with her mother
☐　　Bride with her father
☐　　Bride with mother and father
☐　　Bride with her entire family and/or any combination thereof
☐　　Bride with her maid of honor
☐　　Bride with her bridesmaids
☐　　Bride with the flower girl and/or ring bearer
☐　　Bride's mother putting on her corsage
☐　　Groom leaving his house
☐　　Groom putting on his boutonniere
☐　　Groom with his mother
☐　　Groom with his father
☐　　Groom with mother and father
☐　　Groom with his entire family and/or any combination thereof
☐　　Groom with his best man
☐　　Groom with his ushers
☐　　Groom shaking hands with his best man while looking at his watch
☐　　Groom with the bride's father
☐　　Bride and her father getting out of the limousine
☐　　Special members of the family being seated
☐　　Groom waiting for the bride before the processional
☐　　Bride and her father just before the processional

Other pre-ceremony photos you would like:

☐ _____
☐ _____
☐ _____
☐ _____
☐ _____

Ceremony Photos:

☐   The processional
☐   Bride and groom saying their vows
☐   Bride and groom exchanging rings
☐   Groom kissing the bride at the altar
☐   The Recessional

Other ceremony photos you would like:

☐ _____
☐ _____
☐ _____
☐ _____
☐ _____

Post-Ceremony Photos:

☐   Bride and groom
☐   Newlyweds with both of their families
☐   Newlyweds with the entire wedding party
☐   Bride and groom signing the marriage certificate
☐   Flowers and other decorations

Other post-ceremony photos you would like:

☐ _____
☐ _____
☐ _____
☐ _____
☐ _____

Reception Photos:

- ❑ Entrance of newlyweds and wedding party into the reception site
- ❑ Receiving line
- ❑ Guests signing the guest book
- ❑ Toasts
- ❑ First dance
- ❑ Bride and her father dancing
- ❑ Groom and his mother dancing
- ❑ Bride dancing with groom's father
- ❑ Groom dancing with bride's mother
- ❑ Wedding party and guests dancing
- ❑ Cake table
- ❑ Cake-cutting ceremony
- ❑ Couple feeding each other cake
- ❑ Buffet table and its decoration
- ❑ Bouquet-tossing ceremony
- ❑ Garter-tossing ceremony
- ❑ Musicians
- ❑ The wedding party table
- ❑ The family tables
- ❑ Candid shots of your guests
- ❑ Bride and groom saying good-bye to their parents
- ❑ Bride and groom looking back, waiving good-bye in the getaway car

Other reception photos you would like:

- ❑ _____
- ❑ _____
- ❑ _____
- ❑ _____
- ❑ _____
- ❑ _____
- ❑ _____
- ❑ _____
- ❑ _____
- ❑ _____
- ❑ _____
- ❑ _____
- ❑ _____
- ❑ _____

WHEN YOU LOVE SOMEONE ALL YOUR
SAVED UP WISHES START COMING OUT

Elizabeth Bowen

V I D E O G R A P H Y

PHOTO: KAREN FRENCH

$\mathscr{V}$IDEOGRAPHY

$\mathscr{M}$AIN VIDEO

Next to your photo album, videography is the best way to preserve your wedding memories. Unlike photographs, videography captures the mood of the wedding day in motion and sound. You have the option of selecting one, two, or three cameras. The more cameras used, the more action captured and the more expensive. An experienced videographer, however, can do a good job with just one camera.

A good videographer is unobtrusive and knows how to capture all the most important moments of your wedding. Cameras no longer have to be giant bulky things, as many videographers are switching to digital format. Digital technology also now means that you may receive a dvd instead of a video!

You will need to choose the type of video you want – do you want the footage edited down to a 30 minute film, or do you want an "as it happened" replay? You may wish to have both of these so you can see all the details, but have a shorter version that flows nicely as well. Remember, a short format video requires a lot of time in the editing room and will cost considerably more. Your personal film can take as much as 15-30 hours to put together!

Things to Consider: Be sure to hire a videographer who specializes in weddings, and ask to see samples of his or her work. Pay particular attention to details such as special effects, titles, and background music. Find out what's included in the cost of your package so there are no surprises at the end!

Beware: As in photography, there are many companies with more than one videographer. These companies may use the work of their best videographer to sell their packages and then send a less experienced videographer to the wedding. Again, don't get caught in this trap! Be sure to interview the videographer who will shoot your wedding so you can get a good idea of his/her style and personality. Ask to see his/her own work.

Tips to Save Money: Compare videographers' quality, value and price. There is a wide range, and the most expensive is not necessarily the best. One camera is the most cost effective and may be all you need. Consider hiring a company that offers both videography and photography. You may save overall.

Ask a family member or close friend to videotape your wedding. However, realize that without professional equipment and expertise the final product may not be quite the same.

Price Range: $600 - $4,000

*T*ITLES

Titles and subtitles can be edited into your video before or after the filming. Titles are important since twenty years from now you may not remember the exact time of your wedding or the names of your bridal party members. Some videographers charge more for titling. Make sure you discuss this with your videographer and get in writing exactly what titles will be included.

Options: Titles may include the date, time and location of the wedding, the bride and groom's names, and names of special family members and/or the bridal party. Titles may also include special thanks to those who helped with the wedding. You can them send these people a copy of your video after the wedding, which would be a very appropriate and inexpensive gift!

Tips to Save Money: Consider asking for limited titles, such as the only names of the bride and groom and the date and time of the wedding.

Price Range: $50 - $300

*E*XTRA HOURS

Find out how much your videographer would charge to stay longer than contracted for in case your reception lasts longer than expected. Don't forget to get this in writing.

Tips to Save Money: Avoid paying extra hours beyond what's included in your selected package. You can do this by calculating the number of hours you think you'll need and negotiating that into your package price. Consider taping the ceremony only.

Price Range: $35 - $150/hour

*P*HOTO MONTAGE

A photo montage is a series of photographs set to music on video. The number of photographs depends on the length of the songs and the amount of time allotted for each photograph. A typical song usually allows for approximately 30 to 40 photographs. Photo montages are a great way to display and reproduce your photographs. Copies of this video can be made for considerably less than the cost of reproducing photographs.

Options: Photo montages can include photos of you and your fiancé growing up, the rehearsal, the wedding day, the honeymoon, or any combination thereof.

Things to Consider: Send copies of your photo montage video to close friends and family members as a mementos of your wedding.

Tips to Save Money: Consider making a photo montage yourself. This is very easily done with any video camera, a tripod, and a good stereo. The secret is in holding the camera very still and having the proper lighting while videotaping the photographs. Digital technology has made this even easier; with easy-to-use software you can create a beautiful, professional-looking photo montage that can be saved onto a recordable cd and transferred onto video or dvd in a studio. If you own a dvd-recorder, you can make your own copies!

Price Range: $50 - $500

*E*XTRA COPIES

A professional videographer can reproduce your video much better than you can. Ask your videographer how much s/he charges. You'll certainly want to give your parents a copy!

Tips to Save Money: Borrow a VCR from a friend and make copies yourself. Before considering this, be sure to ask your videographer if that is acceptable – many contracts prohibit this and doing this could be copyright infringement, as with copying any tape.

Price Range: $35- $150

VIDEOGRAPHER COMPARISON CHART

QUESTIONS	POSSIBILITY 1	POSSIBILITY 2
What is the name & phone number of the videographer?		
What is the website & email address of the videographer?		
What is the address of the videographer?		
How many years of experience do you have as a videographer?		
Approximately how many weddings have you videotaped?		
Are you the person who will video-tape my wedding?		
Will you bring an assistant with you to my wedding?		
What type of equipment do you use?		
Do you have a wireless microphone?		
What format do you use (Digital, VHS, Super VHS, 8mm)?		
Do you bring backup equipment with you?		
Do you visit the ceremony and reception sites before the wedding?		
Do you edit the tape after the event? Who keeps the raw footage?		
When will I receive the final product?		
Cost of the desired package: What does it include?		
Can you make a photo montage? If so, what is your price?		
What is your payment policy? What is your cancellation policy?		
Do you offer a money-back guarantee?		

Videographer Comparison Chart

POSSIBILITY 3	POSSIBILITY 4	POSSIBILITY 5

Personal Notes

THE BEST WAY TO SHOW OUR LOVE IS TO
GIVE A PIECE OF OURSELVES TO OTHERS
Anonymous

PHOTO: KAREN FRENCH

S T A T I O N E R Y

Jessica René
and
Timothy Edward Brand...

Community Church, C...
Corona de...

Alicia and Thomas
July 19, 2003

Appetizer
Crab and Avocado Timbale with Cucumber Carpaccio
served with Bell Pepper Confetti and
Cayenne Crème Fraiche

Salad
Butter Lettuce with marinated artichokes served
with Crimini Mushroom, Feta, Roasted Shallot Crepe
dressed with White Balsamic Vinaigrette

Entrée
Filet Medallion with
Green Peppercorn Currant Sauce

Fresh Ono Filet served with a Coriander
Harissa Semolina Crust dressed in a
Beurre Blanc Sauce

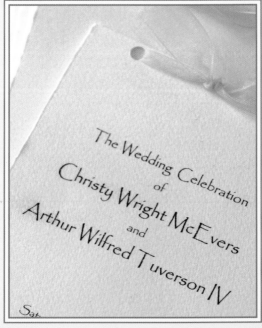

The Wedding Celebration
of
Christy Wright McEvers
and
Arthur Wilfred Tuverson IV

Sat...

$\mathscr{S}$TATIONERY

$\mathscr{I}$NVITATIONS

Begin creating your guest list as soon as possible. Ask your parents and the groom's parents for a list of the people they would like to invite. You and your fiancé should make your own list. Make certain that all names are spelled correctly and that all addresses are current. Determine if you wish to include children; if so, add their names to your list. All children over the age of 16 should receive their own invitation.

Order your invitations at least 4 months before the wedding. Allow an additional month for engraved invitations. Invitations are traditionally issued by the bride's parents; but if the groom's parents are assuming some of the wedding expenses, the invitations should be in their names also. Mail all invitations at the same time, 6 - 8 weeks before the wedding.

Options: There are three types of invitations: traditional/formal, contemporary, and informal. The traditional/formal wedding invitation is white, soft cream, or ivory with raised black lettering. The printing is done on the top page of a double sheet of thick quality paper; the inside is left blank. The contemporary invitation is typically an individualized presentation that makes a statement about the bride and groom. Informal invitations are often printed on the front of a single, heavyweight card and may be handwritten or preprinted.

There are three types of printing: engraved, thermography, and offset printing. Engraving is the most expensive, traditional and formal type of printing. It also takes the longest to complete. In engraved printing, stationery is pressed onto a copper plate, which makes the letters rise slightly from the page. Thermography is a process that fuses powder and ink to create a raised letter. This takes less time than engraving and is less expensive because copper plates do not have to be engraved. Offset printing, the least expensive, is the quickest to produce and offers a variety of styles and colors. It is also the least formal.

Things To Consider: If all your guests are to be invited to both the ceremony and the reception, a combined invitation may be sent without separate enclosure cards. Order one invitation for each married or cohabiting couple that you plan to invite. The officiant and his/her spouse as well as your attendants should receive an invitation.

Order approximately 20% more stationery than your actual count. Allow a minimum of two weeks to address and mail the invitations, longer if using a calligrapher or if your guest list is very large. You may also want to consider ordering invitations to the rehearsal dinner, as these should be in the same style as the wedding invitation.

SAMPLES OF TRADITIONAL/FORMAL INVITATIONS

1)   When the bride's parents sponsor the wedding:

Mr. and Mrs. Alexander Waterman Smith
request the honor of your presence
at the marriage of their daughter
Carol Ann
to
Mr. William James Clark
on Saturday, the fifth of August
two thousand six
at two o'clock in the afternoon
Saint James by-the-Sea
La Jolla, California

2)   When the groom's parents sponsor the wedding:

Mr. and Mrs. Michael Burdell Clark
request the honor of your presence
at the marriage of
Miss Carol Ann Smith
to their son
Mr. William James Clark

3)   When both the bride and groom's parents sponsor the wedding:

Mr. and Mrs. Alexander Waterman Smith
and
Mr. and Mrs. Michael Burdell Clark
request the honor of your presence
at the marriage of their children
Miss Carol Ann Smith
to
Mr. William James Clark

OR

Mr. and Mrs. Alexander Waterman Smith
request the honor of your presence
at the marriage of their daughter
Carol Ann Smith
to
William James Clark
son of Mr. and Mrs. Michael Burdell Clark

4)   **When the bride and groom sponsor their own wedding:**

The honor of your presence is requested
at the marriage of
Miss Carol Ann Smith
and
Mr. William James Clark

OR

Miss Carol Ann Smith
and
Mr. William James Clark
request the honor of your presence
at their marriage

5)   **With divorced or deceased parents:**

a) When the bride's mother is sponsoring the wedding and is not remarried:

Mrs. Julie Hurden Smith
requests the honor of your presence
at the marriage of her daughter
Carol Ann

*For additional wording suggestions, log on to www.WeddingSolutions.com

b) When the bride's mother is sponsoring the wedding and has remarried:

Mrs. Julie Hurden Booker
requests the honor of your presence
at the marriage of her daughter
Carol Ann Smith

OR

Mr. and Mrs. John Thomas Booker
request the honor of your presence
at the marriage of Mrs. Booker's daughter
Carol Ann Smith

c) When the bride's father is sponsoring the wedding and has not remarried:

Mr. Alexander Waterman Smith
requests the honor of your presence
at the marriage of his daughter
Carol Ann

d) When the bride's father is sponsoring the wedding and has remarried:

Mr. and Mrs. Alexander Waterman Smith
request the honor of your presence
at the marriage of Mr. Smith's daughter
Carol Ann

6)   Deceased parents:

a) When a close friend or relative sponsors the wedding:

Mr. and Mrs. Brandt Elliott Lawson
request the honor of your presence
at the marriage of their granddaughter
Carol Ann Smith

7)   In military ceremonies, the rank determines the placement of names:

a) Any title lower than sergeant should be omitted. Only the branch of service should
be included under that person's name:

Mr. and Mrs. Alexander Waterman Smith
request the honor of your presence
at the marriage of their daughter
Carol Ann
United States Army
to
William James Clark

b) Junior officers' titles are placed below their names and are followed by their branch of
service:

Mr. and Mrs. Alexander Waterman Smith
request the honor of your presence
at the marriage of their daughter
Carol Ann
to
William James Clark
First Lieutenant, United States Army

c) If the rank is higher than lieutenant, titles are placed before names, and the branch of
service is placed on the following line:

Mr. and Mrs. Alexander Waterman Smith
request the honor of your presence
at the marriage of their daughter
Carol Ann
to
Captain William James Clark
United States Navy

SAMPLE OF A LESS FORMAL MORE CONTEMPORARY INVITATION

Mr. and Mrs. Alexander Waterman Smith
would like you to
join with their daughter
Carol Ann
and
William James Clark
in the celebration of their marriage

Tips To Save Money: Thermography looks like engraving and is one-third the cost. Choose paper stock that is reasonable and yet achieves your overall look. Select invitations that can be mailed using just one stamp. Order at least 25 extra invitations, just in case you add people to your list or you mess some up. To reorder this small number of invitations later would cost nearly three times the amount you'll spend up front.

Price Range: $0.75 - $6.00 per invitation

$\mathcal{R}$ESPONSE CARDS

Response cards are enclosed with the invitation to determine the number of people who will be attending your wedding. They are the smallest card size accepted by the postal service and should be printed in the same style as the invitation. An invitation to only the wedding ceremony does not usually include a request for a reply. However, response cards should be used when it is necessary to have an exact head count for special seating arrangements. Response cards are widely accepted today. If included, these cards should be easy for your guests to understand and use. Include a self-addressed and stamped return envelope to make it easy for your guests to return the response cards.

Things To Consider: You should not include a line that reads "number of persons" on your response cards because only those whose names appear on the inner and outer envelopes are invited. Each couple, each single person, and all children over the age of 16 should receive their own invitation. Indicate on the inner envelope if they may bring an escort or guest. The omitting of children's names from the inner envelope infers that the children are not invited.

Samples of wording for response cards:

M_____

(The M may be eliminated from the line, especially if many Drs. are invited)

___ accepts

___ regrets

Saturday the fifth of July

Oceanside Country Club

OR

The favor of your reply is requested
by the twenty-second of May

M_____

will _____ attend

Price Range: $0.40 - $1.00 each

*R*ECEPTION CARDS

If the guest list for the ceremony is larger than that for the reception, a separate card with the date, time and location for the reception should be enclosed with the ceremony invitation for those guests also invited to the reception. Reception cards should be placed in front of the invitation, facing the back flap and the person inserting them. They should be printed on the same quality paper and in the same style as the invitation itself.

Sample of a formally-worded reception card:

Mr. and Mrs. Alexander Waterman Smith
request the pleasure of your company
Saturday, the third of July
at three o'clock
Oceanside Country Club
2020 Waterview Lane
Oceanside, California

Sample of a less formal reception card:

Reception immediately following the ceremony
Oceanside Country Club
2020 Waterview Lane
Oceanside, California

*For additional wording suggestions, log on to www.WeddingSolutions.com

Things To Consider: You may also include a reception card in all your invitations if the reception is to be held at a different site than the ceremony.

Tips To Save Money: If all people invited to the ceremony are also invited to the reception, include the reception information on the invitation and eliminate the reception card. This will save printing and postage costs.

Price Range: $0.40 - $1.00 each

*C*EREMONY CARDS

If the guest list for the reception is larger than the guest list for the ceremony, a special insertion card with the date, time and location for the ceremony should be enclosed with the reception invitation for those guests also invited to the ceremony.

Ceremony cards should be placed in front of the invitation, facing the back flap and the person inserting them. They should be printed on the same quality paper and in the same style as the invitation itself.

Price Range: $0.40 - $1.00 each

*P*EW CARDS

Pew cards may be used to let special guests and family members know they are to be seated in the reserved section on either the bride's side or the groom's side. These are most typically seen in large, formal ceremonies. Guests should take this card to the ceremony and show it to the ushers, who should then escort them to their seats.

Options: Pew cards may indicate a specific pew number if specific seats are assigned, or may read "Within the Ribbon" if certain pews are reserved but no specific seat is assigned.

Things To Consider: Pew cards may be inserted along with the invitation, or may be sent separately after the RSVPs have been returned. It is often easier to send them after you have received all RSVPs so you know how many reserved pews will be needed.

Tips To Save Money: Include the pew card with the invitation to special guests and just say "Within the Ribbon." After you have received all your RSVPs, you will know how many pews need to be reserved   This will save you the cost of mailing the pew cards separately.

Price Range: $0.25 - $1.00 each

*S*EATING / PLACE CARDS

Seating/place cards are used to let guests know where they should be seated at the reception and are a good way of putting people together so they feel most comfortable. Place cards should be laid out alphabetically on a table at the entrance to the reception. Each card should correspond to a table -- either by number, color, or other identifying factor. Each table should be marked accordingly.

Options: Select a traditional or contemporary design for your place cards, depending on the style of your wedding.

Regardless of the design, place cards must contain the same information: the bride and groom's names on the first line; the date on the second line; the third line is left blank for you to write in the guest's name; and the fourth line is for the table number, color, or other identifying factor.

Price Range: $0.25 - $1.00 each

*R*AIN CARDS

These cards are enclosed when guests are invited to an outdoor ceremony and/or reception, informing them of an alternate location in case of bad weather. As with other enclosures, rain cards should be placed in front of the invitation, facing the back flap and the person inserting them. They should be printed on the same quality paper and in the same style as the invitation itself.

Price Range: $0.25 - $1.00 each

*M*APS

Maps to the ceremony and/or reception are becoming frequent inserts in wedding invitations. They need to be drawn and printed in the same style as the invitation and are usually on a small, heavier card. If they are not printed in the same style or on the same type of paper as the invitation, they should be mailed separately.

Options: Maps should include both written and visual instructions, keeping in mind the fact that guests may be coming from different locations.

Things To Consider: Order extra maps to hand out at the ceremony if the reception is at a different location.

Tips To Save Money: If you are comfortable with computers, you can purchase software that allows you to draw your own maps. Print a map to both the ceremony and reception on the same sheet of paper, perhaps one on each side. This will save you the cost of mailing two maps. Or have your ushers hand out maps to the reception after the ceremony.

Price Range: $0.50 - $1.00 each

CEREMONY PROGRAMS

Ceremony programs are printed documents showing the sequence of events during the ceremony. These programs add a personal touch to your wedding and are a convenient way of letting guests know who your attendants, officiant, and ceremony musicians are.

Options: Ceremony programs can be handed out to guests by the ushers, or they can be placed at the back of the church for guests to take as they enter.

Price Range: $0.75 - $3.00 each

ANNOUNCEMENTS

Announcements are not obligatory but serve a useful purpose. They may be sent to friends who are not invited to the wedding because the number of guests must be limited, or because they live too far away. They may also be sent to acquaintances who, while not particularly close to the family, might still wish to know of the marriage.

Announcements are also appropriate for friends and acquaintances who are not expected to attend and for whom you do not want to give an obligation of sending a gift. They should include the day, month, year, city, and state where the ceremony took place.

Things To Consider: Announcements should never be sent to anyone who has received an invitation to the ceremony or the reception. They are printed on the same paper and in the same style as the invitations. They should be addressed before the wedding and mailed the day of or the day after the ceremony.

Price Range: $0.75 - $2.00

*T*HANK-YOU NOTES

Regardless of whether the bride has thanked the donor in person or not, she must write a thank-you note for every gift received.

Things To Consider: Order thank-you notes along with your other stationery at least four months before your wedding. You should order some with your maiden initials for thank-you notes sent before the ceremony, and the rest with your married initials for notes sent after the wedding and for future use. Send thank-you notes within two weeks of receiving a gift that arrives before the wedding, and within two months after the honeymoon for gifts received on or after your wedding day. Be sure to mention the gift you received in the body of the note and let the person know how much you like it and what you plan to do with it.

Price Range: $.40 - $.75

*S*TAMPS

Don't forget to budget stamps for response cards as well as for invitations!

Things To Consider: Don't order stamps until you have had the post office weigh your completed invitation. It may exceed the size and weight for one stamp. Order commemorative stamps that fit the occasion.

Price Range: $0.37 - $1.00

*C*ALLIGRAPHY

Calligraphy is a form of elegant handwriting often used to address invitations for formal occasions. Traditional wedding invitations should be addressed in black or blue fountain pen.

Options: You may address the invitations yourself, hire a professional calligrapher, or have your invitations addressed using calligraphy by computer. Make sure you use the same method or person to address both the inner and outer envelopes.

Tips To Save Money: You may want to consider taking a short course to learn the art of calligraphy so that you can address your own invitations. If you have a computer with a laser printer, you can address the invitations yourself using one of many beautiful calligraphy fonts.

Price Range: $.50 - $3.00 each

*N*APKINS AND MATCHBOOKS

Napkins and matchbooks may also be ordered from your stationer. These are placed around the reception room as decorative items and mementos of the event.

Things To Consider: Napkins and matchbooks can be printed in your wedding colors or white with gold or silver lettering. Include both of your names and the wedding date. You may consider including a phrase or thought, or a small graphic design above your names.

Price Range: $.50 - $1.50 each

*S*TATIONERY *C*HECKLIST

		QTY.	COST
❑	Invitations	_____	_____
❑	Envelopes	_____	_____
❑	Response Cards/Envelopes	_____	_____
❑	Reception Cards	_____	_____
❑	Ceremony Cards	_____	_____
❑	Pew Cards	_____	_____
❑	Seating/Place Cards	_____	_____
❑	Rain Cards	_____	_____
❑	Maps	_____	_____
❑	Ceremony Programs	_____	_____
❑	Announcements	_____	_____
❑	Thank-You Notes	_____	_____
❑	Stamps	_____	_____
❑	Personalized Napkins	_____	_____
❑	Personalized Matchbooks	_____	_____

Sample Ceremony Program

The Marriage of
Carol Ann Smith and William James Clark
the eleventh of March, 2006
San Diego, California

OUR CEREMONY

Prelude:
All I Ask of You, by Andrew Lloyd Webber

Processional:
The Canon, by Pachelbel

Rite of Marriage

Welcome guests

Statement of intentions

Marriage vows

Exchange of rings

Blessing of bride and groom

Pronouncement of marriage

Presentation of the bride and groom

Recessional:
Trumpet Voluntary, by Jeromiah Clarke

*S*AMPLE *C*EREMONY *P*ROGRAM (CONT.)

OUR WEDDING PARTY

Maid of Honor:
Susan Smith, Sister of Bride

Best Man:
Brandt Clark, Brother of Groom

Bridesmaids:
Janet Anderson, Friend of Bride
Lisa Bennett, Friend of Bride

Ushers:
Mark Gleason, Friend of Groom
Tommy Olson, Friend of Groom

Officiant:
Father Henry Thomas

OUR RECEPTION

Please join us after the ceremony
in the celebration of our marriage at:
La Valencia Hotel
1132 Prospect Street
La Jolla, CA

Stationery Comparison Chart

QUESTIONS	POSSIBILITY 1	POSSIBILITY 2
What is the name & phone number of the stationery provider?		
What is the website & email address of the stationery provider?		
What is the address of the stationery provider?		
How many years of experience do you have?		
What lines of stationery do you carry?		
What types of printing process do you offer?		
How soon in advance does the order have to be placed?		
What is the turn around time?		
What is the cost of the desired invitation? Announcement?		
What is the cost of the desired response card? Reception card?		
What is the cost of the desired thank-you note?		
What is the cost of the desired party favors?		
What is the cost of the desired wedding program?		
What is the cost of addressing the envelopes in calligraphy?		
What is your payment policy?		
What is your cancellation policy?		

STATIONERY COMPARISON CHART

POSSIBILITY 3	POSSIBILITY 4	POSSIBILITY 5

Stationery Description

Stationer _____   Date Ordered _____

Sales Person _____   Phone No. _____

Address _____

Invitations (Paper, Style, Color, Font, Printing)   _____

_____

Reception Cards (Paper, Style, Color, Font, Printing)   _____

_____

Response Cards (Paper, Style, Color, Font, Printing)   _____

_____

Announcements (Paper, Style, Color, Font, Printing)   _____

_____

Seating/Pew Cards (Paper, Style, Color, Font, Printing)   _____

_____

Napkins/Matchbooks (Paper, Style, Color, Font, Printing)   _____

_____

*S*TATIONERY *W*ORDING

Invitation

_____
_____
_____
_____
_____
_____
_____
_____
_____
_____
_____
_____

Announcements

_____
_____
_____
_____
_____

Reception Cards

_____
_____
_____

Response Cards

_____
_____
_____

Seating/Pew Cards

_____
_____

Napkins/Matchbooks

_____
_____

Guest and Gift List

(Make as many copies of this form as needed to accommodate the size of your guest list.)

Name Telephone No. Email Address Street Address City, State, Zip Code	Table # ——— Pew #	RSVP How Many?	Shower Gift ——————— Wedding Gift	Thank You Sent
——————— ——————— ——————— ———————	———		———————	———
——————— ——————— ——————— ———————	———		———————	———
——————— ——————— ——————— ———————	———		———————	———
——————— ——————— ——————— ———————	———		———————	———
——————— ——————— ——————— ———————	———		———————	———
——————— ———————	———		———————	———

ANNOUNCEMENT LIST

(Make as many copies of this form as needed to accommodate the size of your list.)

Name Telephone No. Email Address Street Address City, State, Zip Code	Name Telephone No. Email Address Street Address City, State, Zip Code

Guest Accommodation List

(Make as many copies of this form as needed to accommodate the size of your guest list.)

Name_____   Arrival Date _____ Time _____
Airline/Train_____   Flight/Train No. _____
Pick Up By _____   Will Stay At _____
Address _____   Phone No. _____
Cost Per Room _____   Confirmation No. _____
Departure Date _____ Time _____   Taken By _____
Airline/Train _____   Flight/Train No. _____

Name_____   Arrival Date _____ Time _____
Airline/Train_____   Flight/Train No. _____
Pick Up By _____   Will Stay At _____
Address _____   Phone No. _____
Cost Per Room _____   Confirmation No. _____
Departure Date _____ Time _____   Taken By _____
Airline/Train _____   Flight/Train No. _____

Name_____   Arrival Date _____ Time _____
Airline/Train_____   Flight/Train No. _____
Pick Up By _____   Will Stay At _____
Address _____   Phone No. _____
Cost Per Room _____   Confirmation No. _____
Departure Date _____ Time _____   Taken By _____
Airline/Train _____   Flight/Train No. _____

Name_____   Arrival Date _____ Time _____
Airline/Train_____   Flight/Train No. _____
Pick Up By _____   Will Stay At _____
Address _____   Phone No. _____
Cost Per Room _____   Confirmation No. _____
Departure Date _____ Time _____   Taken By _____
Airline/Train _____   Flight/Train No. _____

Name_____   Arrival Date _____ Time _____
Airline/Train_____   Flight/Train No. _____
Pick Up By _____   Will Stay At _____
Address _____   Phone No. _____
Cost Per Room _____   Confirmation No. _____
Departure Date _____ Time _____   Taken By _____
Airline/Train _____   Flight/Train No. _____

ADDRESSING ENVELOPES

GUIDELINES FOR ADDRESSING INVITATIONS

We recommend that you start addressing your envelopes at least three months before your wedding, and preferably four months if you are using calligraphy or if your guest list is above 200.

You may want to ask your maid of honor or bridesmaids to help you with this time-consuming task, as this is traditionally part of their responsibilities. Organize a luncheon or late afternoon get-together with hors d'oeuvres and make a party out of it! If you are working with a wedding consultant, she can also help you address invitations.

There are typically two envelopes that need to be addressed for wedding invitations: an inner envelope and an outer envelope. The inner envelope is placed unsealed inside the outer envelope, with the flap away from the person inserting it.

The invitation and all enclosures are placed inside the inner envelope facing the back flap. The inner envelope contains the name (or names) of the person (or people) who are invited to the ceremony and/or reception. The address is not included on the inner envelope.

The outer envelope contains the name (or names) and address of the person (or people) to whom the inner envelope belongs.

Use the guidelines on the following page to help you properly address both the inner and outer envelopes.

GUIDELINES FOR ADDRESSING INVITATIONS

SITUATION	INNER ENVELOPE (no first name or address)	OUTER ENVELOPE (has first name and address)
Husband and Wife (with same surname)	Mr. and Mrs. Smith	Mr. and Mrs. Thomas Smith (use middle name, if known)
Husband and Wife (with different surnames)	Ms. Banks and Mr. Smith (wife first)	Ms. Anita Banks Mr. Thomas Smith (wife's name above husband's)
Husband and Wife (wife has professional title)	Dr. Smith and Mr. Smith	Dr. Anita Smith Mr. Thomas Smith (wife's name & title above husband's)
Husband and Wife (with Children under 16)	Mr. and Mrs. Smith John, Mary, and Glen (in order of age)	Mr. and Mrs. Thomas Smith
Single Woman (regardless of age)	Miss/Ms. Smith	Miss/Ms. Beverly Smith
Single Woman and Guest	Miss/Ms. Smith Mr. Jones (or "and Guest")	Miss/Ms. Beverly Smith
Single Man	Mr. Jones (Master for a young boy)	Mr. William Jones
Single Man and Guest	Mr. Jones Miss/Ms. Smith (or "and Guest")	Mr. William Jones
Unmarried Couple Living Together	Mr. Knight and Ms. Orlandi (names listed alphabetically)	Mr. Michael Knight Ms. Paula Orlandi
Two Sisters (over 16)	The Misses Smith	The Misses Mary and Jane Smith (in order of age)
Two Brothers (over 16)	The Messrs. Smith	The Messrs. John and Glen Smith (in order of age)
Brothers & Sisters (over 16)	Mary, Jane, John & Glen (name the girls first, in order of age)	The Misses Smith The Messrs. Smith (name the girls first)
A Brother and Sister (over 16)	Jane and John (name the girl first)	Miss Jane Smith and Mr. John Smith (name the girl first)
Widow	Mrs. Smith	Mrs. William Smith
Divorcee	Mrs. Smith	Mrs. Jones Smith (maiden name and former husband's surname)

TO GET THE FULL VALUE OF JOY YOU MUST
HAVE SOMEONE TO DIVIDE IT WITH

Mark Twain

PHOTO: JON BARBER

R · E · C · E · P · T · I · O · N

*R*ECEPTION

*R*ECEPTION SITE FEE

The reception is a party where all your guests come together to celebrate your new life as a married couple. It should reflect and complement the formality of your ceremony. The selection of a reception site will depend on its availability, price, proximity to the ceremony site, and the number of people it will accommodate.

There are two basic types of reception sites. The first type charges a per person fee which includes the facility, food, tables, silverware, china, and so forth. Examples: hotels, restaurants and catered yachts. The second type charges a room rental fee and you are responsible for providing the food, beverages, linens, and possibly tables and chairs. Examples: clubs, halls, parks, museums, and private homes.

The advantage of the first type is that most everything is done for you. The disadvantage, however, is that your choices of food, china, and linen are limited. Usually you are not permitted to bring in an outside caterer and must select from a predetermined menu.

Options: Private homes, gardens, hotels, clubs, restaurants, halls, parks, museums, yachts, and wineries are some of the more popular choices for receptions.

Things To Consider: When comparing the cost of different locations, consider the rental fee, food, beverages, parking, gratuity, set-up charges and the cost of rental equipment needed such as tables, chairs, canopies, and so forth. If you are planning an outdoor reception, be sure to have a backup site in case of rain.

Beware: Some hotels are known for double booking. A bride may reserve the largest or most elegant room in a hotel for her reception, only to find out later that the hotel took the liberty to book a more profitable event in the room she had reserved and moved her reception over to a smaller or less elegant room.

Also be careful of hotels that book events too close together. You don't want your guests to wait outside while your room is being set up for the reception. And you don't want to be "forced out" before you are ready to leave because the hotel needs to arrange the room for the next reception. Get your rental hours and the name of your room in writing.

Tips To Save Money: Since the cost of the reception is approximately 35% of the total cost of your wedding, you can save the most money by limiting your guest list. If you hire a wedding consultant, s/he may be able to cut your cake and save you the cake-cutting fee. Check this out with your facility or caterer. Reception sites that charge a room rental fee may waive this fee if you meet minimum requirements on food and beverages consumed. But try to negotiate this before you book the facility.

Price Range: $300 - $5,000

*H*ORS D' OEUVRES

At receptions where a full meal is to be served, hors d' oeuvres may be offered to guests during the first hour of the reception. However, at a tea or cocktail reception, hors d' oeuvres will be the "main course."

Options: There are many options for hors d' oeuvres, depending on the formality of your reception and the type of food to be served at the meal. Popular items are foods that can easily be picked up and eaten with one hand. Hors d' oeuvres may be set out on tables "buffet style" for guests to help themselves, or they may be passed around on trays by waiters and waitresses.

Things To Consider: When selecting hors d' oeuvres for your reception, consider whether heating or refrigeration will be available and choose your food accordingly. When planning your menu, consider the time of day. You should select lighter hors d' oeuvres for a midday reception and heavier hors d' oeuvres for an evening reception.

Tips To Save Money: Tray pass hors d' oeuvres during cocktail hour and serve a lighter meal. Avoid serving hors d' oeuvres that are labor intensive or that require expensive ingredients. Compare two or three caterers; there is a wide price range between caterers for the same food. Compare the total cost of catering (main entrée plus hors d' oeuvres) when selecting a caterer. Consider serving hors d' oeuvres "buffet style." Your guests will eat less this way than if waiters and waitresses are constantly serving them hors d' oeuvres.

Price Range: $3.00 - $20/person

*M*AIN MEAL / CATERER

If your reception is going to be in a hotel, restaurant or other facility that provides food, you will need to select a meal to serve your guests. Most of these facilities will have a predetermined menu from which to select your meal. If your reception is going to be in a facility that does not provide food, you will need to hire an outside caterer. The caterer will be responsible for preparing, cooking, decorating and serving the food.

The caterer will also be responsible for beverages and for cleaning up after the event. Before signing a contract, make sure you understand all the services the caterer will provide. Your contract should state the amount and type of food and beverages that will be served, the way in which they will be served, the number of servers who will be available, the cost per item or person,

Options: Food can be served either buffet style or as a sit-down meal. It should be chosen according to the time of day, year, and formality of the wedding. Although there are many main dishes to choose from, chicken and beef are the most popular selections for a large event. Ask your facility manager or caterer for their specialty. If you have a special type of food you would like to serve at your reception, select a facility or caterer who specializes in preparing it.

Things To Consider: When hiring a caterer, check to see if the location for your reception provides refrigeration and cooking equipment. If not, make sure your caterer is fully self supported with portable refrigeration and heating equipment. A competent caterer will prepare much of the food in his/her own kitchen and should provide an adequate staff of cooks, servers, and bartenders. Ask for references and look at photos from previous parties so you know how the food will be presented; or better yet, visit an event they are catering.

Beware: Avoid mayonnaise, cream sauces, or custard fillings if food must go unrefrigerated for any length of time.

Tips To Save Money: Give only 85 to 95 percent of your final guest count to your caterer or facility manager, depending on how certain you are that all of your guests who have responded will come. Chances are that several, if not many, of your guests will not show up. If they do, your caterer should have enough food for all of them. This is especially true with buffet style receptions, in which case the facility or caterer will charge extra for each additional guest. However, if you give a complete count of your guests to your caterer and some of them don't show up, you will still have to pay for their plates. If offering a buffet meal, have the catering staff serve the food onto guests' plates rather than allowing guests to serve themselves. This will help to regulate the amount of food consumed.

Select food that is not too time-consuming to prepare, or food that does not have expensive ingredients. Also, consider a brunch or early afternoon wedding so the reception will fall between meals, allowing you to serve hors d' oeuvres instead of a full meal. Or tray pass hors d' oeuvres during cocktail hour and choose a lighter meal.

Price Range: $20 - $100/person

LIQUOR / BEVERAGES

Prices for liquor and beverages vary greatly, depending on the amount and brand of alcohol served. Traditionally, at least champagne or punch should be served to toast the couple.

Options: White and red wines, scotch, vodka, gin, rum, and beer are the most popular alcoholic beverages. Sodas and fruit punch are popular nonalcoholic beverages served at receptions. And of course, don't forget coffee or tea. There are a number of options and variations for serving alcoholic beverages: a full open bar where you pay for your guests to drink as much as they wish; an open bar for the first hour, followed by a cash bar where guests pay for their own drinks; cash bar only; beer and wine only; nonalcoholic beverages only; or any combination thereof.

Things To Consider: If you plan to serve alcoholic beverages at a reception site that does not provide liquor, make sure your caterer has a license to serve alcohol and that your reception site allows alcoholic beverages. If you plan to order your own alcohol, do so three or four weeks before the event. If you plan to have a no-host or "cash" bar, consider notifying your guests so they know to bring cash with them. A simple line that says "No-Host Bar" on the reception card should suffice.

In selecting the type of alcohol to serve, consider the age and preference of your guests, the type of food that will be served, and the time of day your guests will be drinking.

On the average, you should allow 1 drink per person per hour at the reception. A bottle of champagne will usually serve six glasses. Never serve liquor without some type of food. Use the following chart to plan your beverage needs:

Beverages	Amount based on 100 guests
Bourbon	3 Fifths
Gin	3 Fifths
Rum	2 Fifths
Scotch	4 Quarts
Vodka	5 Quarts
White Wine	2 Cases
Red Wine	1 Case
Champagne	3 Cases
Other	2 Cases each: Club Soda, Seltzer Water, Tonic Water, Ginger Ale, Cola, Beer

If you are hosting an open bar at a hotel or restaurant, ask the catering manager how they charge for liquor: by consumption or by number of bottles opened. Get this in writing before the event and then ask for a full consumption report after the event.

Beware: In today's society, it is not uncommon for the hosts of a party to be held legally responsible for the conduct and safety of their guests. Keep this in mind when planning the quantity and type of beverages to serve. Also, be sure to remind your bartenders not to serve alcohol to minors.

Tips To Save Money: To keep beverage costs down, serve punch, wine, or nonalcoholic drinks only. If your caterer allows it, consider buying liquor from a wholesaler who will let you return unopened bottles. Also, avoid salty foods such as potato chips, pretzels or ham. These foods will make your guests thirstier so they will tend to drink more.

Host alcoholic beverages for the first hour, then go to a cash bar. Or host beer, wine, and soft drinks only and have mixed drinks available on a cash basis. The bartending fee is often waived if you meet the minimum requirements on beverages consumed. For the toast, tray pass champagne only to those guests who want it, not to everyone. Many people will make a toast with whatever they are currently drinking. Consider serving sparkling cider in place of champagne.

Omit waiters and waitresses. Instead, have an open bar in which your guests have to get their own drinks. People tend to drink almost twice as much if there are waiters and waitresses constantly asking them if they would like another drink and then bringing drinks to them.

Price Range: $8.00 - $35

BARTENDING / BAR SET-UP FEE

Some reception sites and caterers charge an extra fee for bartending and for setting up the bar.

Tips To Save Money: The bartending fee could be and often is waived if you meet a minimum requirement on beverages consumed. Try to negotiate this with your caterer prior to hiring him/her.

Price Range: $75 - $500

CORKAGE FEE

Many reception sites and caterers make money by marking up the food and alcohol they sell. You may wish to provide your own alcohol for several reasons. First, it is more cost effective. Second, you may want to serve an exotic wine or champagne that the reception site or caterer does not offer. In either case, and if your reception site or caterer allows it, be prepared to pay a corkage fee. This is the fee for each bottle brought into the reception and opened by a member of their staff.

Things To Consider: You need to consider whether the expenses saved after paying the corkage fee justify the hassle and liability of bringing in your own alcohol.

Price Range: $5.00 - $20/bottle

FEE TO POUR COFFEE

In addition to the corkage and cake-cutting fees, some facilities also charge extra to pour coffee with the wedding cake.

Things To Consider: Again, when comparing the cost of various reception sites, don't forget to add up all the extra miscellaneous costs, such as the fee for pouring coffee.

Price Range: $0.25 - $1.00/person

SERVICE PROVIDERS' MEALS

Things To Consider: It is considered a courtesy to feed your photographer, videographer, and any other "service provider" at the reception. Check options and prices with your caterer or reception site manager. Make sure you allocate a place for your service providers to eat. You may want them to eat with your guests, or you may prefer setting a place outside the main room for them to eat. Your service providers may be more comfortable with the latter.

Tips To Save Money: You don't need to feed your service providers the same meal as your guests. You can order sandwiches or another less expensive meal for them. If the meal is a buffet, there should be enough food left after all your guests have been served for your service providers to eat. Tell them they are welcome to eat after all your guests have been served. Be sure to discuss this with your catering manager.

Price Range: $10 - $30

GRATUITY

It is customary to pay a gratuity fee to your caterer. The average gratuity is 15% to 20% of your food and beverage bill.

Tips To Save Money: Gratuities can range from 15% to 25%. Ask about these costs up front and select your caterer or reception site accordingly.

Price Range: 15% - 25%

PARTY FAVORS

Party favors are little gift items given to your guests as mementos of your wedding. They add a very special touch to your wedding and can become keepsakes for your guests.

Options: White matchboxes engraved with the couple's names and wedding date; cocktail napkins marked in the same way; individually wrapped and marked chocolates, almonds, or fine candy are all popular party favors. Wine or champagne bottles marked with the bride and groom's names and wedding date on a personalized label are also very popular. These come in different sizes and can be purchased by the case.

If you can afford it, you may also consider porcelain or ceramic party favors. These can be custom-fired with your name and wedding date on them. A new idea that's gaining in popularity among environmentally conscientious couples is to present each guest with a tiny shoot of an endangered tree to be planted in honor of the bride and groom.

Things To Consider: Personalized favors need to be ordered several weeks in advance.

Price Range: $1.00 - $25/person

DISPOSABLE CAMERAS

A great way to inexpensively obtain many candid photographs of your wedding day is to place a disposable 35 mm camera loaded with film on each table at your reception, and to have your guests take shots of the event! Disposable cameras come pre-loaded with film. Your guests can leave the cameras at their table or drop them in a basket or other labeled container near the entrance to the reception site. Arrange for someone to collect the cameras after the event. Tell your DJ, musician, or wedding coordinator to encourage your guests to take photographs with the disposables. You will end up with many beautiful, memorable and candid photographs of your reception.

Things To Consider: Disposable cameras are sold with and without flash. Disposable cameras with flash are more expensive but necessary if your reception is going to be held indoors or in the evening. If you are planning a large reception, consider buying cameras with only 12 exposures. Otherwise, you may end up with too many photographs. For example, if 200 guests attend your reception and you seat 8 guests per table, you will need to purchase 25 cameras. If each camera has 36 exposures, you will end up with 825 photographs. If the cameras have only 12 exposures, you will end up with 300 photographs, which is a more reasonable quantity!

Tips To Save Money: Instead of developing these photographs into print and then placing them into a big album, have your videographer transfer the negatives directly onto video set to your favorite music. You can then reproduce this "photo montage" and send it as a gift to your friends and family members. You can later decide which of these photographs you want to develop into print.

Price Range: $4.00 - $20

𝓡OSE PETALS / RICE

Rose petals or rice are traditionally tossed over the bride and groom as they leave the church after the ceremony or when they leave the reception. These are usually handed out to guests in little sachet bags while the bride and groom are changing into their going away clothes. This tradition was initiated in the Middle Ages whereby a handful of wheat was thrown over the bridal couple as a symbol of fertility. Rose petals are used to symbolize happiness, beauty, and prosperity.

Options: Rose petals, rice, or confetti is often used. However, an environmentally correct alternative is to use grass or flower seeds, which do not need to be "cleaned up" if tossed over a grassy area. These come wrapped in attractive, recycled packages with the couple's names and wedding date printed on the front.

Things To Consider: Rose petals can stain carpets; rice can sting faces, harm birds and make stairs dangerously slippery; confetti is messy and hard to clean. Clubs and hotels seldom permit the use of any of these. Ask about their policy.

Price Range: $0.35 - $2.00/person

GIFT ATTENDANT

The gift attendant is responsible for watching over your gifts during the reception so that no one walks away with them. This is necessary only if your reception is held in a public area such as a hotel or outside garden where other people may be walking by. It is not proper to have a friend or family member take on this duty as s/he would not enjoy the reception. The gift attendant should also be responsible for transporting your gifts from the reception to your car or bridal suite.

Tips To Save Money: Hire a young boy or girl from your neighborhood to watch over your gifts at the reception.

Price Range: $20 - $100

PARKING FEE / VALET SERVICES

Many reception sites such as hotels, restaurants, etc. charge for parking. It is customary, although not necessary, for the host of the wedding to pay this charge. At a large home reception, you should consider hiring a professional, qualified valet service if parking could be a problem. If so, make sure the valet service is fully insured.

Things To Consider: When comparing the cost of reception sites, don't forget to add the cost of parking to the total price.

Tips To Save Money: To save money, let your guests pay their own parking fees.

Price Range: $3.00 - $10/car

Reception Site Comparison Chart

QUESTIONS	POSSIBILITY 1	POSSIBILITY 2
What is the name of the reception site?		
What is the website & email address of the reception site?		
What is the address of the reception site?		
What is the name & phone number of my contact person?		
What dates & times are available?		
What is the maximum number of guests for a seated reception?		
What is the maximum number of guests for a cocktail reception?		
What is the reception site fee?		
What is the price range for a seated lunch?		
What is the price range for a buffet lunch?		
What is the price range for a seated dinner?		
What is the price range for a buffet dinner?		
What is the corkage fee?		
What is the cake-cutting fee?		
What is the ratio of servers to guests?		
How much time will be allotted for my reception?		
What music restrictions are there, if any?		
What alcohol restrictions are there, if any?		

RECEPTION SITE COMPARISON CHART

POSSIBILITY 3	POSSIBILITY 4	POSSIBILITY 5

Reception Site Comparison Chart (CONT.)

QUESTIONS	POSSIBILITY 1	POSSIBILITY 2
Are there any restrictions for rice or rose petal-tossing?		
What room and table decorations are available?		
Is a changing room available?		
Is there handicap accessibility?		
Is a dance floor included in the site fee?		
Are tables, chairs, and linens included in the site fee?		
Are outside caterers allowed?		
Are kitchen facilities available for outside caterers?		
Does the facility have full liability insurance?		
What "perks" or giveaways are offered?		
How many parking spaces are available for my wedding party?		
How many parking spaces are available for my guests?		
What is the cost for parking, if any?		
What is the cost for sleeping rooms, if available?		
What is the payment policy?		
What is the cancellation policy?		
Are credit cards accepted?		

*R*ECEPTION *S*ITE *C*OMPARISON *C*HART (CONT.)

POSSIBILITY 3	POSSIBILITY 4	POSSIBILITY 5

Reception Information Sheet

RECEPTION SITE _____

Site Coordinator _____ Cost _____

Phone No. _____ Fax. No. _____

Website _____ Email _____

Address _____

Name of Room _____ Room Capacity _____

Date Confirmed _____ Confirm Head Count By _____

Beginning Time _____ Ending Time _____

Cocktails/Hors d'oeuvres Time _____ Meal Time _____

Color of Linens _____ Color of Napkins _____

TOTAL COST _____ Deposit _____ Date _____

Balance _____ Date Due_____

Cancellation Policy _____

EQUIPMENT INCLUDES:

❏ Tables   ❏ Chairs   ❏ Linens   ❏ Tableware
❏ Barware   ❏ Heaters   ❏ Electric Outlet   ❏ Musical Inst.

SERVICE INCLUDES:

❏ Waiters   ❏ Bartenders   ❏ Valet   ❏ Main Meal
❏ Cleanup   ❏ Setup   ❏ Security   ❏ Free Parking

CATERER INFORMATION SHEET

CATERER _____

Contact Person _____   Cost Per Person _____

Phone No. _____   Fax. No. _____

Website _____   Email _____

Address _____

Confirmed Date _____   Confirm Head Count By _____

Arrival Time _____   Departure Time _____

Cocktails/Hors d'oeuvres Time _____   Meal Time _____

Color of Linens _____   Color of Napkins _____

TOTAL COST _____   Deposit _____   Date _____

Balance _____   Date Due_____

Cancellation Policy _____

EQUIPMENT INCLUDES:

❑ Tables	❑ Chairs	❑ Linens	❑ Tableware
❑ Barware	❑ Heaters	❑ Lighting	❑ Candles

SERVICE INCLUDES:

❑ Waiters	❑ Bartenders	❑ Setup	❑ Cleanup
❑ Security	❑ Hors d'oeuvres	❑ Buffet Meal	❑ Seated Meal
❑ Cocktails	❑ Champagne	❑ Wine	❑ Beer
❑ Punch	❑ Soft Drinks	❑ Coffee/Tea	❑ Cake

TABLE SEATING ARRANGEMENT

(Complete this form only after finalizing your guest list.)

HEAD TABLE	BRIDE'S FAMILY TABLE	GROOM'S FAMILY TABLE
_____	_____	_____
_____	_____	_____
_____	_____	_____
_____	_____	_____
_____	_____	_____
_____	_____	_____
_____	_____	_____
_____	_____	_____

TABLE 1	TABLE 2	TABLE 3
_____	_____	_____
_____	_____	_____
_____	_____	_____
_____	_____	_____
_____	_____	_____
_____	_____	_____
_____	_____	_____

TABLE 4	TABLE 5	TABLE 6
_____	_____	_____
_____	_____	_____
_____	_____	_____
_____	_____	_____
_____	_____	_____
_____	_____	_____
_____	_____	_____

TABLE SEATING ARRANGEMENT

(Complete this form only after finalizing your guest list).

TABLE 7   TABLE 8   TABLE 9

_____   _____   _____
_____   _____   _____
_____   _____   _____
_____   _____   _____
_____   _____   _____
_____   _____   _____
_____   _____   _____

TABLE 10   TABLE 11   TABLE 12

_____   _____   _____
_____   _____   _____
_____   _____   _____
_____   _____   _____
_____   _____   _____
_____   _____   _____
_____   _____   _____

TABLE 13   TABLE 14   TABLE 15

_____   _____   _____
_____   _____   _____
_____   _____   _____
_____   _____   _____
_____   _____   _____
_____   _____   _____

Liquor Order Form

Liquor Store   _____   Date Ordered   _____

Salesperson   _____   Phone No. _____

Address   _____   Cost   _____

Delivered by   _____   Delivery Date   _____

Type of Liquor	**# of Bottles Needed**	**Price**
_____	_____	_____
_____	_____	_____
_____	_____	_____
_____	_____	_____
_____	_____	_____
_____	_____	_____
_____	_____	_____
_____	_____	_____
_____	_____	_____
_____	_____	_____
_____	_____	_____

PARTY FAVORS COMPARISON CHART

	QUANTITY	PRICE
White matchboxes engraved with names of bride and groom and date of the wedding	_____	_____
Cocktail napkins engraved with names of the bride and groom and date of the wedding	_____	_____
Almonds, chocolates or other fine candy	_____	_____
Customized wine or champagne labels with bride and groom's names and wedding date	_____	_____
Porcelain or ceramic favors with bride and groom's names and wedding date	_____	_____
Plant or tree shoot to be planted in honor of the bride and groom	_____	_____

Caterer Comparison Chart

QUESTIONS	POSSIBILITY 1	POSSIBILITY 2
What is the name of the caterer?		
What is the website & email address of the caterer?		
What is the address of the caterer?		
What is the name & phone number of my contact person?		
How many years have you been in business?		
What percentage of your business is dedicated to wedding receptions?		
Do you have liability insurance? Are you licensed to serve alcohol?		
When is the final head-count needed?		
What is your ratio of servers to guests?		
How do your servers dress for wedding receptions?		
What is your price range for a seated lunch/ buffet lunch?		
What is your price range for a seated/buffet dinner?		
How much gratuity is expected?		
What is your labor fee per employee?		
What is your cake-cutting fee?		
What is your bartending fee?		
What is your fee to clean-up after the reception?		
What is your payment/cancellation policy?		

CATERER COMPARISON CHART

POSSIBILITY 3	POSSIBILITY 4	POSSIBILITY 5

Menu Worksheet

HORS D'OEUVRES

_____
_____
_____

SALADS/APPETIZERS

_____
_____
_____

SOUPS

_____
_____
_____

MAIN ENTRÉE

_____
_____
_____

DESSERTS

_____
_____
_____

WEDDING CAKE

_____
_____
_____

LOVE IS FRIENDSHIP SET
TO MUSIC
Anonymous

· M U S I C ·

PHOTO: KAREN FRENCH

$\mathcal{M}$USIC

$\mathcal{C}$EREMONY MUSIC

Ceremony music is the music played during the ceremony; i.e., prelude, processional, ceremony, recessional, and postlude. Prelude music is played 15 to 30 minutes before the ceremony begins and while guests are being seated. Processional music is played as the wedding party enters the ceremony site. Ceremony music is played during the ceremony. Recessional music is played as the wedding party leaves the ceremony site. Postlude music is played while guests leave the ceremony site.

Options: The most traditional musical instrument for wedding ceremonies is the organ. But guitars, pianos, flutes, harps and violins are also popular today.

Popular selections for a Christian wedding:

Trumpet Voluntary by Purcell
The Bridal Chorus by Wagner
Wedding March by Mendelssohn
Postlude in G Major by Handel
Canon in D Major by Pachelbel
Adagio in A Minor by Bach

Popular selections for a Jewish wedding:

Erev Shel Shoshanim
Erev Ba
Hana' Ava Babanot

Things To Consider: Music may or may not be included as part of the ceremony site fee. Be sure to check with your ceremony site about restrictions pertaining to music and the availability of musical instruments for your use. Discuss the selection of ceremony music with your officiant and musicians. Make sure the musicians know how to play the selections you request.

When selecting ceremony music, keep in mind the formality of your wedding, your religious affiliation, and the length of the ceremony. Also consider the location and time of day. If the ceremony is outside where there may be other noises such as traffic, wind, or people's voices, or if a large number of guests will be attending your ceremony, consider having the music, your officiant, and your vows amplified. Make sure there are electrical outlets close to where the instruments will be set up.

Tips To Save Money: Hire student musicians from your local university or high school. Ask a friend to sing or play at your ceremony; they will be honored. If you're planning to hire a band for your reception, consider hiring a scaled-down version of the same band to play at your ceremony, such as a trio of flute, guitar, and vocals. This could enable you to negotiate a "package" price. If you're planning to hire a DJ for your reception, consider hiring him/her to play pre-recorded music at your ceremony.

Price Range: $100 - $900

RECEPTION MUSIC

Music is a major part of your reception, and should be planned carefully. Music helps create the atmosphere of your wedding. Special songs will make your reception unique. When you select music for your reception, keep in mind the age and musical preference of your guests, your budget, and any restrictions that the reception site may have. Bands and musicians are typically more expensive than DJ's.

Options: There are many options for reception music: you can hire a DJ, a band, an orchestra, or any combination of one or more instruments and vocalists.

Things To Consider: Consider hiring an entertainment agency that can help you choose a reliable DJ or band that will play the type of music you want. Whoever you choose should have experience performing at wedding receptions.

If you want your musician to act as a master of ceremonies, make sure s/he has a complete timeline for your reception so s/he knows when to announce the various events such as the toasts, first dance, and cutting of the cake. Consider watching your musicians perform at another event before booking their services.

If you need a large variety of music to satisfy all your guests, consider hiring a DJ. A professional DJ can play any type of music and may even offer a light show. Make sure you give him/her a list of the songs you want played at your reception and a timeline for playing each one. Make sure there are electrical outlets at the reception site close to where the musicians will be performing.

Tips To Save Money: You will probably get a better price if you hire a band or DJ directly than if you hire them through an entertainment agency.   Check the music department of local colleges and universities for names of student musicians and DJs. You may be able to hire a student for a fraction of the price of a professional musician or DJ. A DJ is typically less expensive than a "live" musician, saving $200 - $1,000. Some facilities have contracts with certain DJ's, and you may be able to save money by hiring one of them.

Price Range: $500 - $5,000

Bonus Tip: For suggestions about appropriate music for each moment of the wedding, to listen to an audio CD containing excerpts from 99 of the most popular classical music for weddings, or to read the lyrics for 100 of the most popular songs for weddings, simply purchase a copy of the best-selling book...*The Ultimate Guide to Wedding Music.*

And, to hear samples of hundreds of the most popular wedding music, log on to *www.WeddingSolutions.com.*

Ceremony Music Comparison Chart

QUESTIONS	POSSIBILITY 1	POSSIBILITY 2
What is the name of the musician or band?		
What is the website & email address of the musician or band?		
What is your address?		
What is the name & phone number of my contact person?		
How many years of professional experience do you have?		
What percentage of your business is dedicated to weddings?		
Are you the person who will perform at my wedding?		
What instrument(s) do you play?		
What type of music do you specialize in?		
What are your hourly fees?		
What is the cost of a soloist?		
What is the cost of a duet?		
What is the cost of a trio?		
What is the cost of a quartet?		
How would you dress for my wedding?		
Do you have liability insurance?		
Do you have a cordless microphone?		
What is your payment/cancellation policy?		

CEREMONY MUSIC COMPARISON CHART

POSSIBILITY 3	POSSIBILITY 4	POSSIBILITY 5

Reception Music Comparison Chart

QUESTIONS	POSSIBILITY 1	POSSIBILITY 2
What is the name of the musician? Band? DJ?		
What is the website & email address of the musician? Band? DJ?		
What is your address?		
What is the name & phone number of my contact person?		
How many years of professional experience do you have?		
What percentage of your business is dedicated to wedding receptions?		
How many people are in your band?		
What type of music do you specialize in?		
What type of sound system do you have?		
Can you act as a master of ceremonies? How do you dress?		
Can you provide a light show?		
Do you have a cordless microphone?		
How many breaks do you take? How long are they?		
Do you play recorded music during breaks?		
Do you have liability insurance?		
What are your fees for a 4-hour reception?		
What is your cost for each additional hour?		
What is your payment/cancellation policy?		

RECEPTION MUSIC COMPARISON CHART

POSSIBILITY 3	POSSIBILITY 4	POSSIBILITY 5

RECEPTION MUSIC SELECTIONS

(Make a copy of this form and give it to your musicians.)

WHEN	SELECTION	SONGWRITER	PLAYED BY
Receiving Line			
During Hors D'Oeuvres			
During Dinner			
During Dinner			
First Dance			
Second Dance			
Third Dance			
Bouquet Toss			
Garter Removal			
Garter Toss			
Cutting of the Cake			
Couple Leaving			
Other			

WHEN YOU LOVE SOMEONE ALL YOUR
SAVED UP WISHES START COMING OUT

Elizabeth Bowen

· B A K E R Y ·

PHOTO: KAREN FRENCH

AKERY

EDDING CAKE

Wedding cakes may be ordered from a caterer or from a bakery. Some hotels and restaurants may also be able to provide a wedding cake. However, you will probably be better off ordering your cake from a bakery that specializes in wedding cakes. Ask to see photographs of other wedding cakes your baker has created, and by all means, ask for a tasting!

Options: When ordering your cake, you will have to decide not only on a flavor, but also on a size, shape and color. Size is determined by the number of guests. You can choose from one large tier to two, three, or more smaller tiers. The cake can be round, square or heart-shaped. The most common flavors are chocolate, carrot, lemon, rum, and "white" cakes. You can be creative by adding a filling to your cake, such as custard, strawberry, or chocolate. You may also want to consider having tiers of different flavors.

Things To Consider: Price, workmanship, quality, and taste vary considerably from baker to baker. In addition to flavor, size, and cost, consider decoration and spoilage (sugar keeps longer than cream frostings). The cake should be beautifully displayed on its own table decorated with flowers or greenery. Make sure the baker, caterer, or reception site manager can provide you with a pretty cake-cutting knife. If not, you will need to purchase or rent one. When determining the size of the cake, don't forget that you'll be saving the top tier for your first anniversary. This top tier should be removed before the cake is cut, wrapped in several layers of plastic wrap or put inside a plastic container, and kept frozen until your anniversary.

Tips To Save Money: Some bakers have set-up and delivery fees, some don't. Check for individuals who bake from their home. They are usually more reasonable, but you should check with your local health department before hiring one of these at-home bakers. Also, some caterers have contracts with bakeries and can pass on savings to you.

Some bakeries require a deposit on columns and plates. Other bakeries use disposable columns and plates, saving you the rental fee and the hassle of returning these items.

Price Range: $2.00 - $12/piece

GROOM'S CAKE

The groom's cake is an old southern tradition whereby this cake is cut up and distributed to guests in little white boxes engraved with the bride and groom's names. Today the groom's cake, if offered, is cut and served along with the wedding cake.

Options: Usually a chocolate cake decorated with fruit.

Tips To Save Money: Because of its cost and the labor involved in cutting and distributing the cake, very few people offer this delightful custom any more.

Price Range: $1.00 - $2.00/piece

CAKE DELIVERY & SET-UP FEE

This is the fee charged by bakers to deliver and set up your wedding cake at the reception site. It usually includes a deposit on the cake pillars and plate which will be refunded upon their return to the baker.

Tips To Save Money: Have a friend or family member get a quick lesson on how to set up your cake. Have them pick it up and set it up the day of your wedding, then have the florist decorate the cake and/or cake table with flowers and greenery.

Price Range: $40 - $100

CAKE-CUTTING FEE

Most reception sites and caterers charge a fee for each slice of cake they cut if the cake is brought in from an outside bakery. This fee will probably shock you. It is simply their way of enticing you to order the cake through them. And unfortunately, many sites and caterers will not allow a member of your party to cut the cake.

Tips To Save Money: Many hotels and restaurants include a dessert in the cost of their meal packages. If you forego this dessert and substitute your cake as the dessert, they may be willing to waive the cake-cutting fee. Be sure to ask them.

Price Range: $0.75 - $2.50/person

*C*AKE TOP

The bride's cake is often topped and surrounded with fresh flowers, but traditional cake tops are also very popular.

Options: Bells, love birds, a bridal couple or replica of two wedding rings are popular choices for cake tops and can be saved as mementos of your wedding day.

Beware: Some porcelain and other heavier cake tops need to be anchored down into the cake. If you're planning to use a cake top other than flowers, be sure to discuss this with your baker.

Tips To Save Money: Borrow a cake top from a friend or a family member as "something borrowed," an age-old wedding tradition (see page 230.)

Price Range: $20 - $150

*C*AKE KNIFE / TOASTING GLASSES

Your cake knife and toasting glasses should compliment your overall setting; these items will bring you happy memories of your wedding day every time you use them. The cake knife is used to cut the cake at the reception. The bride usually cuts the first two slices of the wedding cake with the groom's hand placed over hers. The groom feeds the bride first, then the bride feeds the groom. This tradition makes beautiful wedding photographs.

You will need toasting glasses to toast each other after you cut the cake. They are usually decorated with ribbons or flowers and kept near the cake. This tradition also makes beautiful wedding photographs.

Things To Consider: Consider having your initials and wedding date engraved on your wedding knife as a memento. Consider purchasing crystal or silver toasting glasses as a keepsake of your wedding. Have your florist decorate your knife and toasting glasses with flowers or ribbons.

Tips To Save Money: Borrow your cake knife or toasting glasses from a friend or family member as "something borrowed," an age-old wedding tradition. See "Wedding Traditions" on page 229. Use the reception facility's glasses and knife, and decorate them with flowers or ribbon.

Price Range: $15 - $120/knife; $10 - $100/toasting glasses

Bakery Comparison Chart

QUESTIONS	POSSIBILITY 1	POSSIBILITY 2
What is the name of the bakery?		
What is the website & email address of the bakery?		
What is the address of the bakery?		
What is the name & phone number of my contact person?		
How many years have you been making wedding cakes?		
What are your wedding cake specialties?		
Do you offer free tasting of your wedding cakes?		
Do you freeze your wedding cakes?		
How far in advance should I order my cake?		
Can you make a groom's cake?		
Do you lend, rent or sell cake knives?		
What is the cost per serving of my desired cake?		
What is your cake pillar and plate rental fee, if any?		
Is this fee refundable upon the return of these items?		
When must these items be returned?		
What is your cake delivery and set-up fee?		
What is your payment policy?		
What is your cancellation policy?		

*B*AKERY *C*OMPARISON *C*HART

POSSIBILITY 3	POSSIBILITY 4	POSSIBILITY 5

Personal Notes

_____

_____

_____

_____

_____

_____

_____

_____

_____

_____

_____

_____

_____

_____

_____

_____

_____

_____

_____

_____

_____

_____

_____

_____

_____

_____

_____

LIFE IS THE FLOWER FOR WHICH
LOVE IS THE HONEY
Victor Hugo

PHOTO: KAREN FRENCH

*F*LOWERS

*B*RIDE'S BOUQUET

The bridal bouquet is one of the most important elements of the bride's attire and deserves special attention. Start by selecting the color and shape of the bouquet. The bridal bouquet should be carried low enough so that all the intricate details of your gown are visible.

Options: There are many colors, scents, sizes, shapes and styles of bouquets to choose from. Popular styles are the cascade, cluster, contemporary and hand-tied garden bouquets. The traditional bridal bouquet is made of white flowers. Stephanotis, gardenias, white roses, orchids and lilies of the valley are popular choices for an all-white bouquet.

If you prefer a colorful bouquet, you may want to consider using roses, tulips, stock, peonies, freesia, and gerbera, which come in a wide variety of colors. Using scented flowers in your bouquet will evoke memories of your wedding day whenever you smell them in the future. Popular fragrant flowers for bouquets are gardenias, freesia, stephanotis, bouvardia, and narcissus. Select flowers that are in season to assure availability (see page 155).

Things To Consider: Your flowers should complement the season, your gown, your color scheme, your attendants' attire, and the style and formality of your wedding. If you have a favorite flower, build your bouquet around it and include it in all your arrangements. Some flowers carry centuries of symbolism. Consider stephanotis -- tradition regards it as the bridal good-luck flower! Pimpernel signifies change; white flowers radiate innocence; forget-me-nots indicate true love; and ivy stands for friendship, fidelity, and matrimony -- the three essentials for a happy marriage.

No flower, however, has as much symbolism for brides as the orange blossom, having at least 700 years of nuptial history. Its unusual ability to simultaneously bear flowers and produce fruit symbolizes the fusion of beauty, personality, and fertility.

Whatever flowers you select, final arrangements should be made well in advance of your wedding date to insure availability. Confirm your final order and delivery time a few days before the wedding. Have the flowers delivered before the photographer arrives so that you can include them in your pre-ceremony photos.

In determining the size of your bouquet, consider your gown and your overall stature. Carry a smaller bouquet if you're petite or if your gown is fairly ornate. A long, cascading bouquet complements a fairly simple gown or a tall or larger bride. Arm bouquets look best when resting naturally in the crook of your arm.

For a natural, fresh-picked look, have your florist put together a cluster of flowers tied together with a ribbon. For a Victorian appeal, carry a nosegay or a basket filled with flowers. Or carry a Bible or other family heirloom decorated with just a few flowers. For a contemporary look, you may want to consider carrying an arrangement of calla lilies or other long-stemmed flower over your arm. For a dramatic statement, carry a single stem of your favorite flower!

Beware: If your bouquet includes delicate flowers that will not withstand hours of heat or a lack of water, make sure your florist uses a bouquet holder to keep them fresh. If you want to carry fresh-cut stems without a bouquet holder, make sure the flowers you select are hardy enough to go without water for the duration of your ceremony and reception.

Tips To Save Money: The cost of some flowers may be significantly higher during their off-season. So try to select flowers which are in bloom and plentiful at the time of your wedding. Avoid exotic, out-of-season flowers. Allow your florist to emphasize your colors using more reasonable, seasonal flowers to achieve your total look. If you have a favorite flower that is costly or out of season, consider using silk for that one flower.

Avoid scheduling your wedding on holidays such as Valentine's Day and Mother's Day when the price of flowers is higher. Because every attendant will carry or wear flowers, consider keeping the size of your wedding party down to accommodate your floral budget.

Price Range: - $75 - $400

*T*OSSING BOUQUET

If you want to preserve your bridal bouquet, consider having your florist make a smaller, less expensive bouquet specifically for tossing. This will be the bouquet you toss to your single, female friends toward the end of the reception. Tradition has it that the woman who catches the bouquet is the next to be married. Have your florist include a few sprigs of fresh ivy in the tossing bouquet to symbolize friendship and fidelity.

Tips To Save Money: Use the floral cake top or guest book table "tickler bouquet" as the tossing bouquet. Or omit the tossing bouquet altogether and simply toss your bridal bouquet.

Price Range: $25 - $100

*M*AID OF HONOR'S BOUQUET

The maid of honor's bouquet can be somewhat larger or of a different color than the rest of the bridesmaids' bouquets. This will help to set her apart from the others.

Price Range: $25 - $100

*B*RIDESMAIDS' BOUQUETS

The bridesmaids' bouquets should complement the bridal bouquet but are generally smaller in size. The size and color should coordinate with the bridesmaids' dresses and the overall style of the wedding. Bridesmaids' bouquets are usually identical.

Options: To personalize your bridesmaids' bouquets, insert a different flower in each of their bouquets to make a statement. For example, if one of your bridesmaids has been sad, give her a lily of the valley to symbolize the return of happiness. To tell a friend that you admire her, insert yellow jasmine. A pansy will let your friend know that you are thinking of her.

Things To Consider: Choose a bouquet style (cascade, cluster, contemporary, hand-tied) that compliments the formality of your wedding and the height of your attendants. If your bridesmaids will be wearing floral print dresses, select flowers that complement the floral print.

Tips To Save Money: Have your attendants carry a single stemmed rose, lily or other suitable flower for an elegant look that also saves money.

Price Range: $25 - $100

*M*AID OF HONOR / BRIDESMAIDS' HAIRPIECE

For a garden-look, have your maid of honor and bridesmaids wear garlands of flowers in their hair. If so, provide your maid of honor with a slightly different color or variety of flower to set her apart from the others.

Options: You may consider using artificial flowers for the hairpieces as long as they are in keeping with the flowers carried by members of the bridal party. Since it is not always easy to find good artificial blooms, other types of hairpieces may be more satisfactory, durable, and attractive.

Things To Consider: Flowers used for the hairpiece must be a sturdy and long-lived variety.

Price Range: $8.00 - $100

FLOWER GIRL'S HAIRPIECE

Flower girls often wear a wreath of flowers as a hairpiece.

Options: This is another place where artificial flowers may be used, but they must be in keeping with the flowers carried by members of the bridal party. Since it is not always easy to find good artificial blooms, other types of hairpieces may be more satisfactory, durable, and attractive.

Things To Consider: If the flowers used for the hairpiece are not a sturdy and long-lived variety, a ribbon, bow, or hat might be a safer choice.

Price Range: $8.00 - $75

BRIDE'S GOING AWAY CORSAGE

You may want to consider wearing a corsage on your going-away outfit. This makes for pretty photos as you and your new husband leave the reception for your honeymoon. Have your florist create a corsage which echoes the beauty of your bouquet.

Beware: Put a protective shield under lilies when using them as a corsage, as their anthers will easily stain fabric. Be careful when using Alstroemeria as a corsage, as its sap can be harmful if it enters the human bloodstream.

Tips To Save Money: Ask your florist if s/he can design your bridal bouquet in such a way that the center flowers may be removed and worn as a corsage. Or omit this corsage altogether.

Price Range: $10 - $50

OTHER FAMILY MEMBERS' CORSAGES

The groom is responsible for providing flowers for his mother, the bride's mother, and the grandmothers. The officiant, if female, may also be given a corsage to reflect her important role in the ceremony. The corsages don't have to be identical, but they should be coordinated with the color of their dresses.

Options: The groom may order flowers that can be pinned to a pocketbook or worn around a wrist. He should ask which style the women prefer, and if a particular color is needed to coordinate with their dresses. Gardenias, camellias, white orchids, or cymbidium orchids are excellent choices for corsages, as they go well with any outfit.

Things To Consider: The groom may also want to consider ordering corsages for other close family members, such as sisters and aunts. This will add a little to your floral expenses, but will make these female family members feel more included in your wedding and will let guests know that they are related to the bride and groom. Many women do not like to wear corsages, so the groom should check with the people involved before ordering the flowers.

Beware: Put a protective shield under lilies when using them as corsages, as their anthers will easily stain fabric. Be careful when using Alstroemeria as corsages, as its sap can be harmful if it enters the human bloodstream.

Tips To Save Money: Ask your florist to recommend reasonable flowers for corsages. Dendrobium orchids are reasonable and make lovely corsages.

Price Range: $10 - $35

*G*ROOM'S BOUTONNIERE

The groom wears his boutonniere on the left lapel, nearest to his heart.

Options: Boutonnieres are generally a single blossom such as a rosebud, stephanotis, freesia or a miniature carnation. If a rosebud is used for the wedding party, have the groom wear two rosebuds, or add a sprig of baby's breath to differentiate him from the groomsmen.

Things To Consider: Consider using a small cluster of flowers instead of a single bloom for the groom's boutonniere.

Beware: Be careful when using Alstroemeria as a boutonniere, as its sap can be harmful if it enters the human bloodstream.

Tips To Save Money: Use mini-carnations rather than roses.

Price Range: $4.00 - $25

$\mathscr{U}$SHERS AND OTHER FAMILY MEMBERS' BOUTONNIERES

The groom gives each man in his wedding party a boutonniere to wear on his left lapel. The officiant, if male, may also be given a boutonniere to reflect his important role in the ceremony. The ring bearer may or may not wear a boutonniere, depending on his outfit. A boutonniere is more appropriate on a tuxedo than on knickers and knee socks.

Options: Generally, a single blossom such as a rosebud, freesia, or miniature carnation is used as a boutonniere.

Things To Consider: The groom should also consider ordering boutonnieres for other close family members such as fathers, grandfathers, and brothers. This will add a little to your floral expenses, but will make these male family members feel more included in your wedding and will let guests know that they are related to the bride and groom.

Beware: Be careful when using Alstroemeria as boutonnieres, as its sap can be harmful if it enters the human bloodstream.

Tips To Save Money: Use mini-carnations rather than roses.

Price Range: $3.00 - $15

$\mathscr{M}$AIN ALTAR

The purpose of flowers at the main altar is to direct the guests' visual attention toward the front of the church or synagogue and to the bridal couple. Therefore, they must be seen by guests seated in the back. The flowers for the ceremony site can be as elaborate or as simple as you wish. Your officiant's advice, or that of the altar guild or florist, can be most helpful in choosing flowers for the altar and chancel.

Options: If your ceremony is outside, decorate the arch, gazebo, or other structure serving as the altar with flowers or greenery. In a Jewish ceremony, vows are said under a Chuppah, which is placed at the altar and covered with greens and fresh flowers.

Things To Consider: In choosing floral accents, consider the decor of your ceremony site. Some churches and synagogues are ornate enough and don't need extra flowers. Too many arrangements would get lost in the architectural splendor. Select a few dramatic showpieces that will complement the existing decor. Be sure to ask if there are any restrictions on flowers at the church or synagogue. Remember, decorations should be determined by the size and style of the building, the formality of the wedding, the preferences of the bride, the cost, and the regulations of the particular site.

Tips To Save Money: Decorate the ceremony site with greenery only. Candlelight and greenery are elegant in and of themselves. Use greenery and flowers from your garden. Have your ceremony outside in a beautiful garden or by the water, surrounded by nature's own splendor.

Price Range: $50 - $3,000

ALTAR CANDELABRA

In a candlelight ceremony, the candelabra may be decorated with flowers or greens for a dramatic effect.

Options: Ivy may be twined around the candelabra, or flowers may be strung to them.

Price Range: $50 - $200

AISLE PEWS

Flowers, candles or ribbons are often used to mark the aisle pews and add color.

Options: A cluster of flowers, a cascade of greens, or a cascade of flowers and ribbons are all popular choices. Candles with adorning greenery add an elegant touch.

Things To Consider: Use hardy flowers that can tolerate being handled as pew ornaments. Gardenias and camellias, for example, are too sensitive to last long.

Beware: Avoid using Allium in your aisle pew decorations as they have an odor of onions.

Tips To Save Money: It is not necessary to decorate all of the aisle pews, or any at all. To save money, decorate only the reserved family pews. Or decorate every second or third pew.

Price Range: $5.00 - $75

RECEPTION SITE

Flowers add beauty, fragrance, and color to your reception. Flowers for the reception, like everything else, should fit your style and color scheme. Flowers can help transform a stark reception hall into a warm, inviting and colorful room.

Things To Consider: Consider renting indoor plants or small trees to give your reception a garden-like atmosphere. Decorate them with twinkle lights to achieve a magical effect.

Tips To Save Money: You can save money by taking flowers from the ceremony to the reception site for decorations. However, you must coordinate this move carefully to avoid having your guests arrive at an undecorated reception room. Use greenery rather than flowers to fill large areas. Trees and garlands of ivy can give a dramatic impact for little money. Use greenery and flowers from your garden. Have your reception outside in a beautiful garden or by the water, surrounded by nature's own beauty.

Price Range: $300 - $3,000

HEAD TABLE

The head table is where the wedding party will sit during the reception. This important table should be decorated with a larger or more dramatic centerpiece than the guest tables.

Things To Consider: Consider using a different color or style of arrangement to set the head table apart from the other tables.

Beware: Avoid using highly fragrant flowers, such as narcissus, on tables where food is being served or eaten, as their fragrance may conflict with other aromas.

Tips To Save Money: Decorate the head table with the bridal and attendants' bouquets.

Price Range: $100 - $600

GUEST TABLES

At a reception where guests are seated, a small flower arrangement may be placed on each table.

Things To Consider: The arrangements should complement the table linens and the size of the table, and should be kept low enough so as not to hinder conversation among guests seated across from each other.

Beware: Avoid using highly fragrant flowers, like Narcissus, on tables where food is being served or eaten, as their fragrance may conflict with other aromas.

Tips To Save Money: To keep the cost down and for less formal receptions, use small potted flowering plants placed in white baskets, or consider using dried or silk arrangements that you can make yourself and give later as gifts. Or place a wreath of greenery entwined with colored ribbon in the center of each table. Use a different colored ribbon at each table and assign your guests to tables by ribbon color instead of number.

Price Range: $10 - $100

BUFFET TABLE

If buffet tables are used, have some type of floral arrangement on the tables to add color and beauty to your display of food.

Options: Whole fruits and bunches of berries offer a variety of design possibilities. Figs add a festive touch. Pineapples are a sign of hospitality. Vegetables offer an endless array of options to decorate with. Herbs are yet another option in decorating. A mixture of rosemary and mint combined with scented geraniums makes a very unique table decoration.

Things To Consider: Depending on the size of the table, place one or two arrangements at each side.

Beware: Avoid placing certain flowers, such as carnations, snapdragons, or the star of Bethlehem, next to buffet displays of fruits or vegetables, as they are extremely sensitive to the gasses emitted by these foods.

Price Range: $50 - $500

PUNCH TABLE

Put an assortment of greens or a small arrangement of flowers at the punch table. See "Buffet Table."

Price Range: $10 - $100

CAKE TABLE

The wedding cake is often the central location at the reception. Decorate the cake table with flowers.

Tips To Save Money: Have your bridesmaids place their bouquets on the cake table during the reception, or decorate the cake top only and surround the base with greenery and a few loose flowers.

Price Range: $30 - $300

CAKE

Flowers are a beautiful addition to a wedding cake and are commonly seen spilling out between the cake tiers.

Things To Consider: Use only nonpoisonous flowers, and have your florist – not the caterer – design the floral decorations for your cake. A florist will be able to blend the cake decorations into your overall floral theme.

Price Range: $20 - $100

CAKE KNIFE

Decorate your cake knife with a white satin ribbon and/or flowers.

Things To Consider: Consider engraving the cake knife with your names and wedding date.

Price Range: $5.00 - $35

TOASTING GLASSES

Tie small flowers with white ribbons on the stems of your champagne glasses. These wedding accessories deserve a special floral touch since they will most likely be included in your special photographs.

Things To Consider: Consider engraving your toasting glasses with your names and wedding date.

Price Range: $10 - $35

FLORAL DELIVERY & SET-UP

Most florists charge a fee to deliver flowers to the ceremony and reception sites and to arrange them on site.

Things To Consider: Make sure your florist knows where your sites are and what time to arrive for set-up.

Price Range: $25 - $200

Florists Comparison Chart

QUESTIONS	POSSIBILITY 1	POSSIBILITY 2
What is the name of the florist?		
What is the website & email address of the florist?		
What is the address of the florist?		
What is the name & phone number of my contact person?		
How many years of professional floral experience do you have?		
What percentage of your business is dedicated to weddings?		
Do you have access to out-of-season flowers?		
Will you visit my wedding sites to make floral recommendations?		
Can you preserve my bridal bouquet?		
Do you rent vases and candleholders?		
Can you provide silk flowers?		
What is your cost of a bridal bouquet made of a dozen white		
What is your cost of a boutonniere made of a single white rose?		
What is your cost of a corsage made with two gardenias?		
Do you have liability insurance? fee? Do you accept credit cards?		
What are your delivery/set-up fees?		
What is your payment/cancellation policy?		

*F*LORISTS *C*OMPARISON *C*HART

POSSIBILITY 3	POSSIBILITY 4	POSSIBILITY 5

BOUQUETS AND FLOWERS

BRIDE'S BOUQUET

COLOR SCHEME _____

STYLE _____

FLOWERS _____

_____

_____

GREENERY _____

OTHER (Ribbons, Etc.) _____

MAID OF HONOR'S BOUQUET

COLOR SCHEME _____

STYLE _____

FLOWERS _____

_____

_____

GREENERY _____

OTHER (Ribbons, Etc.) _____

BRIDESMAIDS' BOUQUETS

COLOR SCHEME _____

STYLE _____

FLOWERS _____

_____

GREENERY
OTHER (Ribbons, Etc.) _____

BOUQUETS AND FLOWERS (CONT.)

FLOWER GIRL'S BOUQUET

COLOR SCHEME _____

STYLE _____

FLOWERS _____

_____

_____

GREENERY _____

OTHER (Ribbons, Etc.) _____

OTHER

GROOM'S BOUTONNIERE _____

_____

USHERS AND OTHER BOUTONNIERES _____

_____

MOTHER OF THE BRIDE CORSAGE _____

_____

MOTHER OF THE GROOM CORSAGE _____

_____

ALTAR OR CHUPPAH _____

_____

STEPS TO ALTAR OR CHUPPAH _____

_____

BOUQUETS AND FLOWERS (CONT.)

PEWS _____

_____

ENTRANCE TO THE CEREMONY _____

_____

ENTRANCE TO RECEPTION _____

_____

RECEIVING LINE _____

_____

HEAD TABLE _____

_____

PARENTS' TABLE _____

_____

GUEST TABLES _____

_____

CAKE TABLE _____

_____

SERVING TABLES (BUFFET, DESSERT) _____

_____

GIFT TABLE _____

_____

FLOWERS AND THEIR SEASONS

Flower	Winter	Spring	Summer	Fall
Allium		x	x	
Alstroemeria	x	x	x	x
Amaryllis	x		x	
Anemone	x	x		x
Aster	x	x	x	x
Baby's Breath	x	x	x	x
Bachelor's Button	x	x	x	x
Billy Buttons		x	x	
Bird of Paradise	x	x	x	x
Bouvardia	x	x	x	x
Calla Lily	x	x	x	x
Carnation	x	x	x	x
Celosia		x	x	
Chrysanthemum	x	x	x	x
Daffodils		x		
Dahlia			x	x
Delphinium			x	x
Eucalyptus	x	x	x	x
Freesia	x	x	x	x
Gardenia	x	x	x	x
Gerbera	x	x	x	x
Gladiolus	x	x	x	x
Iris	x	x	x	x
Liatris		x	x	x
Lily	x	x	x	x

Flowers and their Seasons

Flower	Winter	Spring	Summer	Fall
Lily of the Valley		x		
Lisianthus		x	x	x
Narcissus	x	x		x
Nerine	x	x	x	x
Orchid (Cattleya)	x	x	x	x
Orchid (Cymbidium)	x	x	x	x
Peony		x		
Pincushion			x	
Protea	x			x
Queen Anne's Lace			x	
Ranunculus		x		
Rose	x	x	x	x
Saponaria			x	
Snapdragon		x	x	x
Speedwell			x	
Star of Bethlehem	x			x
Statice	x	x	x	x
Stephanotis	x	x	x	x
Stock	x	x	x	x
Sunflower		x	x	
Sweet Pea		x		
Tuberose			x	x
Tulip	x	x		
Waxflower	x	x		

*P*OPULAR *W*EDDING *F*LOWERS

This section contains information on the most popular flowers used in weddings. Each floral description is listed alphabetically by the flower's most commonly used name and includes the flower's historical significance in weddings, its main usage, proper care, durability, things to beware of and much more. We have also included 90 color photographs of these flowers. We hope this section gives you a better understanding of these flowers and helps you make the appropriate floral selections and coordinate your overall color scheme.

The photographs are displayed in alphabetical order by the flower's common name in bold type to coincide with the floral descriptions. We have also included the flower's botanical name and its class under each photo.

*A*LLIUM

There are two types of Allium: the giant Allium and the miniature Allium. The giant variety is a fluffy looking, bubble-shaped purple flower which is 4-10 inches in diameter and sits on a stem that is at least 2 feet long. The smaller Allium is egg-shaped with flowers that are only 1-2 inches across and sit atop a stem that is half the size of its giant brother.

These flowers, which come from the mountains in ancient China, are excellent for banquet table arrangements because of their striking appearance. Warning: it is best to use these flowers on a table from which you are offering food such as hors d'oeuvres, because they do have an odor of onions. But if you place these flowers in water 24 hours before the wedding, much of the odor will be eliminated.

Historically, these flowers are used at weddings because onions were a sign of good luck and health. The smaller varieties are available throughout most of the year, but the giant Allium are only available in the late spring and early summer. They will keep for about 10 days.

*A*LSTROEMERIA

Native to South America, Alstroemeria is named for the Swedish jurist Clas Alstroemer. This automatically makes the flower appropriate for weddings since marriage is an official act.

Also known as a Peruvian Lily, there are more than 50 varieties within the Alstroemeria assortment in popular colors and shades. Alstroemeria are available year-round in hues of pink, salmon, orange, red, lavender and yellow. During the winter, spring and fall, they may be purchased in white. The whitest varieties currently available are "Bianca," "Paloma" and "Casablanca." The orchid-like "Casablanca" has large, beautiful white flowers with less striping on the petals.

The flowers typically are multicolored clusters on a stalk. They are excellent and economical for wedding table arrangements because one stem contains many clusters, which makes the table arrangement look like it contains lots of flowers. The Alstroemeria's worldwide popularity is attributed to its versatility and long life. It is ideal for use in mixed bouquets, arrangements, corsages, and on its own or by the bunch in a vase. With proper care, Alstroemeria will last from 2-3 weeks. A word of warning: Alstroemeria contains a chemical that may cause dermatitis in susceptible people, and sap from the Alstroemeria can be harmful if it enters the human bloodstream. So handle these cut flowers with care!

AMARYLLIS

Amaryllis, botanically known as Hippeastrum, is sometimes called the Belladonna Lily. It is a bulb flower which originated in South Africa. Its unusual star shaped flowers sit majestically atop a large, hollow stem. Shaded in colors of crimson, pink and white, this flower makes an excellent focal point for a table arrangement or an altar arrangement. Amaryllis first becomes available in the late summer and is readily available until year's end. The flower is odorless. If you are getting married at Christmas time, we recommend using a few "Christmas Gift" white Amaryllis within your flower decor. The flower will remain open for five days.

ANEMONES

The Anemone has many names in many different parts of the country. It is sometimes called a windflower, sometimes a poppy, and also a lily of the field. The Anemone was first discovered in China in the early 1900's by Italian explorers who brought the flower back with them because they were so impressed by its texture and regal coloration. In Italy these flowers were made into a crown and worn by the bride at weddings.

The Anemone's vibrant purple, pink, red, blue and white flowers often come with a contrasting center. They stand on a long, bending stem which makes it useful in incorporating the flower into hair ornaments.

The average Anemone will keep for a week. It has no scent. A word of caution: do not mix this flower with Narcissus; the Anemone is sensitive to the gasses emitted from Narcissus' stem.

ASTERS

The aster is a long-lasting perennial with American roots. It was first discovered by the early settlers and was originally called "The Ancestor Flower." It acquired this name because it was passed along from one generation to another. This gives its place at a wedding particular significance as family members witness a major step in their next generation.

The white "Monte Cassino" aster is a bushy, double flower variety with a diameter of 2-4 inches. There are also single flowered varieties, notably the "Pink Star," "Blue Star," and "White Star," which are becoming increasingly popular. These flowers are generally available year-round and are excellent in both bouquets and table arrangements to add fullness to the design. One of the sparser varieties is the "Climax," which is available only in late September and October. Asters will frequently last up to one week after the wedding.

*B*ABY'S BREATH

Baby's Breath is botanically named Gypsophila and contains hundreds of tiny white or pink flowers covering a multitude of intertwining stems. This wonderful filler flower is perfect as a backdrop to any arrangement or bouquet. Because the flowers are less than 1/4 inch in diameter, they set off the top note flower in a bridal bouquet. It is also possible to dye them other colors to match your wedding decor without harming them. Baby's Breath, sometimes referred to as "gyp," is available year-round.

Baby's Breath is an excellent flower to use at weddings because Gypsophila is derived from the Greek word Philein which means "to love." The plant was first discovered in the Mediterranean. Shortly thereafter, species were discovered as far away as Siberia. The Dutch and Israelis have been growing this long-lasting flower for the last 200 years. It has a life-span of up to 3 weeks and has no scent.

*B*ACHELOR'S BUTTON

What more appropriate flower for a wedding than a Bachelor's Button? Botanically it is called Centaurea. It is one of the rare, strikingly blue flowers. It is appropriately used at weddings since the groom is no longer a bachelor and no longer blue. Ushers frequently wear this flower in their lapels.

In many parts of the U.S. this flower is more commonly known as a cornflower, so called because it was originally a weed found in cornfields. The flower has been actively grown as a commercial product since the mid-1400's. Lately the Dutch have produced different colors of this 2 inch diameter flower. You can purchase the variety in pure white, scarlet, and pink from early spring into early winter. The normal keeping period of a Bachelor's Button is about 5 days.

*B*ILLY BUTTONS

Craspedia globosa originated in the Outback of Australia. Its common name is "drumsticks" but native Aussies gave it the nickname Billy Buttons.

The Billy Button is a globular flower which grows atop an unbranched and leafless stem. The stems are approximately 6 inches long and its pom pom like flower gives it the look of a drum stick used to beat a bass drum.

The flowers are yellow and are used to add interest to a table arrangement. If properly cared for, they will last up to two weeks.

𝓑IRD OF PARADISE

The Bird of Paradise is the common name for Strelitzia. The flower was named after King George III of England's wife, Charlotte von Mecklenburg-Strelitz. The royal lady was admired for her elegance and color, so it was most appropriate that this elegant, colorful flower be named in her honor. Strelitzia originated in South Africa.

The flower sits atop a 3 foot stalk. It is 2-toned: orange and blue. It received its common Bird of Paradise name because it actually gives the appearance of a beautiful bird perched on a stalk.

Available year-round, the Bird of Paradise is used primarily at weddings to project a note of elegance in table decorations. It is best to use this scentless flower sparingly in floral design so as not to detract from its impact. It will last about 2 weeks.

𝓑OUVARDIA

A fragrant bloom often used for weddings, Bouvardia seems to have everything going for it. It has a characteristic scent, making it especially appealing for bouquet work and small arrangements. It has an incredibly long vase life of three weeks and is available year-round.

The flowers are delicate and grow in clusters. Each tubular Bouvardia blossom is star shaped. The flower is formed by a cluster of these regularly shaped stars and is set off by simple leaves, which make an excellent frame for the blossoms. Each flower in the cluster is about 1 inch in diameter. The Bouvardia blossom comes in shades of white, pink, salmon and red.

Historically, the Bouvardia was known for its curative abilities. It was named in honor of Dr. Charles Bouvard, who was the physician to King Louis XII. He created hundreds of different medicines using the flower. The King thought this flower was responsible for his long life. Symbolically, Bouvardia is welcome at weddings as brides and grooms are toasted for a long life. This extremely fragrant variety will last in excess of 2 weeks.

𝓒ALLA LILY

Although the Calla lily isn't really a lily, it shares many of the lily's qualities. It first became popular in the U.S. when Katherine Hepburn recited this famous movie line, "The Calla lilies are blooming again." The elegant Ms. Hepburn has long been associated with this traditional, long-lasting and elegant flower, which is grown primarily in England and Holland.

Calla lilies, botanically named Zantedeschia, are named after an Italian botanist Zantedeschi, who discovered them in South Africa. They were given the name "calla" from the Greek word "Kallos," meaning beautiful.

Sitting regally above its 2-3 foot stalk, the Calla is an extremely decorative flower. Its trumpet-like shape captivates the eye and is frequently used in wedding receptions and at the church to herald the bride.

Calla lilies are available year-round in white, yellow, red and pink coloration. Although they are dominating in appearance, their scent is insignificant.

$\mathcal{C}$ARNATIONS

Even the most demanding bride will be satisfied by the vast selection of Carnations available. No other flower offers a better selection of colors, shades and types. The botanical name for Carnation is Dianthus. Appropriately, this name translates from the Greek as "divine flower." It is the perfect flower for such a divine event as a wedding ceremony or reception. Available year-round in every size, from standard to giant to mini-spray Carnations, they are extremely popular. First discovered on the west coast of Europe, Carnations truly bloomed as a favorite when they were brought to America in the early 1900s. Fascinated by its exceedingly large variety, Americans adopted the flower as their own, and Europeans soon began referring to it as the "American Carnation."

Through breeding techniques, the variations of this sweet smelling flower were so great that their numbers swelled by the dozens each year. Available in either full-size or miniature varieties, Carnations are grown in large numbers in California, Holland and South America and are available year-round. Because of their abundance, except for rare varieties, they will be affordable on any wedding budget. Each stem contains multiple flowers which makes them even more attractive from an economic as well as a visual standpoint. Carnations are commonly used to frame the walkway in the church, as a bridal canopy, as boutonnieres, and in floral arrangements. One note of caution: avoid placing Carnation arrangements next to buffet displays of fruit or vegetables as the flower is quite sensitive to the gasses they emit.

$\mathcal{C}$HRYSANTHEMUM

The Chrysanthemum, or Mum, is one of the most abundant and popular flowers in the world. One can trace its origin to the western part of Russia. The botanical and the common name are identical and come from the Latin word meaning "yellow flower." Although yellow Chrysanthemum are among the most common color, they are available in many different colors as well as color combinations. The giant version of the flower is also referred to as a Pom Pom and is the flower of choice at football games.

Available year-round in a multitude of shapes and sizes, the Chrysanthemum is a preferred flower at weddings. A white variety, the "Marguerite," was used by French, Italian and English royalty at weddings to signify that the choice of bride by the groom was purely correct. In the U.S., two varieties with special meaning names, the "Happy" and the "Funshine," are frequently chosen for table decorations and wedding aisle arrangements.

The shapes of the Mum vary from puff-ball to daisy-like, tubular, and spider-like varieties. Even though many different colored Mums can be obtained from a florist, the hearty nature of Chrysanthemum makes it possible for the flowers to be successfully dyed to match a particular wedding color scheme. Except for Mums that are dyed, arrangements usually last 2 to 3 weeks after the final toast to the bride and groom.

CELOSIA

The Celosia is known by many names in many lands. It is sometimes called a Crested Cocks-comb; sometimes a Burnt Plume; a Plume Celosia; a Chinese Wool Flower or a Plumed Brain Flower...the latter because its ruffled flowers resemble the focal point of the mind. This flower was first used at weddings to symbolize the joining of one's mind to one's mate.

The foliage comes in deep shades of orange, red, yellow, purple and creamy white. The flame varieties appear as compact spikes, while the cockscomb varieties have compact heads like the comb on a rooster's head. The coarse flowers sit atop a thick, fleshy stalk and become the focal point of any arrangement in which they are included. The heads of the flowers are 2-8 inches across and, when cut to size, they make an exciting and attractive decoration for the bride and groom's place setting. After the wedding, they can easily be dried and kept as a remembrance.

These flowers first originated in Africa, but the first known cultivated varieties came from Japan. They are available from May until September. They have no scent and are best used at indoor functions since they have a tendency to react to atmospheric differences and spot easily.

DAFFODIL

Daffodil, although common, is unusual in that its common name and its scientific name, Narcissus, are equally well known by the general public. Legend has it that the name of the flower comes from a youth who was so in love with his own beauty that the gods turned him into this beautiful Narcissus flower. To this day, self love is still referred to by the term "narcissistic." You can find Daffodils in white, pink and multi-colors; the overwhelming majority, however, are yellow.

The flower is trumpet shaped with star-like petals projecting from the center. Its leaves are strap-shaped. You are best off getting your Daffodils from a greenhouse. An easy way to tell if your Daffodils are from a greenhouse is that greenhouse grown Narcissus are generally delivered with their leaves, while field grown are typically delivered without their leaves.

In planning wedding arrangements, remember that this flower is quite fragrant so make sure it is placed in areas where it will not conflict with other aromas. The "Paper White" variety is very attractive, but be aware that this particular variety has an extremely pungent odor. Another word of caution: the stems tend to get slimy in water, but this can easily be counteracted with preservative. Daffodils generally last more than a week. Although some varieties are available between November and April, keep in mind that this sunny yellow bulb flower is least expensive during its growing season in the Spring.

DAHLIA

The Dahlia was first discovered in the plains of Mexico nearly 400 years ago, where it was called acoctli. Although quite beautiful in appearance, nothing was done to bring about its cultivation until 200 years later. At that time, botanical experts in Mexico sent a gift of Dahlia seeds to the royal gardens in Madrid where they were cultivated and given as a gift to the wife of the Mexican ambassador to the Spanish court.

The flower was named in honor of a noted botanical author from Sweden, A. Dahl. Dahlias immediately became popular for use in royal functions, and members of the royal court sought them out to establish their position in society.

Dahlias have a strong, spicy smell and are available in a broad range of shapes, from fluffy to cactus to pom-pom to peony flower. Most of the Dahlias today are cultivated in Holland, but Californians have recently become more interested in developing hybrids. Dahlias are increasingly available from July through November.

Dahlias come in a variety of colors that include purple, lavender, red, yellow, pink and even bronze and white. The newest varieties include two-tone flowers. Dahlias measure 4-8 inches across and sit on stems that are 1-3 feet in length. When the Dahlia is in full bloom, it makes an excellent decorative hair piece or bridal bouquet adornment. Its average vase life is 1-2 weeks. These flowers are similar in appearance to Chrysanthemums and, when feasible, may be used in their place in arrangements.

DELPHINIUM

A summer wedding is the perfect time to feature Delphinium. Although most varieties are available year-round, all varieties are readily available from June through November. Also known as Larkspur, this multi-bloomed flower is regal yet soft in appearance. It has spike-shaped flower clusters of 1-2 inch disc shaped flowers towering in 8-20 inch spikes on stems 1 1/2 to 4 feet long. Useful alone in vases or for decoration, they will last at least one week. They are popularly used in Flemish-style bouquets.

A perfect variety for an "old fashioned wedding" theme, Delphinium originated in Asia, although today they can be found in cultivation on most continents. Delphinium consolida was named by the Greeks after the god of the city of Delphi. In Greek, Consolida means "to strengthen" which adds meaning to a wedding where one hopes the matrimonial bond will strengthen the betrothed's commitment to each other.

Pink, white and blue varieties are the most dominant and most traditional, although red and mixed types can also be obtained. One of the pink varieties, the "Princess Caroline," so named because it was used at Princess Caroline of Monaco's wedding, is characterized by outstanding uniformity in both color and length. Like other pure and hybrid varieties, these Delphinium have no scent.

EUCALYPTUS

The common name "Eucalyptus" is the same as its botanical name. There are several varieties of Eucalyptus available in either a green-gray or blue-green color. All are very aromatic. "Silver Dollar" is the type of Eucalyptus traditionally used at weddings. Romantics believe that placing branches of this tree at a wedding will bring good fortune to the newlyweds.

Eucalyptus originated in Australia. It is available year-round and makes an interesting setting for many other varieties of flowers. Today Eucalyptus is cultivated primarily in the United States and Israel. Eucalyptus oil was historically used in medication. It is considered good luck to have it at weddings as a symbol that the couple will enjoy good health together.

FREESIA

Freesia is one of the most popular flowers, possibly because it is so distinctive. The flower was named after a German doctor, F.F. Freese, who discovered it in Cape Colony in South Africa.

Freesia have long, narrow sword-shaped leaves which grow in two rows. The flower stalk is branched with 8-14 flowers growing from the top of the stalk at a 90 degree angle, forming a comb. Some compare this comb of flowers to a wedding party, with the two largest blooms signifying the bride and groom and the remaining buds the attendants.

A note of caution: handle Freesia delicately. Like a bride, they must be treated gently and with respect if they are to flourish.

You can determine how fresh your Freesia is by the numbers of flowers along the comb that are open. Remember, for a wedding it is best to have your flowers at their fullest bloom on that day. This is one flower that appreciates some sugar in its water. Freesia can last for more than 2 weeks.

Freesia come in a wide palette of colors and are available throughout the year. White and yellow varieties predominate, although Freesia are also available in shades of blue, red, purple, orange and pink. Freesia are often added to other, larger flowers in long cascading bouquets. Its blooms can also be separated and wired to headpieces or used in tight cluster designs.

GARDENIA

If ever there was a flower suited for a wedding party corsage, it is the Gardenia. Its small and spotless white blooms appear to have been strategically placed against shiny leaves. This flower is dainty enough to complement any member of the bridal group's gown but impressive enough to make a statement. The fragrance of the Gardenia flower is jasmine-like and projects a pleasant but not overpowering scent. Some bridal parties also use potted Gardenia plants to set off the tables on which the reception seating arrangement cards are placed.

The Gardenia was discovered in Asia by botanist A. Garden who brought them with him to England in the mid-1700s. Although these flowers are somewhat available in all parts of the world throughout the year, the great majority of the cut flowers are used in America. Since Gardenias are primarily used in small personal carrying arrangements at weddings and then either pressed or dried as memories, their keeping time is unimportant.

GERBERA DAISY

The Gerbera Daisy is sometimes known as the African Daisy or Transvaal Daisy because of its origination in South Africa, where it was discovered by Dutch botanist Gronovius in 1737. He named the Gerbera in honor of his Danish colleague Traugott Gerber. The flower is very similar in appearance to a field daisy but comes in a large variety of colors and sizes. The most popular colors are yellow, red, orange, pink, white and two tone. There are more than 41 different varieties available from Holland throughout the year.

With their bright and splashy appearance, Gerbera are wonderful for informal weddings. Because of their broad range of sizes from standard to micro to mini, they are particularly attractive in table arrangements. One intriguing new standard variety is the "Fire Ball" which has a two foot stem, is almost 5 inches in diameter and appears to be an amazing mass of orange flames. Since Gerbera have a long vase life of 2 to 3 weeks, wedding party guests can enjoy them long after the wedding.

GLADIOLUS

This flower adds majesty to any large arrangement at a wedding. Gladiolus are often used in tall fabric covered vases to line the bridal aisle to the altar. Since they have no scent, they make excellent decorative flowers to enhance the look of food serving areas at the reception. Experienced floral designers can also take individual blooms from the Gladiolus and create a camellia-like flower known as a "glamellia" for use as corsages and boutonnieres.

The species was discovered growing wild in Africa. It was brought back to Europe in bulb form by amateur horticulturists and was later improved and domesticated by professional breeders. Today, the Gladiolus is known as a Glad in some parts of the USA and as a Sword Lily in other areas.

The color palette of the flower and its gradations of shading are so varied that it can easily fit into any wedding color scheme. You can choose from reds, whites, yellows, pinks, violets, orange and purple varieties. The flowers grow in clusters up its sword-like stem, with the larger flowers appearing closer to the bottom. This makes it an excellent flower for table settings since the beauty of the flower can easily be enjoyed at eye level. Glads are available year-round but are most plentiful in the summer.

*I*RIS

The Iris, in its undeveloped form, was discovered in Africa in the late-1800s. However, once it was brought to Holland and cross hybridized, it truly took a position in the world of flowers. That importance was recognized in the scientific name given to the flower Iris Hollandica. The name Iris itself translates into "rainbow," as strong multiple colors are among the flower's top notes of interest.

The Iris has an unusual leaf-colored stem that runs up its entire 2 foot stem. Atop this stem is a single blossom which features turned back petals and a contrasting color comb. Dutch Iris will keep for an entire week. The most popular Iris is of a blazing dark blue color, however there is growing interest in the yellow, white and two-tone varieties. Make note of the strength of color in buying Iris. If the color is faint, it may indicate that the buds will have difficulty opening in time for the ceremony.

There are many legends surrounding the significance of Iris at weddings. Perhaps the most interesting is that a blue Iris and a white Iris were placed in a bud vase at the bride's table to remind her that her marriage would have both vibrant and pale times. It is said that this started the traditional pledge that marriages are for better or for worse.

*L*IATRIS

The Liatris grows to as much as 16 inches and features a lavender-pink flower. The flower spike is tube-like and opens from the top down. Depending on where in the United States you are from, the Liatris is also called a Gayfeather, a Blazing Star, or a Button Snakeroot. The flower was originally grown in the eastern section of America but was formally cultivated in England around 1734.

The vertical erectness of the Liatris and its long vase life of about 2 weeks make this flower popular for vase and floral arrangements at weddings. The Liatris is odorless and best used in modern floral arrangements.

*L*ILIES (ASIATIC AND ORIENTAL)

No flower is more frequently used at weddings than this hybrid. These lilies were originally found in China and Japan. The first known use of lilies at weddings was by the Ming dynasty in China.

Asiatics come in a wider color selection than the Orientals. These include yellow, pink, peach, ivory and white as well as combinations of these colors. The Asiatic is smaller than the Oriental lily, although each contains 3-7 flowers per stem.

Two of the most popular lilies are the "Stargazer" and the "Casablanca." The "Stargazer" is noted for its red accent marks which highlight the white throat of this orchid-like flower. The "Casablanca" is a huge white flower which takes its name from the Spanish "Casa" (house) and "Blanca" (white). They are found throughout the world.

Lilies are strongly scented. The Oriental hybrids are more heavily scented than the Asiatic varieties. One must be careful to keep them separate and apart from other fragrant flowers. They are versatile enough to be used in bouquets, floral arrangements, altar decorations and church aisle decorations.

There are over 4,000 different lily varieties. Among the new popular varieties used in American weddings is the "La Rive" which has a very soft pink coloration. White lilies are often used as a single flower placed upon a white wedding Bible. Because they vary so greatly in color and are available to some extent throughout the year, there is a lily for every bride.

Warning: Put a protective shield under the lily when using them as corsages. The anthers which project from the center of the flower will easily stain fabric. It is safest to remove the anther prior to using them in this manner.

LILY OF THE VALLEY

Wedding Bells traditionally proclaim a marriage. Perhaps this explains why the Lily of the Valley is found at most weddings. It is popularly used in bridal bouquets and other arrangements because its flowers are reminiscent of wedding bells. Like a bride and groom, its oval basal leaves stand in pairs around a pendulous stalk. The flower cluster of 4-10 white, bell-shaped blooms sits atop the stalk much as church bells are at the top of the steeple.

Botanically known as Convallaria majalis, this delicate looking perennial was first seen growing in Western Europe in May, 1420. This makes sense since May is the only month in which it blooms naturally. Today most of the supply is still from Western Europe, however current technology permits bridal parties to obtain it year round.

If Lily of the Valley is to be used in vases, it is best to put the whole flower, including the roots, in the water. This will allow you to enjoy it for about 5 days.

LISIANTHUS

Lisianthus is more commonly referred to as Eustoma. Part of its appeal is its large size. In fact, its very name means wide open mouth. The 4 petaled blossom presents itself in a saucer shape with a single stamen and seed capsule apparent in its center. The ornamental flower sits atop a 30-32 inch stem with opposing oval leaves. Some are single flowered varieties, others double.

The Eustoma found its way to Europe and the United States from Japan. It is available in dark purple, pink, white and two-tone. The flowers make a dramatic addition to arrangements. Since each flower is very large, just a few can add drama to entry way and table displays. While most varieties are available from May through December, some varieties, such as "Dark Blue Fuji," can be obtained year-round. Lisianthus can last from 3-4 weeks.

Narcissus

See description for daffodil.

Nerine

The Nerine, also known as the Spider Lily, is primarily available in pink, although it is also available in red, orange and white. It is a bulbous plant which originated in the coastal regions of South Africa. Its botanical name is after the Greek sea-god, Nereus. Legend has it that the bulb was placed aboard ships to be traded and that some of them were hijacked to the Isle of Guernsey where they proliferate today.

The leaves of Nerine are about 10 inches long. The average 16 inch flower stalk bears a cluster of 6-10 trumpet-shaped blooms with rather undulating flower lobes. Each flower is 1-3 inches in diameter.

As a complete flower, Nerine's height, erectness, and rather open, airy appearance make it a good choice for those wishing a more contemporary look to their wedding design. Individually, its flowers can be used for corsages for the wedding party. It is available year- round. The flowers last for more than one week.

The most popular varieties are "Favoriet" and "Pink Triumph." Perhaps the Nerine is used to symbolize the triumph of the young girl winning her favorite guy.

Orchid (CATTLEYA)

The variety of orchid most commonly seen in the United States is a hybrid called Cattleya. Named after a British merchant, the Cattleya is a relatively expensive and fragile flower. For this reason, it has traditionally been reserved for very special occasions, such as weddings, where it is commonly used as the focal point for the bridal bouquet or as a corsage for the mother of the bride and the mother of the groom.

Native to South America and grown worldwide today, this variety is available year-round in lavender, white, yellow and orange. The flower itself makes a statement. Its lip, with beautiful markings, is usually a darker color than the other petals.
The flower grows on a stalk that is 4-6 inches in length, although most times the stem is cut and the flower is worn as a corsage. Since the flower itself is about 8 inches in diameter, it can be

worn alone and still look impressive. Although orchids can last about a week, they are sensitive to damaging.

ORCHID (CYMBIDIUM)

There are many varieties of orchids. Some varieties, such as the Cymbidium and Dendrobian, are very versatile. Both are excellent for arrangements, corsages and bouquets. Cymbidiums are particularly spectacular when used in a hand-tied bouquet or in a slight cascade for the bridal attendants. The regal Dendrobian works well when incorporated into the ceremony design.

Cymbidium orchids are ancestors of the orchid hybrids. They come in both large and small flowered varieties. Large flowered varieties originated in Burma, India and the Himalayas while small flowered varieties are native to Taiwan and China. The Dendrobian orchid was originally discovered in Australia and eastern Indonesia.

Cymbidiums stand 12-32 inches high. Large flowered varieties carry 8-18 flowers on the stem, each measuring 4-6 inches in diameter, while 2/3 of the stem of the small flowered varieties is crowded with flowers. Dendrobian orchid stalks are at least a foot long and each contains 8-12 flowers measuring 3 1/2 to almost 5 inches in diameter. This variety is butterfly shaped on a long stem. The flower is generally lavender or white.

Available year-round, Cymbidium and Dendrobian orchids have no scent. In order to ensure a 2-5 week life for Cymbidiums, they should be kept out of the sun. Dendrobians are particularly sensitive to pollution. They last 8-12 days.

PEONY

Peonies give spring weddings a unique, elegant look and aroma. The cultivation of peonies began in China more than 1,000 years ago; however, its name is derived from the doctor of the Greek gods and alludes to its medicinal qualities.

There is only a six week window, between May and June, during which Peonies can be purchased, although this time frame is expanding somewhat. Its limited availability period adds to its uniqueness in wedding centerpiece arrangements. Its soft yet elegant composition imparts dignity and femininity to wedding designs. Peonies retain their beauty for up to 2 weeks.

Peonies are usually double flowered with a diameter of about 6 inches. The 30 varieties generally available are most popularly found in white, red and pink. By far the most popular peony is the pink "Sarah Bernhardt," which accounts for half of all peonies. Other popular varieties are the white "Shirley Temple," the bright pink "Dr. Arthur Fleming," and the red "Karl Rosenfield." The white "Duchesse de Nemours" variety has a strong fragrance. New early flowering varieties are being introduced in salmon-orange, orange-red and cream-white. These too are named for famous people.

𝓟INCUSHION

The Pincushion Flower is so-named because its center appears to be a pincushion filled with pins. A perennial summer bloom, it contains 3 inch round flowers on 2 foot long stems. At one time the flower stems were weak, impacting their usability, but this problem has been overcome through breeding.

Its botanical name, Scabiosa, derives from the skin disease "scabies" for which it was thought to be a remedy. Originally cultivated in the Mediterranean regions, it requires a temperate climate or summer temperatures. Perhaps part of its decorative appeal is that it is available for only 3-4 months of the year.

Scabiosa is primarily purchased in shades of lavender blue, violet blue and white, although it originally was found naturally in a crimson color. The flower has a frilly looking petal which is very feminine. It is frequently used in table arrangements because of its pleasing shape and striking blue color. It has no scent. Its vase life is 3-7 days.

𝓟ROTEA

Brides and grooms are the king and queen of their night. Perhaps this is well symbolized by using Protea in wedding arrangements. The king Protea (cynaroides) and queen Protea (magnifica) are large, with well-formed flower heads. As with people, the king is often taller than his queen; the king achieving 2-3 feet in length and the queen 1 1/2 to 2 feet. There are also smaller varieties.

A Protea is a Honeypot or Sugar bush. It is a woody plant which was originally cultivated in Australia, Israel and southern parts of Africa. Its leaves are simple and alternate. The shape of the flower is irregular with 4 external segments which grow alternately with the petals. The flowers are somewhat arched inwards. The center is double and surrounded by hairy bracts. Some varieties are black topped. Some have a woolly appearance.

The long-lasting Protea makes a dramatic statement when used in low table arrangements. They are most appropriately used in contemporary wedding design. Protea's eye-catching appeal will be wasted if your arrangement is elevated, as its beauty lies in its compact form and coloration, which is best appreciated at low levels.

𝓠UEEN ANNE'S LACE

The name says it all. Delicate and lacy, Queen Anne's Lace looks like the lace used in bridal gown design. It is a white, flat flower comprised of hundreds of small florets on a straight 1 1/2 to 3 foot stem. Actually, it is a summer wildflower that grows in the field, and most florists do not carry it. But do not gather it directly from a field as it may bear chiggers or other small critters. Once picked, it has a life-span of only about 3 days. Apart from informal wildflower arrangements, it can also be used in the hair to complement the wedding gown.

*R*ANUNCULUS

A Ranunculus is like a very full peony. This early spring flower originated in the Persian Gulf and is sometimes called a Persian Buttercup or Iranian Peony. The Ranunculus name is from the latin rana, meaning "frog." It was so named because the flower grows best in swampy areas.

This flower is extremely full and tightly packed with petals. It is available in multiple shades of orange, red, pink, yellow and white.

Ranunculus are up to 4 inches across and sit on 10-18 inch stems. The flower was frequently used by Persian shahs to decorate the bridal suite. These brightly colored, unscented flowers will last more than a week with proper care.

*R*OSES

No flower symbolizes love more than the rose, making it the perfect wedding flower. Fittingly, among the more than 130 popular varieties are the "Bridal Pink," "Darling," "Kiss," "Flirt" and "Only Love."

Many varieties are named for women, although roses today are often given to men by women as a symbol of their love. Perhaps due to their names, " Purple Prince" and "Idole" are popular choices for men. Rose varieties can be categorized as large flowered, medium flowered, small flowered or cluster. Some are heavily scented; some moderately; some lightly and some have no scent at all. Depending upon the variety, roses can last up to 3 weeks.

The rose is from the family Rosaceae. It is naturally a prickly shrub with feathery leaves and showy flowers having five petals in the wild state but often being doubled or partly doubled under cultivation. The thorns on the stalks vary depending on the variety. The stalk length runs between 12 inches and 40 inches, depending upon variety and quality. The leaves are compound and may consist of five leaflets. They can be obtained in reds, pinks, salmon, orange, lavender, cream, white and two-tone colors.

Some rose varieties were first seen in Asia; others in Central Europe, the Middle East and Asia Minor. They can easily be used for any phase of wedding design: altar and church decorations, corsages and bouttonieres, hand bouquets, and centerpieces. Roses can be used to complement any wedding decor. For example, the "Porcelina" rose, which is a large, ivory colored flower, can be used to create an elegant bridal bouquet, eliciting a formal atmosphere.

The softly-colored "Champagne" rose, singly wrapped in a napkin at each dinner plate, is a nice touch to symbolize your affection and appreciation for your guests. Warning: make sure to remove all thorns!

So remember, when you want to have a perfect wedding, make sure to seal your vows with a kiss...a "Kiss" rose!

Saponaria

The name of this flower is derived from the Latin word for soap because the sap of the plant is said to have a cleansing effect. It was originally used in weddings as a sign that the bride was cleansed or pure.

Although first found in the Mediterranean region, Saponaria today is primarily field grown in The Netherlands. It is a very delicate, small flower on long, flowing stems. It is used as a filler in bouquets because of the abundance of flowers on each stalk. Deep pink is the most commonly used variety, but it is also available in pure white. Both its colors and its delicate scent make this flower popular for use in weddings. It is only available in June, July and August, but the flower can be forced indoors for weddings in late May.

Snapdragon

The botanical name for Snapdragon is Antirrhinum majus. It originated in the Mediterranean region of France and Spain more than 400 years ago. It is now one of the most popular flowers around. The flowers sit in graduated clusters atop a spike that is between 8 and 12 inches in length and along a stem that can grow as long as 45 inches. Snapdragons are available in shades of red, orange, lavender, pink, salmon and white. They have no scent.

Because of their abundance of color and their vertical shape, Snapdragons are extremely useful in vase arrangements. These flowers are readily available in May and June and then again in late summer until the end of October. Snapdragons can also be found in limited supply in late winter and early spring. Properly cared for, they can last about a week.

Note of warning: these flowers require sufficient water supply at all times. They are also extremely sensitive to ethylene gas and should be kept far away from fruits and vegetables on food table displays. If kept too close, they will start to drop their buds on the table.

Speedwell

The scientific name of Speedwell is Veronica longifolia. It's a very old plant and the first record of its cultivation was in Switzerland/France in the mid 1500's.

The flower itself is primarily blue and grows cone-shaped sitting above heart-shaped leaves. It must be carefully cared for, otherwise it has the tendency to dry out and become limp. There are some pink and white varieties grown in Virginia. These flowers have the same tendency to dry out and must be carefully pre-treated.

Speedwell is available only in the heat of the summer. The flower is primarily used in mixed bouquets and basic floral arrangements. The Veronica longifolia has a limited vase life of about 5 days.

STAR OF BETHLEHEM

The Star of Bethlehem, botanically known as Ornithogalum, features white flowers with either a white-green or a black-grey center. A series of 2 dozen or more flowers sit pyramid shape atop a stem that is approximately 15 inches long. These flowers originated in Africa but were formally cultivated in Holland 450 years ago.
The Star of Bethlehem was so named because it reminded the priests of flowers that were found in churches of the sacred city of Bethlehem. In medieval times this flower was used to signify the religious commitment of the bride to the groom.

The Star of Bethlehem was a rarely used flower until about 50 years ago, when florists discovered that its flowers easily adapted to dying in a variety of shades. These flowers are strong, and will maintain their presence for up to a month. Although this flower is normally long lived, it is particularly sensitive to fruits and vegetables. Therefore it is advisable not to use it on tables that feature edibles. These flowers look particularly nice in small bud vases and are frequently used to decorate cocktail tables.

STATICE

Statice or limonium gives the appearance of a sea of color. Perhaps that is why it is also known as Sea Lavender. Statice used to be predominantly yellow, but today most varieties are seen in shades of blue. They are also available in purple, lavender, white, and pink.

Statice originated in Turkestan and areas in the Mediterranean. Botanically, blue Sea Lavender is called Statice perezii. It was named after the Dutch baron P.J.R. de Perez who was Governor of the Dutch West Indies 1803-1859. This variety is distinguished by its smooth, bare foot stalk, comprised of multi-branching stems of small, star-shaped flower clusters.

The other major variety consists primarily of purple flowers with a splash of white. Both are used as filler flowers in large arrangements and are the perfect addition to any natural-looking wedding design. Statice lasts about 2 weeks and dries well, so the bride can have a beautiful keepsake of her wedding. It is available year-round.

STEPHANOTIS

Pure white and fragrant, this traditional wedding flower has been used in bridal bouquets, corsages, and wedding decorations for centuries. Sometimes referred to as Madagascar Jasmine, it is delicately fragranced and has a pure white waxy color. Although it is relatively expensive and must be handled carefully to avoid bruising, Stephanotis is perfect for wedding use any time of the year.

Originally from Madagascar and first introduced in England at the beginning of the 19th century, Stephanotis is actually an evergreen climbing shrub with long tendrils and shiny dark green leaves that average 2 1/2 inches. Each star shaped flower cluster is formed from five tips of petals sitting atop a tube which protrudes from a short stem. Each individual flower itself is under two inches.

Stock

Stock traces its origins to ancient times. This extremely fragrant, spiked flower has a hairy clustered appearance. The flowers are available in white, red, pink, salmon, lavender and yellow. It is extremely useful in mixed bridal bouquets and large arrangements because its blooms are so tightly packed. A skilled floral designer can also transform this inexpensive flower into a wisteria-looking vine to drape an arch or trellis.

Stock, also called Gillyflowers, are botanically identified as Matthiola. They are available throughout most of the year, with lesser amounts of the assortment during the Thanksgiving and Christmas seasons. Matthiola will last at least one week.

Sunflower

Americans have fallen in love with sunflowers. Botanically, a sunflower is called Helianthus, coming from the Greek words "Helio," meaning sun, and "Anthos," meaning flowers.

The flower is self descriptive. From its dark colored center, yellow ray-like petals project out much like the sun's rays. Helianthus is one of the few major flowers that found its origin in the United States. These flowers grow wild in the southwest and are now professionally cultivated throughout the world.

Giant varieties can have flower heads that are 15 inches in diameter. Because of their huge size, giant helianthus are best suited to single placement or in large arrangements. Smaller varieties measuring 3-4 inches across make excellent filler and can be worn in the hair during informal ceremonies. These fragrant-free flowers will last up to 12 days.

Sweet Pea

This vividly colored, climbing flower is a native of Italy. Its scientific name is Lathyrus. Since its colors are strong oranges, lilacs and purples and its flowers are extremely fragrant, Italian royalty used this as part of the altar setting at weddings. One common variety identifies this wedding connection through the name "Royal Family."

Once the flowers were cultivated professionally, breeders eliminated much of their scent. Now smaller Sweet Peas have absolutely no fragrance. Most varieties of Sweet Peas are readily available in the spring.

TUBEROSE

Often confused with Snapdragon, Tuberose is a small, rose-like bud flower which grows atop 3 foot long stems. This flower has many fragrant florets which grow and open from the bottom up and look a bit like stephanotis. The maximum size of each white, star-shaped flower is 2 1/2 inches when fully opened.

Tuberose originated in southern Mexico and is now grown primarily in Israel, Africa and the south of France. An extremely fragrant flower, it is frequently used for corsages and small bouquets. It can also be used to decorate small cocktail tables at the wedding reception.

In fact, Tuberose flowers are so fragrant that they are greatly in demand by the perfume industry in France. Due to their limited availability and perfume industry demands, they can be quite expensive.

TULIPS

For variety of shape and color, few flowers surpass the tulip. Hundreds of species of tulips originally grew wild in Turkey and Iran. They were first formally cultivated in The Netherlands in the 1500's.
At one time this flower was so highly valued that it was used as money. At that period of time, extremely wealthy Holland traders used tulips at weddings as a sign of affluence.

Botanically called "Tulipa," its name is derived from the turban shape of the flower. Today there are thousands of different species available at different times of the year. They are cupped, fringed, spiked, single-colored, multicolored, large and small. All are stately adornments in large and small floral arrangements.

A popular and yet unusual tulip is the "Parakeet" tulip which has irregularly shaped, two-tone streaked petals on flowers that are so large that they have to be braced so as not to collapse their stems. Another is the "Kees Nelis Triumph" tulip which features a dramatic red cup petal that appears to change instantly into a flaming yellow border. Since tulips are available in greatest abundance in the spring, they are sought after as wedding decor to symbolize a new beginning.

Since limited life span does not adversely affect wedding use, the tulip is a wedding standard. However, their hollow stems restrict them to floral designs with a water source. A special note of care: avoid mixing tulips with daffodils in the same arrangement. These flowers are allergic to each other.

WAXFLOWER

The waxflower, or Chamelaucium ciliatum, is sometimes known as the Pink Tea Tree. It is a very small, light, airy flower with a diameter that is less than an inch. Each branching stem contains a lot of buds. Its foliage is needle-like.

Because of the delicate nature of its flowers, the Waxflower is frequently used as filler in floral design. Its primary use is in bouquets and as decoration for a bridal table. It is available in pink, lavender and white. It is available starting in December and may be easily obtained through the end of May.

Historically, the waxflower was used as a setting for tea service when the bride-to-be was first introduced formally to the groom's parents.

Allium sphaerocephalon
drumstick Allium

Alstroemeria hybrid
Peruvian lily

Alstroemeria hybrid
Peruvian lily

Alstroemeria hybrid
Peruvian lily

Amaryllis belladonna
belladonna lily

Anemone coronaria
'Mona Lisa' group
Anemone

Aster hybrid
Butterfly series

Callistephus chinensis
'Matsumoto'
Matsumoto **Aster**

Gypsophila paniculata
'Gilboa'
baby's breath

Gypsophila paniculata
miniature **baby's breath**

Centaurea cyanus
bachelor's button

Craspedia globosa
billy buttons

Strelitzia reginae
bird of paradise

Bouvardia hybrid
'Lady Stephanie'

Bouvardia ternifolia
Bouvardia

Zantedeschia elliottiana
yellow mini-**calla**

Zantedeschia rehmannii
burgundy mini-**calla**

Zantedeschia aethiopica
'Alba'
calla

Dianthus caryophyllus
hybrid 'Tapestry'
carnation

Dianthus caryophyllus
nana 'Porcelain'
miniature **carnation**

Chrysanthemum
frutescens
marguerite daisy

Chrysanthemum
morifolium
'Westland Yellow'

Chrysanthemum
morifolium 'Red Rover'
red rover mum

Chrysanthemum
morifolium
'Statesman'

Celosia argentea
v. cristata
crested cockscomb

Narcissus hybrid
daffodil

Dahlia hybrid
formal decorative Dahlia

Delphinium ajacis
pink larkspur

Delphinium
'belladonna' group

Delphinium hybrid
'Pacific Giant'
hybrid Delphinium

Eucalyptus polyanthemos
'Flat Seed'
silver dollar Eucalyptus

Freesia hybrid
pink

Freesia hybrid
red/rust

Freesia hybrid
white

Freesia hybrid
yellow

Gardenia jasminoides
Gardenia

Gerbera jamesonii
Germini 'Foxi'
mini Gerbera

Gerbera jamesonii
'Tamara'
Gerbera

Gerbera jamesonii
'Sensitive'
Gerbera

Gladiolus hybrid
gladiola

Gladiolus hybrid
gladiola

Gladiolus x. colvillei
mini glads

Iris hybrid
'Casa Blanca'
Iris

Iris hybrid
'Professor Blaauw'
Iris

Liatris callilepis
gayfeather

Lilium Asiatic hybrid
'Mercedes'
Asiatic **lily**

Lilium Asiatic hybrid
'Polyanne'
Asiatic **lily**

Lilium speciosum hybrid
'Casa Blanca'
Oriental **Lily**

Lilium speciosum hybrid
'Stargazer'
Oriental **lily**

Convallaria majalis
lily-of-the-valley

Eustoma grandiflorum
Echo series
double white **lisianthus**

Eustoma grandiflorum
pink **lisianthus**

Narcissus hybrid
'Paperwhite'
Paperwhites

Nerine bowdenii
Nerine

Cattleya x. hybrid
'Semi-Alba'
Cattleya **orchid**

Cattleya x. Japhette
Japhette **orchid**

Cymbidium
hybrid mini
mini-Cymbidium **orchid**

Cymbidium hybrid
Cymbidium **orchid**

Cymbidium hybrid
Cymbidium **orchid**

Phalaenopsis amabilis
Phalaenopsis **orchid**

Paeonia officinalis
hybrid
peony

Scabiosa caucasica
perennial **pincushion** flower

Protea cynaroides
King Protea

Protea magnifica
'Rose Queen'
Queen Protea

Ammi majus
Queen Anne's lace

Ranunculus asiaticus
Persian Ranunculus

Ranunculus asiaticus
Persian Ranunculus

Rosa hybrid
'Afterglow'
tea **rose**

Rosa hybrid
'Dolores'
tea **rose**

Rosa hybrid
'Kardinal'
tea **rose**

Rosa hybrid
'Lady Diane'
tea **rose**

Saponaria vaccaria
Saponaria

Antirrhinum majus
white **snapdragon**

Veronica longifolia
speedwell

Ornithogalum
umbellatum
star of Bethlehem

Limonium hybrid
'Misty' series
Misty white **statice**

Limonium sinuatum
blue **statice**

Stephanotis floribunda
Madagascar jasmine

Matthiola incana
lavender **stock**

Matthiola incana
peach **stock**

Matthiola incana
yellow **stock**

Helianthus annuus
'Sunbright'
sunflower

Helianthus annuus
sunflower

Lathyrus odoratus
sweet pea

Polianthes tuberosa
tuberose

Tulipa hybrid
purple **tulip**

Tulipa hybrid
'Flaming Parrot'
French parrot **tulip**

Tulipa hybrid
red **tulip**

Tulipa hybrid
white **tulip**

Chamelaucium uncinatum
'Purple Pride'
waxflower

TO LOVE SOMEONE DEEPLY GIVES

YOU STRENGTH

Lao Tzu

PHOTO: PAUL BARNETT

ECORATIONS

TABLE CENTERPIECES

Each of the tables at your reception, including the head table, should be decorated with a centerpiece.

Options: Candles, mirrors and flowers are popular choices for table centerpieces. However, the options are endless. Just be creative! An arrangement of shells, for example, makes a very nice centerpiece for a seaside reception. Votive candles set on top of a mirror make a romantic centerpiece for an evening reception.

A wreath of greenery woven with colored ribbon makes a delightful centerpiece. Use a different color ribbon at each table and have your guests seated according to ribbon color!

Things To Consider: Select a table centerpiece which complements your colors and/or setting. The centerpiece for the head table should be larger or more elaborate than for the other tables. Make sure that your centerpiece is kept low enough so as not to hinder conversation among guests seated across from each other. Consider using a centerpiece that your guests can take home as a memento of your wedding.

Tips To Save Money: Make your own table centerpieces using materials that are not expensive.

Price Range: $10 - $100

BALLOONS

Balloons are often used to decorate a reception site. A popular idea is to release balloons at the church or reception. This adds a festive, exciting, and memorable touch to your wedding. Balloons can be used to create an arch backdrop for the wedding cake or inexpensive centerpieces for the tables.

Things To Consider: Color coordinate your balloons to match your wedding color scheme. Choose colors from your bouquet or your bridesmaids' dresses. Balloons should be delivered and set-up well in advance — at least before the photographer shows up.

If you are planning to release balloons at the church or reception, check with your city. Releasing balloons in some cities might be illegal. Also make sure there are no wires where balloons can get entangled. If they do, you could be held responsible for damages or cleanup expenses.

Tips To Save Money: Balloons are less expensive than fresh flowers and can be used as a substitute for flowers to decorate the reception site.

Price Range: $75 - $500

WHERE YOU FIND TRUE FRIENDSHIP,
YOU FIND TRUE LOVE

Anonymous

T R A N S P O R T A T I O N

JUST MARRIED

*T*RANSPORTATION

*T*RANSPORTATION

It is customary for the bride and her father to ride to the ceremony site together on the wedding day. You may also include some or all members of your wedding party. Normally a procession to the church begins with the bride's mother and several of the bride's attendants in the first vehicle. If desired, you can provide a second vehicle for the rest of the attendants. The bride and her father will go in the last vehicle. This vehicle will also be used to transport the bride and groom to the reception site after the ceremony.

Options: There are various options for transportation. The most popular choice is a limousine since it is big and open and can accommodate several people as well as your bridal gown. You can also choose to rent a car that symbolizes your personality as a couple.

There are luxury cars such as Mercedes Benz, sports cars such as a Ferraris, and vintage vehicles such as 1950's Thunderbirds or 1930's Cadillacs. If your ceremony and reception sites are fairly close together, and if weather permits, you might want to consider a more romantic form of transportation, such as a horse-drawn carriage.

Things to Consider: In some areas of the country, limousines are booked on a 3-hour minimum basis.

Beware: Make sure the company you choose is fully licensed and has liability insurance. Do not pay the full amount until after the event.

Tips To Save Money: Consider hiring only one large limousine. This limousine can transport you, your parents and your attendants to the ceremony, and then you and your new husband from the ceremony to the reception.

Price Range: $35 - $100/hour

Transportation Comparison Chart

QUESTIONS	POSSIBILITY 1	POSSIBILITY 2
What is the name of the transportation service?		
What is the website & email address of the transportation service?		
What is the address of the transportation service?		
What is the name & phone number of my contact person?		
How many years have you been in business?		
How many vehicles do you have available?		
Can you provide a back-up vehicle in case of an emergency?		
What types of vehicles are available?		
What are the various sizes of vehicles available?		
How old are the vehicles?		
How many drivers are available?		
Can you show me photos of your drivers?		
How do your drivers dress for weddings?		
Do you have liability insurance?		
What is the minimum amount of time required to rent a vehicle?		
What is the cost per hour? Two hours? Three hours?		
What is your payment/cancellation policy?		

*T*RANSPORTATION *C*OMPARISON *C*HART

POSSIBILITY 3	POSSIBILITY 4	POSSIBILITY 5

$\mathcal{W}$EDDING $\mathcal{D}$AY $\mathcal{T}$RANSPORTATION

TO CEREMONY SITE

Name	Pickup Time	Pickup Location	Vehicle/Driver
Bride	_____	_____	_____
Groom	_____	_____	_____
Bride's Parents	_____	_____	_____
Groom's Parents	_____	_____	_____
Bridesmaids	_____	_____	_____
Ushers	_____	_____	_____
Other Guests	_____	_____	_____
Other Guests	_____	_____	_____

TO RECEPTION SITE

Name	Pickup Time	Pickup Location	Vehicle/Driver
Bride & Groom	_____	_____	_____
Bride's Parents	_____	_____	_____
Groom's Parents	_____	_____	_____
Bridesmaids	_____	_____	_____
Ushers	_____	_____	_____
Other Guests	_____	_____	_____

LOVE AND YOU SHALL
BE LOVED

Ralph Waldo Emerson

PHOTO: KAREN FRENCH

THANK YOU
for being a part
of this special day.
CRISTA & KEVIN
05·25·03

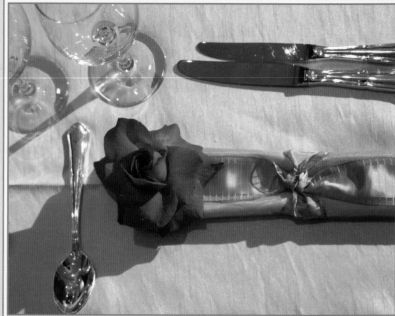

RENTAL ITEMS

RIDAL SLIP RENTAL

The bridal slip is an undergarment which gives the bridal gown its proper shape.

Things To Consider: Be sure to wear the same slip you'll be wearing on your wedding day during your fittings. Many bridal salons rent slips. Schedule an appointment to pick up your slip one week before the wedding; otherwise, you run the risk of not having one available on your wedding day. If rented, the slip will have to be returned shortly after the wedding. Arrange for someone to do this for you within the allotted time.

Tips To Save Money: Rent a slip rather than purchasing one; chances are you will never use it again.

Price Range: $25 - $75

CEREMONY ACCESSORIES

Ceremony rental accessories are additional items needed for the ceremony but not included in the ceremony site fee.

Options: Ceremony rental accessories may include the following items:

Aisle Runner: A thin rug made of plastic, paper or cloth extending the length of the aisle. It is rolled out after the mothers are seated, just prior to the processional. Plastic or paper doesn't work well on grass; but if you must use one of these types of runners, make sure the grass is clipped short.

Kneeling Cushion: A small cushion or pillow placed in front of the altar where the bride and groom kneel for their wedding blessing.

Arch (Christian):   A white lattice or brass arch where the bride and groom exchange their vows, often decorated with flowers and greenery.

Chuppah (Jewish):   A canopy under which a Jewish ceremony is performed, symbolizing cohabitation and consummation.

You may also need to consider renting audio equipment, aisle stanchions, candelabra, candles, candlelighters, chairs, heaters, a gift table, a guest book stand, and a canopy.

Things To Consider: If you plan to rent any accessories for your ceremony, make sure the rental supplier has been in business for a reasonable period of time and has a good reputation. Reserve the items you need well in advance. Find out the company's payment, reservation and cancellation policies.

Some companies allow you to reserve emergency items such as heaters or canopies without having to pay for them unless needed, in which case you would need to call the rental company a day or two in advance to request the items. If someone else requests the items you have reserved, the company should give you the right of first refusal.

Tips To Save Money: When considering a ceremony outside of a church, figure the cost of rental items. Negotiate a package deal, if possible, by renting items for both the ceremony and the reception from the same supplier. Consider renting these items from your florist so you only have to pay one delivery fee.

Price Range: $100 - $500

*T*ENT / CANOPY

A large tent or canopy may be required for receptions held outdoors to protect you and your guests from the sun or rain. Usually rented through party rental suppliers, tents and canopies can be expensive due to the labor involved in delivery and set-up.

Options: Tents and canopies come in different sizes and colors. Depending on the shape of your reception area, you may need to rent several smaller canopies rather than one large one. Contact several party rental suppliers to discuss the options.

Things To Consider: Consider this cost when making a decision between an outdoor and an indoor reception. In cooler weather, heaters may also be necessary.

Tips To Save Money: Shop early and compare prices with several party rental suppliers.

Price Range: $300 - $5,000

DANCE FLOOR

A dance floor will be provided by most hotels and clubs. However, if your reception site does not have a dance floor, you may need to rent one through your caterer or a party rental supplier.

Things To Consider: When comparing prices of dance floors, include the delivery and set-up fees.

Price Range: $100 - $600

TABLES / CHAIRS

You will have to provide tables and chairs for your guests if your reception site or caterer doesn't provide them as part of their package. For a full meal, you will have to provide tables and seating for all guests. For a cocktail reception, you only need to provide tables and chairs for approximately 30 to 50 percent of your guests. Ask your caterer or reception site manager for advice.

Options: There are various types of tables and chairs to choose from. The most common chairs for wedding receptions are white wooden or plastic chairs. The most common tables for receptions are round tables that seat 8 guests. The most common head table arrangement is several rectangular tables placed end-to-end to seat your entire wedding party on one side, facing your guests. Contact various party rental suppliers to find out what types of chairs and tables they carry as well as their price ranges.

Things To Consider: When comparing prices of renting tables and chairs, include the cost of delivery and set-up.

Tips To Save Money: Attempt to negotiate free delivery and set-up with party rental suppliers in exchange for giving them your business.

Price Range: $3 - $10/person

LINEN / TABLEWARE

You will also need to provide linens and tableware for your reception if your reception site or caterer doesn't provide them as part of their package.

Options: For a sit-down reception where the meal is served by waiters and waitresses, tables are usually set with a cloth (usually white, but may be color coordinated with the wedding), a centerpiece, and complete place settings. At a less formal buffet reception where guests serve themselves, tables are covered with a cloth but place settings are not mandatory. The necessary plates and silverware may be located at the buffet table, next to the food.

Things To Consider: Linens and tableware depend on the formality of your reception. When comparing prices of linens and tableware, include the cost of delivery and set-up.

Price Range: $3.00 - $25

*H*EATERS

You may need to rent heaters if your reception will be held outdoors and if the temperature may drop below sixty-five degrees.

Options: There are electric and gas heaters, both of which come in different sizes. Gas heaters are more popular since they do not have unsightly and unsafe electric cords.

Price Range: $25 - $75

*L*ANTERNS

Lanterns are often used at evening receptions.

Options: Many choices are available, from fire lanterns to electric ones.

Things To Consider: Consider the formality of the reception and choose the proper lighting to complement your decorations.

Price Range: $6.00 - $60/lamp

*O*THER RENTAL ITEMS (TRASH CANS, GIFT TABLE, ETC.)

If your reception site or caterer doesn't provide them, you will need to purchase, rent or borrow other miscellaneous items for your reception, such as trash cans, a gift table, trash bags, and so on.

PERSONAL NOTES

Rental Supplier Comparison Chart

QUESTIONS	POSSIBILITY 1	POSSIBILITY 2
What is the name of the party rental supplier?		
What is the website & email address of the party rental supplier?		
What is the address of the party rental supplier?		
What is the name & phone number of my contact person?		
How many years have you been in business?		
What are your hours of operation?		
Do you have liability insurance?		
What is the cost per item needed?		
What is the cost of pick-up and delivery?		
What is the cost of setting up the items rented?		
When would the items be delivered?		
When would the items be picked up after the event?		
What is your payment policy?		
What is your cancellation policy?		

RENTAL SUPPLIER COMPARISON CHART

POSSIBILITY 3	POSSIBILITY 4	POSSIBILITY 5

Ceremony Equipment Checklist

Rental Supplier _____   Contact Person _____

Address _____

Website _____   Email Address _____

Phone Number _____   Hours _____

Payment Policy _____

Cancellation Policy _____

Delivery Time _____   Tear Down Time _____

Setup Time _____   Pickup Time _____

QTY.	ITEM	DESCRIPTION	PRICE	TOTAL
_____	Arch/Altar	_____	_____	_____
_____	Canopy (Chuppah)	_____	_____	_____
_____	Backdrops	_____	_____	_____
_____	Floor Candelabra	_____	_____	_____
_____	Candles	_____	_____	_____
_____	Candlelighters	_____	_____	_____
_____	Kneeling Bench	_____	_____	_____
_____	Aisle Stanchions	_____	_____	_____
_____	Aisle Runners	_____	_____	_____
_____	Guest Book Stand	_____	_____	_____
_____	Gift Table	_____	_____	_____
_____	Chairs	_____	_____	_____
_____	Audio Equipment	_____	_____	_____
_____	Lighting	_____	_____	_____
_____	Heating/Cooling	_____	_____	_____
_____	Umbrellas/Tents	_____	_____	_____
_____	Bug Eliminator	_____	_____	_____
_____	Coat/Hat Rack	_____	_____	_____
_____	Garbage Cans	_____	_____	_____

𝓡ECEPTION 𝓔QUIPMENT 𝓒HECKLIST

Rental Supplier _____   Contact Person _____

Address _____

Website _____   Email Address _____

Phone Number _____   Hours _____

Payment Policy _____

Cancellation Policy _____

Delivery Time _____   Tear Down Time _____

Setup Time _____   Pickup Time _____

QTY.	ITEM	DESCRIPTION	PRICE	TOTAL
_____	Audio Equipment	_____	____	____
_____	Cake Table	_____	____	____
_____	Candelabras/Candles	_____	____	____
_____	Canopies	_____	____	____
_____	Coat/Hat Rack	_____	____	____
_____	Dance Floor	_____	____	____
_____	Bug Eliminator	_____	____	____
_____	Garbage Cans	_____	____	____
_____	Gift Table	_____	____	____
_____	Guest Tables	_____	____	____
_____	Heating/Cooling	_____	____	____
_____	High/Booster Chairs	_____	____	____
_____	Lighting	_____	____	____
_____	Mirror Disk Ball	_____	____	____
_____	Place Card Table	_____	____	____
_____	Tents	_____	____	____
_____	Umbrellas	_____	____	____
_____	Visual Equipment	_____	____	____
_____	Wheelchair Ramp	_____	____	____

Personal Notes

$\mathcal{G}$IFTS

$\mathcal{B}$RIDE'S GIFT

The bride's gift is traditionally given by the groom to the bride. It is typically a personal gift such as a piece of jewelry.

Options: A string of pearls, a watch, pearl earrings, or a gold chain with a heart-shaped charm holding photos of the two of you.

Things To Consider: This gift is not necessary and should be given only if budget allows.

Tips To Save Money: Consider omitting this gift. A pretty card from the groom proclaiming his eternal love for the bride is a very special yet inexpensive gift.

Price Range: $50 - $500

$\mathcal{G}$ROOM'S GIFT

The groom's gift is traditionally given by the bride to the groom.

Options: A nice watch, an elegant pen set, or a dramatic photo of the bride framed in silver or crystal.

Things To Consider: This gift is not necessary and should be given only if budget allows.

Tips To Save Money: Consider omitting this gift. A pretty card from the bride proclaiming her eternal love for the groom is a very special yet inexpensive gift.

Price Range: $50 - $500

BRIDESMAIDS' GIFTS

Bridesmaids' gifts are given by the bride to her bridesmaids and maid of honor as a permanent keepsake of the wedding. The best gifts are those that can be used both during and after the wedding, such as jewelry.

Options: For bridesmaids' gifts, consider items of jewelry that can be worn during the wedding to give your wedding party a coordinated and elegant look. Choose the collection that most fits your style, then select the type and color of stone to match the color of your flowers and/or bridesmaids dresses. We believe this is the perfect bridesmaids' gift!

Things To Consider: Bridesmaids' gifts are usually presented at the bridesmaids' luncheon, if there is one, or at the rehearsal dinner. The gift to the maid of honor may be similar to the bridesmaids' gifts but should be a bit more expensive.

Tips To Save Money: Ask your photographer to take, at no extra charge, professional portraits of each bridesmaid and her escort for use as bridesmaids' gifts. Select a beautiful background that will remind your bridesmaids of the occasion, such as your cake table. Put the photo in a pretty frame. This makes a very special yet inexpensive gift for your attendants.

Price Range: $25 - $200/gift

USHERS' GIFTS

Ushers' gifts are given by the groom to his ushers as a permanent keepsake of the wedding.

Options: For ushers' gifts, consider fancy pen sets, wallets, leather belts, silver frames, watches, and desk clocks.

Things To Consider: The groom should deliver his gifts to the ushers at the bachelor party or at the rehearsal dinner. The gift to the best man may be similar to the ushers' gifts but should be a bit more expensive.

Tips To Save Money: Negotiate with your photographer to take, at no extra charge, professional portraits of each usher and his escort for use as ushers' gifts. Select a beautiful background that will remind your ushers of the occasion, such as your cake table.

Price Range: $25 - 200/gift

PARTIES

BRIDESMAIDS' LUNCHEON

The bridesmaids' luncheon is given by the bride for her bridesmaids. It is not a shower; rather, it is simply a time for good friends to get together formally before the bride changes her status from single to married.

Things To Consider: You can give your bridesmaids their gifts at this gathering. Otherwise, plan to give them their gifts at the rehearsal dinner.

Price Range: $12 - $60/meal

REHEARSAL DINNER

It is customary that the groom's parents host a dinner party following the rehearsal, the evening before the wedding.   The dinner usually includes the bridal party, their spouses or guests, both sets of parents, close family members, the officiant, and the wedding consultant and/or coordinator.

Options: The rehearsal dinner party can be held just about anywhere, from a restaurant, hotel, or private hall to the groom's parents' home. Close relatives and out-of- town guests may be included if budget permits.

Tips To Save Money: Restaurants specializing in Mexican food or pizza are fun yet inexpensive options for a casual rehearsal dinner.

Price Range: $10 - $100/person

Bachelor Party

The bachelor party is a male-only affair typically organized by your best man. He is responsible for selecting the date and reserving the place and entertainment as well as inviting your male friends and family. Your best man should also assign responsibilities to the ushers, as they should help with the organization of this party.

Things To Consider: You often hear wild stories about bachelor parties being nights full of loose women, alcohol, and great fun. However, these stories are actually quite rare. Most of the time, they are all lies or a big exaggeration of what really happened. It is not uncommon for the guys invited to the bachelor party to create these wild stories and make a vow of never telling the truth about how boring the party really was! Whatever you do, make this party a memorable one. Make sure you do something different and enjoy it!

Options: In the past, a typical bachelor party would start with the young bachelor and his friends getting together for dinner and drinking a fair amount of beer. After eating and drinking to their heart's content, they would then go bar-hopping or get together at someone's house to play games or watch X-rated movies. Going to nude dancing locations was also popular for young bachelors. So was hiring a call girl or stripper. As the bachelor age group becomes older (average bachelor age today is 25), this tradition has changed a bit. Now a bachelor party can be as simple as a group of friends getting together for dinner and drinks.

Beware: Your best man should not plan your bachelor party for the night before the wedding, since chances are that you will consume a large amount of alcohol and stay up late. You don't want to have a hangover or be exhausted during your wedding. It is much more appropriate to have the bachelor party two or three nights before the wedding. Tell your best man that you will be busy the night before the wedding, just in case he is planning to surprise you.

Your best man should designate a driver for you and for those who will be drinking alcohol. You don't want to get into an accident days before the wedding or spend your wedding day in jail for drunk driving. Remember, you and your best man are responsible for the well-being of everybody invited to the party.

One word of advice: even though the bachelor party is your last night out as a single man, it does not give you the license to cheat on your fiancée or do something that would upset her. This would be the worst way to begin your married life.

Price Range: It is customary for the best man and ushers to pay for this party.

*M*ISCELLANEOUS

*N*EWSPAPER ANNOUNCEMENTS

There are two types of announcements you can send to your local newspaper: one to announce your engagement, and one to announce your wedding.

For your engagement announcement, send information to the newspapers, along with a photograph, right after your engagement or at least 4 to 6 weeks before the wedding. The photograph is usually the head and shoulders of the engaged couple. The photograph should be wallet-sized or larger, black and white, and glossy. Call your local newspapers to ask about their requirements. Most papers will not take orders over the phone, so you will need to mail the information or deliver it personally.

For your wedding announcement, send information to the newspapers, along with a photograph of either the bride alone or the bridal couple, at least three weeks before the wedding. The photograph should be wallet-sized or larger, black and white, and glossy. Your photograph should show the way you will look the day of your wedding. The announcement should appear the day following the ceremony.

Things To Consider: If you and your fiancé grew up in different towns, consider sending announcements to the local papers of both towns. If either of you is having second thoughts about the wedding, cancel both announcements as soon as possible.

Tips To Save Money: If you don't mind having your wedding announced a few weeks after the wedding, you can send a photo from your actual wedding day. This will save you the cost and hassle of dressing up to have your photo taken before the wedding.

Price Range: $40 - $100 (depending on size)

*M*ARRIAGE LICENSE

Marriage license requirements are state-regulated and may be obtained from the County Clerk in most county courthouses.

Options: Some states (California and Nevada, for example) offer two types of marriage licenses: a public license and a confidential one. The public license is the most common one and requires a health certificate and a blood test. It can only be obtained at the County Clerk's office.

The confidential license is usually less expensive and does not require a health certificate or blood test. If offered, it can usually be obtained from most Justices of the Peace. An oath must be taken in order to receive either license.

Things To Consider: Requirements vary from state to state but generally include the following points:

1. Applying for and paying the fee for the marriage license. There is usually a waiting period before the license is valid and a limited time before it expires.

2. Meeting residency requirements for the state and/or county where the ceremony will take place.

3. Meeting the legal age requirements for both bride and groom or having parental consent.

4. Presenting any required identification, birth or baptismal certificates, marriage eligibility or other documents.

5. Obtaining a medical examination and/or blood test for both the bride and groom to detect communicable diseases.

Price Range: $20 - $100

PRENUPTIAL AGREEMENT

A prenuptial agreement is a legal contract between the bride and groom itemizing the property each brings into the marriage and explaining how those properties will be divided in case of divorce or death. Although you can write your own agreement, it is advisable to have an attorney draw up or review the document. The two of you should be represented by different attorneys.

Things To Consider: Consider a prenuptial agreement if one or both of you have a significant amount of capital or assets, or if there are children involved from a previous marriage. If you are going to live in a different state after the wedding, consider having an attorney from that state draw up or review your document.

Nobody likes to talk about divorce or death when planning a wedding, but it is very important to give these issues your utmost consideration. By drawing a prenuptial agreement, you encourage open communication and get a better idea of each other's needs and expectations. You should also consider drawing up or reviewing your wills at this time.

Tips To Save Money: Some software packages allow you to write your own will and prenuptial agreement, which can save you substantial attorney's fees. However, if you decide to draw either agreement on your own, you should still have an attorney review it.

Price Range: $500 - $3,000

*B*RIDAL GOWN PRESERVATION

The pride and joy you will experience in seeing your daughter and/or granddaughter wear your wedding gown on her wedding day will more than justify the expense of having your gown preserved. Bring your gown to a reputable dry cleaning company which specializes in preserving wedding gowns. They will dry clean your dress, vacuum seal it, and place it in an attractive box. By doing this, your gown will be protected from yellowing, falling apart, or getting damaged over the years. Most boxes have a plastic see-through window where you can show the top part of your dress to friends and family members without having to open the vacuum-sealed container.

Tips To Save Money: Some bridal boutiques offer gown preservation. Try to negotiate having your gown preserved for free with the purchase of a wedding gown. It's well worth the try! But remember, get any agreement in writing and be sure to have it signed by either the owner or the manager of the boutique.

Price Range: $100 - $250

*B*RIDAL BOUQUET PRESERVATION

The bridal bouquet can be preserved to make a beautiful memento of the wedding.

Things To Consider: Have your bouquet dried, mounted, and framed to hang on your wall or to display on an easel in a quiet corner of your home. You can also have an artist paint your bouquet.

Price Range: $100 - $500

WEDDING CONSULTANT

Wedding consultants are professionals whose training, expertise, and contacts will help make your wedding as close to perfect as it can possibly be. They can save you considerable time, money and stress when planning your wedding. Wedding consultants have information on many ceremony and reception sites as well as reliable service providers such as photographers, videographers and florists, which will save you hours of investigation and legwork.

Wedding consultants can provide facilities and service providers to match your budget. They can also save you stress by ensuring that what you are planning is correct and that the service providers you hire are reliable and professional. Most service providers recommended by wedding consultants will go out of their way to do an excellent job for you so that the wedding consultant will continue to recommend their services.

Options: You can have a wedding consultant help you do as much or as little as you think necessary. A consultant can help you plan the whole event from the beginning to the end, helping you formulate a budget and select your ceremony and reception sites, flowers, wedding gown, invitations, and service providers; or s/he can help you at the end by coordinating the rehearsal and the wedding day. Remember, you want to feel like a guest at your own wedding. You and your family should not have to worry about any details on that special day. This is the wedding consultant's job!

Things To Consider: Strongly consider engaging the services of a wedding consultant. Contrary to what many people believe, a wedding consultant is part of your wedding budget, not an extra expense! A good wedding consultant should be able to save you at least the amount of his/her fee by suggesting less expensive alternatives that still enhance your wedding. In addition, many consultants obtain discounts from the service providers they work with. If this is not enough, they are more than worth their fee by serving as an intermediary between you and your parents and/or service providers.

When hiring a wedding consultant, make sure you check his/her references. Ask the consultant if s/he is a member of the Association of Bridal Consultants (ABC) and ask to see a current membership certificate. All ABC members agree to uphold a Code of Ethics and Standards of Membership. Many consultants have formal training and experience in event planning and in other specialties related to weddings, such as flower arranging and catering.

Price Range: $500 - $10,000

*W*EDDING PLANNING SOFTWARE

With a computer, you can ease the process of planning your wedding. A good wedding planning software will help you create a budget, generate a guest list, address invitations, create a wedding timeline or schedule of events, keep track of payments made to service providers, and keep track of invitations sent as well as RSVPs and gifts received.

Options: One of the best wedding planning software programs available is published by Wedding Solutions Publishing and is called *Easy Wedding Planning Software for Windows*. This software is very easy to use and will greatly assist you plan all aspects of your wedding. Please log on to *www.WeddingSolutions.com* to see all the great features available with this invaluable software.

Price Range: $30 - $60

*T*AXES

Don't forget to figure-in the cost of taxes on all taxable items you purchase for your wedding. Many people make a big mistake by not figuring out the taxes they will have to pay for their wedding expenses. For example, if you are planning a reception for 250 guests with an estimated cost of $60/person for food and beverages, your pretax expenses would be $15,000. A sales tax of 7.5% would mean an additional expense of $1,125! Find out what the sales tax is in your area and which items are taxable, and figure this expense into your overall budget.

Wedding Consultants Comparison Chart

QUESTIONS	POSSIBILITY 1	POSSIBILITY 2
What is the name of the wedding consultant?		
What is the website & email address of the wedding consultant?		
What is the address of the wedding consultant?		
What is the name & phone number of my contact person?		
How many years of professional experience do you have?		
How many consultants are in your company?		
Are you a member of the Association of Bridal Consultants?		
What services do you provide?		
What are your hourly fees?		
What is your fee for complete wedding planning?		
What is your fee to oversee the rehearsal and wedding day?		
What is your payment policy?		
What is your cancellation policy?		
Do you have liability insurance?		

*W*EDDING *C*ONSULTANTS *C*OMPARISON *C*HART

POSSIBILITY 3	POSSIBILITY 4	POSSIBILITY 5

CONSULTANT'S INFORMATION FORM

(Make a copy of this form and give it to your wedding consultant.)

THE WEDDING OF _____ & _____

Ceremony Site _____ **Phone No.** _____

Ceremony Address _____

Reception Site _____ **Phone No.** _____

Reception Address _____

Ceremony Services	Contact Person	Arrival Time	Departure Time	Phone
Florist				
Musicians				
Officiant				
Photographer				
Rental Supplier				
Site Coordinator				
Soloist				
Transportation				
Videographer				
Other				
Reception Services	Contact Person	Arrival Time	Departure Time	Phone
Baker				
Bartender				
Caterer				
Florist				
Gift Attendant				
Guest Book Attendant				
Musicians				
Rental Supplier				
Site Coordinator				
Transportation				
Valet Service				
Other				

*N*AME & *A*DDRESS *C*HANGE *F*ORM

To Whom it May Concern:

This is to inform you of my recent marriage and to request a change of name and/or address. The following information will be effective as of _____

My account/policy number is: _____

Under the name of: _____

PREVIOUS INFORMATION

Husband's Name _____   Phone No. _____

Previous Address: _____

Wife's Maiden Name _____   Phone No. _____

Previous Address: _____

PRESENT/FUTURE INFORMATION

Husband's Name _____   Phone No. _____

Wife's Name _____   Phone No. _____

New Address: _____

SPECIAL INSTRUCTIONS

- ❑ Change name
- ❑ Change address/phone
- ❑ Add spouse's name
- ❑ Send necessary forms to include my spouse on my policy/account
- ❑ We plan to continue service
- ❑ We plan to discontinue service after _____

If you have any questions, please feel free to contact us at (   ) _____

Husband's Signature _____

Wife's Signature _____

Change Of Address Worksheet

Company	Account or Policy No.	Phone or Address	Done
Auto Insurance	_____	_____	____
Auto Registration	_____	_____	____
Bank Accounts	_____	_____	____
	_____	_____	____
	_____	_____	____
Credit Cards	_____	_____	____
	_____	_____	____
	_____	_____	____
	_____	_____	____
	_____	_____	____
Dentist	_____	_____	____
Doctors	_____	_____	____
	_____	_____	____
Driver's License	_____	_____	____
Employee Records	_____	_____	____
Insurance: Dental	_____	_____	____
Insurance: Disability	_____	_____	____
Insurance: Homeowner's	_____	_____	____
Insurance: Life	_____	_____	____
Insurance: Renter's	_____	_____	____
Insurance: Other	_____	_____	____
IRA Accounts	_____	_____	____
	_____	_____	____
Leases	_____	_____	____
	_____	_____	____
Loan Companies	_____	_____	____
	_____	_____	____
	_____	_____	____
	_____	_____	____

*C*HANGE *O*F *A*DDRESS *W*ORKSHEET
(CONT.)

Company	Account or Policy No.	Phone or Address	Done
Magazines	_____	_____	_____
Memberships	_____	_____	_____
	_____	_____	_____
	_____	_____	_____
Mortgage	_____	_____	_____
Newspaper	_____	_____	_____
	_____	_____	_____
	_____	_____	_____
Passport	_____	_____	_____
Pensions	_____	_____	_____
Post Office	_____	_____	_____
Property Title	_____	_____	_____
Retirement Accounts	_____	_____	_____
	_____	_____	_____
Safe Deposit Box	_____	_____	_____
School Records	_____	_____	_____
	_____	_____	_____
Social Security	_____	_____	_____
Stock Broker	_____	_____	_____
Subscriptions	_____	_____	_____
	_____	_____	_____
	_____	_____	_____
Taxes	_____	_____	_____
Telephone Co.	_____	_____	_____
Utilities	_____	_____	_____
Voter Registration	_____	_____	_____
Will/Trust	_____	_____	_____
Other	_____	_____	_____
	_____	_____	_____
	_____	_____	_____
	_____	_____	_____
	_____	_____	_____

Personal Notes

_____
_____
_____
_____
_____
_____
_____
_____
_____
_____
_____
_____
_____
_____
_____
_____
_____
_____
_____
_____
_____
_____
_____
_____

$\mathcal{T}$IMELINES

The following section includes two different timelines or schedule of events for your wedding day: one for members of your wedding party, and one for the various service providers you have hired. Use these timelines to help your wedding party and service providers understand their roles and where they need to be throughout your wedding day. This will also give you a much better idea of how your special day will unfold.

When preparing your timeline, first list the time that your wedding ceremony will begin. Then work forward or backwards, using the sample as your guide. The samples included give you an idea of how much time each event typically takes. But feel free to change the amount of time allotted for any event when customizing your own.

Use the space in the description column to write any additional information, such as addresses, or any other comments that will help members of your wedding party understand what their roles are and where they need to be. Once you have created your own timeline, make a copy and give one to each member of your wedding party.

Wedding Party Timeline

(Sample)

This is a sample wedding party timeline. To develop your own, use the form on page 222. Use the extra space in the description column to write additional information such as addresses or any other comments that will help members of your wedding party understand what their roles are. Once you have created your own timeline, make a copy and give one to each member of your wedding party.

TIME	DESCRIPTION	BRIDE	BRIDE'S MOTHER	BRIDE'S FATHER	MAID OF HONOR	BRIDE'S MAIDS	BRIDE'S FAMILY	GROOM	GROOM'S MOTHER	GROOM'S FATHER	BEST MAN	USHERS	GROOM'S FAMILY	FLOWER GIRL	RING BEARER
2:00 PM	Manicurist Appointment:	✓	✓		✓	✓									
2:30 PM	Hair/Makeup Appointment:	✓	✓		✓	✓									
4:15 PM	Arrive at Dressing Site:	✓	✓		✓	✓									
4:30 PM	Arrive at Dressing Site:							✓			✓	✓			
4:45 PM	Pre-Ceremony Photos:							✓	✓	✓	✓	✓	✓		
5:15 PM	Arrive at Ceremony Site:							✓	✓	✓	✓	✓	✓		
5:15 PM	Pre-Ceremony Photos:	✓	✓	✓	✓	✓	✓								
5:20 PM	Give Officiant Marriage License & Fee										✓				
5:20 PM	Ushers receive seating chart											✓			
5:30 PM	Ushers hand out wedding program as guests arrive											✓			
5:30 PM	Arrive at ceremony site:													✓	✓
5:30 PM	Guest book attendant asks guests to sign in:														
5:30 PM	Prelude Music Begins:														
5:35 PM	Begin Seating Guests:											✓			
5:45 PM	Arrive at ceremony site:	✓	✓	✓	✓	✓	✓								
5:45 PM	Honored Guests are Seated:											✓			
5:50 PM	Groom's Parents are Seated								✓	✓		✓			
5:55 PM	Bride's Mother is Seated		✓									✓			
5:55 PM	Attendants line up and get ready for Procession				✓	✓						✓		✓	✓
5:56 PM	Bride's father takes his place next to Bride	✓		✓											
5:57 PM	Aisle Runner is rolled down the aisle											✓			
5:58 PM	Officiant, Groom, and Best Man enter from:							✓			✓				
6:00 PM	Processional music begins:														

WEDDING PARTY TIMELINE
(Sample)

TIME	DESCRIPTION	BRIDE	BRIDE'S MOTHER	BRIDE'S FATHER	MAID OF HONOR	BRIDE'S MAIDS	BRIDE'S FAMILY	GROOM	GROOM'S MOTHER	GROOM'S FATHER	BEST MAN	USHERS	GROOM'S FAMILY	FLOWER GIRL	RING BEARER
6:00 PM	Groom's Mother Stands up								✓						
6:01 PM	Ushers enter from:											✓			
6:02 PM	Bridesmaids, Maid of Honor, RB, FG, Bride & Father march up aisle	✓		✓	✓	✓								✓	✓
6:20 PM	Bride/Groom, FG/RB, Maid of Honor/Best Man march down aisle	✓			✓			✓			✓			✓	✓
6:22 PM	Mother/Father of Bride, Mother/Father of Groom march down aisle		✓	✓					✓	✓					
6:25 PM	Signing of Marriage Certificate:	✓			✓			✓			✓				
6:30 PM	Post ceremony photos taken:	✓	✓	✓	✓	✓	✓	✓	✓	✓	✓	✓	✓	✓	✓
6:30 PM	Cocktails and Hors D'oeuvres served:														
6:30 PM	Gift attendant watches over gifts as guests arrive:														
7:15 PM	Receiving Line is formed, or Band/DJ announces Bride & Groom	✓						✓							
7:45 PM	Guests are seated & meal is served														
8:30 PM	Toasts										✓				
8:40 PM	First Dance	✓						✓							
8:45 PM	Traditional Dances:	✓	✓	✓				✓	✓	✓					
9:00 PM	Open dance floor for all guests														
9:30 PM	Bride & groom toast eachother before cutting cake	✓						✓							
9:40 PM	Cake-cutting ceremony	✓						✓							
10:00 PM	Bride tosses bouquet to single women	✓			✓	✓								✓	
10:10 PM	Groom takes garter from Bride's leg	✓						✓							
10:15 PM	Groom tosses garter to single men							✓				✓	✓		✓
10:20 PM	Man who caught garter puts on woman's leg who caught bouquet														
10:30 PM	Hand out rose petals, rice, or birdseed to toss over bride & groom as they														
10:45 PM	Grand Exit by Bride & Groom	✓						✓							

Wedding Party Timeline

(Create your own timeline using this form, make copies, and give one to each member of your wedding party).

TIME	DESCRIPTION	BRIDE	BRIDE'S MOTHER	BRIDE'S FATHER	MAID OF HONOR	BRIDE'S MAIDS	BRIDE'S FAMILY	GROOM	GROOM'S MOTHER	GROOM'S FATHER	BEST MAN	USHERS	GROOM'S FAMILY	FLOWER GIRL	RING BEARER

WEDDING PARTY TIMELINE
(Continuation)

TIME	DESCRIPTION	BRIDE	BRIDE'S MOTHER	BRIDE'S FATHER	MAID OF HONOR	BRIDE'S MAIDS	BRIDE'S FAMILY	GROOM	GROOM'S MOTHER	GROOM'S FATHER	BEST MAN	USHERS	GROOM'S FAMILY	FLOWER GIRL	RING BEARER

Service Provider Timeline

(Sample)

This is a sample of a service provider timeline. To develop your own, use the form on page 226. Use the extra space in the description column to write additional information such as addresses or any other comments that will help your service providers understand what their roles are and where they should be throughout the day. Once you have created your own timeline, make a copy and give one to each of your service providers.

TIME	DESCRIPTION	BAKERY	CATERER	CEREM. MUSICIAN	OFFICIANT	OTHER	FLORIST	HAIR DRESSER	LIMOUSINE	MAKEUP ARTIST	MANICURIST	PARTY RENTALS	PHOTOGRAPHER	RECEP. MUSICIANS	VIDEOGRAPHER
1:00 PM	Party rental supplier drops off supplies at ceremony site:											✓			
1:30 PM	Party rental supplier drops off supplies at reception site:											✓			
2:00 PM	Manicurist meets bride at:										✓				
2:30 PM	Makeup artist meets bride at:									✓					
3:00 PM	Hair dresser meets bride at:							✓							
4:00 PM	Limousine picks up bridal party at:								✓						
4:15 PM	Caterer begins setting up:		✓												
4:30 PM	Florist arrives at ceremony site:						✓								
4:40 PM	Baker delivers cake to reception site:	✓													
4:45 PM	Florist arrives at reception site:						✓								
4:45 PM	Pre-ceremony photos of groom's family at:												✓		
5:00 PM	Videographer arrives at ceremony site:														✓
5:15 PM	Pre-ceremony photos of bride's family at:												✓		
5:20 PM	Ceremony site decorations are completed (guest book table, flowers, etc)					✓	✓								
5:30 PM	Prelude music begins:			✓											
5:45 PM	Reception site decorations completed (gift table, place cards, flowers, etc)		✓			✓	✓								
5:58 PM	Officiant enters from:				✓										
6:00 PM	Processional music begins:			✓											
6:15 PM	Caterer finishes setting up:		✓												
6:25 PM	Bride & Groom sign marriage certificate				✓								✓		✓
6:30 PM	Post-ceremony photos of wedding party at:												✓		
6:30 PM	Cocktails & Hors D'oeuvres served:		✓												
6:30 PM	Band/DJ starts playing:													✓	

SERVICE PROVIDER TIMELINE

(Sample)

TIME	DESCRIPTION	BAKERY	CATERER	CEREM. MUSICIAN	OFFICIANT	OTHER	FLORIST	HAIR DRESSER	LIMOUSINE	MAKEUP ARTIST	MANICURIST	PARTY RENTALS	PHOTOGRAPHER	RECEP. MUSICIANS	VIDEOGRAPHER
6:30 PM	Move guest book & gifts to reception site					✓									
6:30 PM	Ceremony music ends			✓											
6:45 AM	Move arch/urns/flowers to reception site					✓									
7:00 PM	Limousine picks up Bride & Groom at ceremony site:								✓						
7:15 PM	Band/DJ announces entrance of Bride & Groom													✓	
7:45 PM	Meal is served		✓												
8:10 PM	Band/DJ announces champagne will be served for toasts													✓	
8:15 PM	Champagne is served for toasts		✓												
8:30 PM	Band/DJ announces toast by Best Man													✓	
8:40 PM	Band/DJ announces first dance													✓	
9:00 PM	Transport gifts to:					✓									
9:30 PM	Band/DJ announces cake-cutting ceremony													✓	
10:30 PM	Transport top tier of cake & flowers to:					✓									
10:40 PM	Transport rental items that need to be returned to:					✓									
10:45 PM	Limousine picks up Bride & Groom at reception site:								✓						
11:00 PM	Videographer departs														✓
11:00 PM	Photographer departs												✓		
11:00 PM	Wedding consultant departs					✓									
11:30 PM	Band/DJ stops playing													✓	
11:45 PM	Party rental supplier picks up supplies at ceremony/reception sites											✓			

Service Provider Timeline

(Create your own timeline using this form, make copies, and give one to each of your service providers).

TIME	DESCRIPTION	BAKERY	CATERER	CEREM. MUSICIAN	OFFICIANT	OTHER	FLORIST	HAIR DRESSER	LIMOUSINE	MAKEUP ARTIST	MANICURIST	PARTY RENTALS	PHOTOGRAPHER	RECEP. MUSICIANS	VIDEOGRAPHER

SERVICE PROVIDER TIMELINE
(Continuation)

TIME	DESCRIPTION	BAKERY	CATERER	CEREM. MUSICIAN	OFFICIANT	OTHER	FLORIST	HAIR DRESSER	LIMOUSINE	MAKEUP ARTIST	MANICURIST	PARTY RENTALS	PHOTOGRAPHER	RECEP. MUSICIANS	VIDEOGRAPHER

Personal Notes

WEDDING TRADITIONS

Have you ever wondered why certain things are almost always done at weddings? For example, why the bride carries a bouquet or wears a veil? Or why guests throw rice or rose petals over the newlyweds? In this section we discuss the origin and symbolism of some of the most popular wedding traditions.

This comprehensive list of wedding traditions comes from a delightful little book entitled *The Romance of the Wedding Ceremony* by Rev. Richleigh Hale Powers, Ph.D. This book has helped many couples personalize their wedding ceremony in a format that is both fun and easy to use.

THE BRIDE'S BOUQUET

Bridal bouquets have evolved through the ages. Saracen brides carried bouquets of orange blossoms to symbolize fertility, and Roman brides carried sheaves of wheat to symbolize prosperity for their husbands. In the eighteenth century, the practice of carrying a bouquet of flowers or herbs became a popular tradition which symbolized fragility, purity, and new life. Bouquets of dill were among the most popular herb carried. After the ceremony the dill was eaten to "provoke lust." Today, bridal bouquets are tossed to assembled single women to symbolize new life and to pass on the bride's good fortune.

THE SPECIAL MEANING OF THE BRIDE'S VEIL

The veil represents modesty and respect. It symbolizes the sanctity and exclusiveness of the marriage covenant and reminds the couple and the witnesses that the physical relationship is to be entered into only after the vows are completed.

RICE AND PETALS

In the Middle Ages, handfuls of wheat were thrown over married couples to symbolize the hope for fertility. In modern times, rice is thrown instead of wheat to symbolize fertility. In recent years, flower petals have become another alternative, symbolizing beauty, happiness and prosperity.

SOMETHING OLD, SOMETHING NEW, SOMETHING BORROWED, SOMETHING BLUE

Old and new items jointly symbolize the passage from the old unmarried state to that of the new married union. The wearing of a borrowed belonging demonstrates community participation in and approval of the wedding. Blue is worn because it is the color that signifies purity, love, and fidelity.

WHITE AISLE RUNNER

A white aisle runner symbolizes walking on holy ground. A marriage covenant is not made merely between two people and their witnesses. It is made in the presence of God and He is actively involved in the agreement. The white aisle runner symbolizes God's holiness.

SPECIAL SEATING FOR THE PARENTS

The parents of the bride and groom are part of the marriage covenant. The commitments they make during the ceremony are just as binding as the vows of the couple. The final responsibility of parents for their children is to determine with them God's will for a life partner. Thereafter, they serve in a chain of counsel for them and their children. Parents enter in the line of authority and leave in the line of counsel.

THE GROOM ENTERING FIRST

By this action the groom signifies that he is the covenant initiator. This is important because whoever initiates the covenant assumes greater responsibility for seeing it fulfilled.

THE FATHER OF THE BRIDE WALKING DOWN THE AISLE

This action has two meanings. By doing so, the father is saying to the bride, "I am endorsing this young man as God's very best choice of a husband for you, and I am now bringing you to him." In addition, the father is saying to the young man, "I am presenting to you a daughter who I have earnestly endeavored to raise as a pure bride."

THE BRIDE AND GROOM TAKING EACH OTHER'S RIGHT HAND DURING THE CEREMONY

The open right hand offered by each party symbolizes their strength, resources and purpose. By clasping each other's right hand, they pledge these qualities to each other so that each partner can depend on all the resources that the other brings into the covenant relationship. The handclasp goes far beyond sealing the contract. It symbolizes the cleaving together of lives which is to be accomplished in the marriage covenant.

THE GROOM MAKING THE FIRST MARRIAGE VOW

The groom must be the leader and assume greater responsibility for fulfilling the marriage covenant. As covenant initiator, he must commit himself to the purposes of marriage which God established in the beginning, and these must be reflected in his vows.

THE SYMBOLISM OF THE WEDDING RINGS

The wedding rings symbolize the promises binding two people together in marriage. The unbroken circle of the wedding band represents the continuity of undying love. Greek theory believed the fourth finger of the left hand to be connected to the heart, making this the appropriate finger to be "bound" in romantic attachment.

KISSING THE BRIDE

During the Roman empire, the kiss between a couple symbolized a legal bond. Continued use of the kiss to seal the marriage bond is based on the deeply rooted idea of the kiss as a vehicle for transference of power and souls.

THE COUPLE BEING PRONOUNCED "HUSBAND AND WIFE"

This establishes their change of names and a definite point in time for the beginning of the marriage. These words are to remove any doubt in the minds of the couple or the witnesses concerning the validity of the marriage.

SIGNING THE WEDDING PAPERS

The newlywed couple signs the wedding papers to establish a public document and a continuing public record of the covenant.

SIGNING THE GUEST BOOK

Your wedding guests are official witnesses to the covenant. By signing the guest book, they are saying, "I have witnessed the vows, and I will testify to the reality of this marriage." Because of this significance, the guest book should be signed after the wedding rather than before it.

THE PURPOSE OF THE RECEIVING LINE

The receiving line is for guests to give their blessings to the couple and their parents.

THE MEANING OF SERVING FOOD AT THE RECEPTION

Food is part of the covenant celebration. It further symbolizes the unity of the couple. Entering into a meal itself is a form of covenant.

THE BRIDE AND GROOM FEEDING WEDDING CAKE TO EACH OTHER

This represents the sharing of their body to become one. A New Testament illustration of this symbolism is The Lord's Supper.

*D*o's & *D*on'ts

Your wedding will last only a few hours but will likely take several months to plan. That is why it is so important to enjoy the complete wedding planning process. This is a time to get excited, to fall even more deeply in love with each other, to learn more about each other and how to give and take. If you can handle your wedding planning with your fiancé and parents, you can handle anything! Here is a list of do's and don'ts when planning your special day. If you follow these suggestions, your wedding planning and your wedding day will be much more enjoyable!

*D*o's

- ♦ Read this book completely.

- ♦ Hire a professional wedding consultant.

- ♦ Maintain a sense of humor.

- ♦ Maintain open communication with your fiancé and with both sets of parents, especially if they are financing the wedding.

- ♦ Be receptive to your parents' ideas, especially if they are financing the wedding.

- ♦ Be flexible and keep your overall budget in mind.

- ♦ Maintain a regular routine of exercise and eat a well-balanced diet.

- ♦ Buy the *Indispensable Groom's Guide*, published by Wedding Solution Publishing, and give it to your fiancé. This book is available at most major bookstores.

- ♦ Buy the *Wedding Party Responsibility Cards*, published by Wedding Solutions Publishing, and give a card to each member of your wedding party. This book is available at most major bookstores.

- ♦ Register for gifts; consider a price range that your guests can afford.

- Break-in your shoes well before your wedding day.

- Practice with makeup and various hairstyles for your wedding day.

- Check recent references for all of your service providers.

- Get everything in writing with your service providers.

- Assign your guests to tables and group them together by age, interests, acquaintances, etc.

- Consider drawing-up a prenuptial agreement and a will.

- Send thank-you notes as soon as you receive gifts.

- Give a rose to each of your mothers as you walk down the aisle during the recessional.

- Try to spend some time with each of your guests and personally thank them for coming to your wedding.

- Encourage the bride's parents to introduce their family and friends to the family and friends of the groom's family, and vice-versa.

- Toast both sets of parents at the rehearsal dinner and/or at the reception. Thank them for everything they have done for you and for giving you a beautiful wedding.

- Eat well at the reception, especially if you will be drinking alcohol.

- Keep a smile on your face; there will be many photographs taken of both of you.

- Expect things to go wrong on your wedding day. Most likely something will go wrong, and no one will notice it but yourself. Relax and don't let it bother you.

- Preserve the top tier of your wedding cake for your first year anniversary.

- Send a special gift to both sets of parents, such as a small album containing the best photographs of the wedding. Personalize this gift by having it engraved with your names and the date of your wedding.

*D*ON'TS

- ◆   Don't get involved in other activities; you will be very busy planning your wedding.

- ◆   Don't make any major decisions without discussing it openly with your fiancé.

- ◆   Don't be controlling. Be open to other people's ideas.

- ◆   Don't overspend your budget; this can be extremely stressful.

- ◆   Don't wait until the last minute to hire your service providers. The good ones get booked months in advance.

- ◆   Don't try to make everyone happy; it is impossible and will only make your wedding planning more difficult.

- ◆   Don't try to impress your friends.

- ◆   Don't invite old boyfriends or girlfriends to your wedding; you don't want to make anybody uncomfortable.

- ◆   Don't try to do "everything." Delegate responsibilities to your fiancé, your parents, and to members of your wedding party.

- ◆   Don't rely on friends or family to photograph or videotape your wedding. Hire professionals!

- ◆   Don't assume that members of your wedding party know what to do. Give them direction with your Wedding Party Timeline and the *Wedding Party Responsibility Cards*, available at most major bookstores.

- ◆   Don't assume your service providers know what to do. Give each of them a copy of your detailed Service Provider Timeline.

- ◆   Don't schedule your bachelor party the night before the wedding. You don't want to have a hangover on your special day!

- ◆   Don't arrive late at the ceremony!

- ◆   Don't get drunk during the reception; you don't want to make a fool of yourself on your most special day.

◆   Don't flirt with members of the opposite sex.

◆   Don't allow your guests to drive drunk after the reception; you may be held responsible.

◆   Don't rub cake in the face of your spouse during the cake-cutting ceremony; your spouse might not appreciate it!

◆   Don't overeat; this may upset your stomach or make you sleepy.

◆   Don't leave your reception without saying good-bye to your family and friends.

◆   Don't drive if you have had too much to drink!

WEDDING PARTY RESPONSIBILTIES

Each member of your wedding party has his/her own individual duties and responsibilities. The following is a list of the most important duties for each member of your wedding party.

The most convenient method for conveying this information to members of your wedding party is by purchasing a set of the *Wedding Party Responsibility Cards,* published by Wedding Solutions Publishing.

These cards are very attractive and contain all the information your wedding party needs to know to assure a smooth wedding: what to do, how to do it, when to do it, when to arrive, and much more. They also include financial responsibilities as well as the processional, recessional and altar line-up. These cards are available at most major bookstores. But you can purchase them directly from Wedding Solutions Publishing by sending $9.95 plus $2.95 for shipping and handling to Wedding Solutions Publishing, Inc., 6347 Caminito Tenedor, San Diego, CA 92120.

MAID OF HONOR

- ♦ Helps bride select attire and address invitations.
- ♦ Plans bridal shower for bride.
- ♦ Arrives at dressing site 2 hours before ceremony to assist bride in dressing.
- ♦ Arrives dressed at ceremony site 1 hour before the wedding for photographs.
- ♦ Arranges the bride's veil and train before the processional and recessional.
- ♦ Holds bride's bouquet and groom's ring, if no ring bearer, during the ceremony.
- ♦ Witnesses the signing of the marriage license.
- ♦ Keeps bride on schedule.
- ♦ Dances with best man during the bridal party dance.
- ♦ Helps bride change into her going away clothes.
- ♦ Mails wedding announcements after the wedding.
- ♦ Returns bridal slip, if rented.

Best Man

◆ Responsible for organizing ushers' activities.
◆ Organizes bachelor party for groom.
◆ Drives groom to ceremony site and sees that he is properly dressed before the wedding.
◆ Arrives dressed at ceremony site 1 hour before the wedding for photographs.
◆ Brings marriage license to wedding.
◆ Pays the clergyman, musicians, photographer, and any other service providers the day of the wedding.
◆ Holds the bride's ring for the groom, if no ring bearer, until needed by officiant.
◆ Witnesses the signing of the marriage license.
◆ Drives newlyweds to reception if no hired driver.
◆ Offers first toast at reception, usually before dinner.
◆ Keeps groom on schedule.
◆ Dances with maid of honor during the bridal party dance.
◆ May drive couple to airport or honeymoon suite.
◆ Oversees return of tuxedo rentals for groom and ushers, on time and in good condition.

Bridesmaids

◆ Assist maid/matron of honor in planning bridal shower.
◆ Assist bride with errands and addressing invitations.
◆ Participate in all pre-wedding parties.
◆ Arrive at dressing site 2 hours before ceremony.
◆ Arrive dressed at ceremony site 1 hour before the wedding for photographs.
◆ Walk behind ushers in order of height during the processional, either in pairs or in single file.
◆ Sit next to ushers at the head table.
◆ Dance with ushers and other important guests.
◆ Encourage single women to participate in the bouquet-tossing ceremony

USHERS

- Help best man with bachelor party.
- Arrive dressed at ceremony site 1 hour before the wedding for photographs.
- Distribute wedding programs and maps to the reception as guests arrive.
- Seat guests at the ceremony as follows:
     -- If female, offer the right arm.
     -- If male, walk along his left side.
     -- If couple, offer right arm to female; male follows a step or two behind.
     -- Seat bride's guests in left pews.
     -- Seat groom's guests in right pews.
     -- Maintain equal number of guests in left and right pews, if possible.
     -- If a group of guests arrive at the same time, seat the eldest woman first.
     -- Just prior to the processional, escort groom's mother to her seat; then escort bride's mother to her seat.
- Two ushers may roll carpet down the aisle after both mothers are seated.
- If pew ribbons are used, two ushers may loosen them one row at a time after the ceremony.
- Direct guests to the reception site.
- Dance with bridesmaids and other important guests.

BRIDE'S MOTHER

- Helps prepare guest list for bride and her family.
- Helps plan the wedding ceremony and reception.
- Helps bride select her bridal gown.
- Helps bride keep track of gifts received.
- Selects her own attire according to the formality and color of the wedding.
- Makes accommodations for bride's out of town guests.
- Arrives dressed at ceremony site 1 hour before the wedding for photographs.
- Is the last person to be seated right before the processional begins.
- Sits in the left front pew to the left of bride's father during the ceremony.
- May stand up to signal the start of the processional.
- Can witness the signing of the marriage license.
- Dances with the groom after the first dance.
- Acts as hostess at the reception.

Bride's Father

- Helps prepare guest list for bride and her family.
- Selects attire that complements groom's attire.
- Rides to the ceremony with bride in limousine.
- Arrives dressed at ceremony site 1 hour before the wedding for photographs.
- After giving bride away, sits in the left front pew to the right of bride's mother. If divorced, sits in second or third row unless financing the wedding.
- When officiant asks, "Who gives this bride away?" answers, "Her mother and I do" or something similar.
- Can witness the signing of the marriage license.
- Dances with bride after first dance.
- Acts as host at the reception.

Groom's Mother

- Helps prepare guest list for groom and his family.
- Selects attire that complements mother of the bride's attire.
- Makes accommodations for groom's out-of-town guests.
- With groom's father, plans rehearsal dinner.
- Arrives dressed at ceremony site 1 hour before the wedding for photographs.
- May stand up to signal the start of the processional.
- Can witness the signing of the marriage license.

GROOM'S FATHER

♦ Helps prepare guest list for groom and his family.
♦ Selects attire that complements groom's attire.
♦ With groom's mother, plans rehearsal dinner.
♦ Offers toast to bride at rehearsal dinner.
♦ Arrives dressed at ceremony site 1 hour before the wedding for photographs.
♦ Can witness the signing of the marriage license.

FLOWER GIRL

♦ Usually between the ages of four and eight.
♦ Attends rehearsal to practice but is not required to attend pre-wedding parties.
♦ Arrives dressed at ceremony site 45 minutes before the wedding for photos.
♦ Carries a basket filled with loose rose petals to strew along bride's path during processional, if allowed by ceremony site.
♦ If very young, may sit with her parents during ceremony.

RING BEARER

♦ Usually between the ages of four and eight.
♦ Attends rehearsal to practice but is not required to attend pre-wedding parties.
♦ Arrives at ceremony site 45 minutes before the wedding for photographs.
♦ Carries a white pillow with rings attached.
♦ If younger than 7 years, carries artificial rings.
♦ If very young, may sit with his parents during ceremony.
♦ After ceremony, carries ring pillow upside down so artificial rings do not show.

Wedding Party Form

(Make a copy of this form and give it to your wedding consultant.)

Parents	Home No.	Work No.	Responsibilities
Bride's Mother			
Bride's Father			
Groom's Mother			
Groom's Father			

Bride's Attendants	Home No.	Work No.	Responsibilities
Maid of Honor			
Matron of Honor			
Bridesmaid			
Bridesmaid			
Bridesmaid			
Bridesmaid			
Bridesmaid			
Bridesmaid			
Flower Girl			
Flower Girl			
Other			

Groom's Attendants	Home No.	Work No.	Responsibilities
Best Man			
Usher			
Usher			
Usher			
Usher			
Usher			
Usher			
Ring Bearer			
Ring Bearer			
Other			

Who Pays For What

BRIDE AND/OR BRIDE'S FAMILY

- Engagement party
- Wedding consultant's fee
- Bridal gown, veil and accessories
- Wedding stationery, calligraphy and postage
- Wedding gift for bridal couple
- Groom's wedding ring
- Gifts for bridesmaids
- Bridesmaids' bouquets
- Pre-wedding parties and bridesmaids' luncheon
- Photography and videography
- Bride's medical exam and blood test
- Wedding guest book and other accessories
- Total cost of the ceremony, including location, flowers, music, rental items and accessories
- Total cost of the reception, including location, flowers, music, rental items, accessories, food, beverages, cake, decorations, favors, etc.
- Transportation for bridal party to ceremony and reception
- Own attire and travel expenses

GROOM AND/OR GROOM'S FAMILY

- Own travel expenses and attire
- Rehearsal dinner
- Wedding gift for bridal couple
- Bride's wedding ring
- Gifts for groom's attendants
- Medical exam for groom including blood test
- Bride's bouquet and going away corsage
- Mothers' and grandmothers' corsages
- All boutonnieres
- Officiant's fee

♦ Marriage license
♦ Honeymoon expenses

ATTENDANTS

♦ Own attire except flowers
♦ Travel expenses
♦ Bridal shower paid for by maid of honor and bridesmaids
♦ Bachelor party paid for by best man and ushers

WEDDING FORMATIONS

The following section illustrates the typical ceremony formations (processional, recessional and altar line up) for both Christian and Jewish weddings, as well as the typical formations for the receiving line, head table, and parents' tables at the reception.

These ceremony formations are included in the *Wedding Party Responsibility Cards,* published by Wedding Solutions Publishing. This attractive set of cards makes it very easy for your wedding party to remember their place in these formations. Give one card to each member of your wedding party... they will appreciate it.

These cards are available at most major bookstores. But you can purchase them directly from Wedding Solutions Publishing by sending $9.95 plus $2.95 for shipping and handling to Wedding Solutions Publishing, Inc., 6347 Caminito Tenedor, San Diego, CA 92120.

Christian Ceremony

Altar Line Up

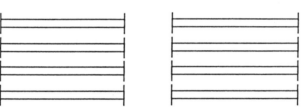

Bride's Pews   Groom's Pews

Abbreviations

B = Bride   GF = Groom's Father
G = Groom   GM = Groom's Mother
BM = Best Man   BMa = Bridesmaids
MH = Maid of Honor   U = Ushers
BF = Bride's Father   FG = Flower Girl
BMo = Bride's Mother   RB = Ring Bearer
                           O = Officiant

CHRISTIAN CEREMONY

PROCESSIONAL   RECESSIONAL

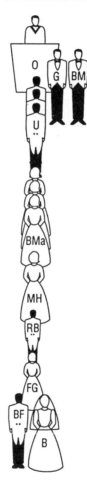
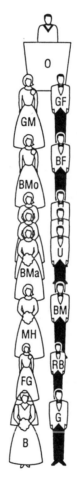

ABBREVIATIONS

B = Bride	GF = Groom's Father
G = Groom	GM = Groom's Mother
BM = Best Man	BMa = Bridesmaids
MH = Maid of Honor	U = Ushers
BF = Bride's Father	FG = Flower Girl
BMo = Bride's Mother	RB = Ring Bearer
	O = Officiant

Jewish Ceremony

Altar Line Up

Groom's Pews   Bride's Pews

ABBREVIATIONS

B = Bride   GF = Groom's Father
G = Groom   GM = Groom's Mother
BM = Best Man   BMa = Bridesmaids
MH = Maid of Honor   U = Ushers
BF = Bride's Father   FG = Flower Girl
BMo = Bride's Mother   RB = Ring Bearer
                             R = Rabbi

Jewish Ceremony

Processional

Recessional

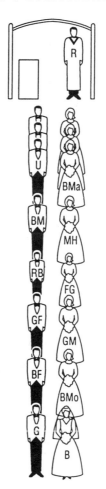

Abbreviations

B = Bride	GF = Groom's Father
G = Groom	GM = Groom's Mother
BM = Best Man	BMa = Bridesmaids
MH = Maid of Honor	U = Ushers
BF = Bride's Father	FG = Flower Girl
BMo = Bride's Mother	RB = Ring Bearer
	R = Rabbi

RECEIVING LINE

HEAD TABLE

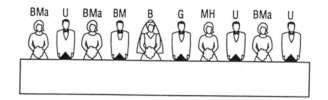

PARENTS' TABLE

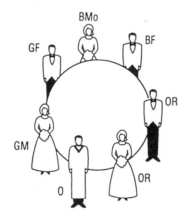

ABBREVIATIONS

B = Bride	GF = Groom's Father
G = Groom	GM = Groom's Mother
BM = Best Man	BMa = Bridesmaids
MH = Maid of Honor	U = Ushers
BF = Bride's Father	OR = Other Relatives
BMo = Bride's Mother	O = Officiant

*T*HINGS *T*O *B*RING

*T*O THE REHEARSAL

BRIDE'S LIST:

- ❑ Wedding announcements (maid of honor to mail after wedding)
- ❑ Bridesmaids' gifts (if not already given)
- ❑ Camera and film
- ❑ Fake bouquet or ribbon bouquet from bridal shower
- ❑ Groom's gift (if not already given)
- ❑ Reception maps and wedding programs
- ❑ Rehearsal information and ceremony formations
- ❑ Flower girl basket and ring bearer pillow
- ❑ Seating diagrams for head table and parents' tables
- ❑ Wedding schedule of events/timeline
- ❑ Tape player with wedding music

GROOM'S LIST:

- ❑ Bride's gift (if not already given)
- ❑ Marriage license
- ❑ Ushers' gifts (if not already given)
- ❑ Service providers' fees to give to best man or wedding consultant so s/he can pay them at the wedding

To the Ceremony

BRIDE'S LIST:

- ❏ Aspirin/Alka Seltzer
- ❏ Bobby pins
- ❏ Breath spray/mints
- ❏ Bridal gown
- ❏ Bridal gown box
- ❏ Cake knife
- ❏ Change of clothes for going away
- ❏ Clear nail polish
- ❏ Deodorant
- ❏ Garter
- ❏ Gloves
- ❏ Groom's ring
- ❏ Guest book
- ❏ Hair brush
- ❏ Hair spray
- ❏ Head piece
- ❏ Iron
- ❏ Jewelry
- ❏ Kleenex
- ❏ Lint brush
- ❏ Luggage
- ❏ Make-up
- ❏ Mirror
- ❏ Nail polish
- ❏ Panty hose
- ❏ Passport
- ❏ Perfume
- ❏ Personal camera
- ❏ Plume pen for guest book
- ❏ Powder
- ❏ Purse
- ❏ Safety pins
- ❏ Scotch tape/masking tape
- ❏ Sewing kit
- ❏ Shoes
- ❏ Something old
- ❏ Something new
- ❏ Something borrowed
- ❏ Something blue
- ❏ Spot remover
- ❏ Straight pins
- ❏ Tampons or sanitary napkins
- ❏ Toasting goblets
- ❏ Toothbrush & paste

GROOM'S LIST:

- ❏ Airline tickets
- ❏ Announcements
- ❏ Aspirin/Alka Seltzer
- ❏ Breath spray/mints
- ❏ Bride's ring
- ❏ Change of clothes for going away
- ❏ Cologne
- ❏ Cuff Links
- ❏ Cummerbund
- ❏ Deodorant
- ❏ Hair comb
- ❏ Hair spray
- ❏ Kleenex
- ❏ Lint brush
- ❏ Luggage
- ❏ Neck tie
- ❏ Passport
- ❏ Shirt
- ❏ Shoes
- ❏ Socks
- ❏ Toothbrush & paste
- ❏ Tuxedo
- ❏ Underwear

AT THE TOUCH OF LOVE EVERYONE

BECOMES A POET

Plato

PHOTO: KAREN FRENCH

H O N E Y M O O N   P L A N N E R

KAREN FRENCH

SOTA PHOTOGRAPHY

KAREN FRENCH

KAREN FRENCH

KAREN FRENCH

Easy

HONEYMOON

Planning

A comprehensive guide
containing all the information
a bride and groom should know when
planning a Honeymoon!

*H*ONEYMOONS

Your honeymoon is the time to celebrate your new life together as a married couple. It should be the vacation of a lifetime. This does not necessarily mean spending your life's earnings, but the vacation should be special and should show your bride how much she means to you.

The honeymoon is traditionally your responsibility. However, you should get your fiancée involved in the planning of your honeymoon as it should be a joint decision as to where to go, how long to stay, and how much money to spend.

You will find many tools and suggestions on the following pages to help you plan this important trip. After reading this book, you will have information on different types of honeymoons, and you should be able to determine the perfect honeymoon destination for you and your bride, research and select a responsible travel agent, gather useful information using the resource leads provided, establish a reasonable budget with confidence, and - most importantly - walk away with the assurance that you are planning the honeymoon of a lifetime! Start planning your honeymoon months before the wedding. Many locations that are popular with honeymooners tend to book fairly quickly, so the earlier you plan your trip, the better values you'll usually find.

There are many choices to make and many plans to be made but most of them seem to fall into place once you've made the toughest decision... where to go.

Many people have a preconceived notion of where a honeymoon should take place. And indeed, these locations are, year after year, some of the places most frequently visited by newly-weds. We'll take a look at some of these "traditional" destinations as well as some that are a little "less traditional."

Think about what you and your fiancée might find appealing (and unappealing) in the following honeymoon vacations. Be careful not to assume what your new bride may be looking for in a honeymoon. Couples are often surprised when they discover what the other partner considers a "vacation." Refer to the section entitled *Choosing A Destination* to determine what each other's ideal vacation includes.

*T*YPES OF *H*ONEYMOONS

Listed on the following pages are sample honeymoon plans -- both traditional and less traditional. A brief description of some of the most popular honeymoon trips (ones that have remained popular with newlyweds for generations) is provided as well.

You can get very helpful information on planning a vacation package in the following brochures from the United States Tour Operator Association, (212) 599-6599, www.ustoa.com.

- *How to Select a Tour Vacation Package*
- *Worldwide Tour and Vacation Package Finder*
- *The Standard for Confident Travel*

*T*RADITIONAL HONEYMOONS

CRUISES

Cruises are a popular retreat for those who want the luxury of a hospitable resort with the added benefit of visiting one or more new areas. There are hundreds of different cruise options available to you. Typically, almost everything is included in the cost of your cruise: extravagant dining, unlimited group and individual activities, relaxing days and lively nights.

Costs vary greatly depending on the location the cruise will visit (if any) and your cabin accommodations. Locations range from traveling the Mississippi River to encircling the Greek Isles. Spend some time choosing your cabin. Most of them are small, but pay attention to distracting things, such as noisy areas and busy pathways, that might be located close by.

Even though most everything is included in your cost, be sure to ask about those items which may not be included (alcoholic beverages, sundries, spa treatments and tips generally are not included.) Request a helpful publication entitled *Answers to Your Most Frequently Asked Questions*, published by Cruise Lines International Association, (212) 921-0066, www.cruising.org.

ALL INCLUSIVE RESORTS

Many newlyweds, tired from the previous months of wedding planning and accompanying stress, opt for the worry-free guarantee of an all-inclusive resort. Some resorts are for the entire family, some are for couples only (not necessarily newlywed), and some are strictly for honeymooners. Most of these resorts are nestled on a picturesque island beach catering to your relaxation needs. Most offer numerous sports, water activities, entertainment, and exceptional service and attention. Your costs will vary depending on the location you choose, and there are many, many to choose from. "All-inclusive" means everything is included in your price. You won't have to worry about meals, drinks, tour fees or even tips.

One way of considering if this is a good option for you is to list all of the activities that the vacation package offers that you are interested in. Add up the individual costs and compare. If you wouldn't be participating much in the activities, food, and drink, you may actually save money by arranging your own trip at an independent resort. Even still, many couples prefer to spend the extra money in exchange for a vacation free of planning and wearying decisions.

Because of its convenience, many couples choose this resort option as the setting for their honeymoon. Some of the most popular all-inclusive resorts are Club Med and Sandals.

THE POCONOS

The Poconos Honeymoon resorts are located in Pennsylvania and are considered to be some of the most popular Honeymoon destinations around. The Poconos offer a variety of individual resorts, each heavily laden with fanciful symbols of romance and sweet desires. The atmosphere is perfect for those who want to be enveloped in a surrounding where you'll never forget you're in love and on your honeymoon. Some travel packages here are considered all-inclusive, but as always, be sure to ask about exclusions and extras. For information about honeymooning in the Poconos, call 1-800- POCONOS.

WALT DISNEY WORLD

Another popular destination for those seeking a "theme" resort are those offered as *Disney's Fairy Tale Honeymoons*. These vacation packages include accommodations at Disney's exclusive resorts and admission to their theme parks. Some packages are also available with accommodations at some of the privately owned resorts at Disney World. Prices for Disney packages can range greatly depending on your tastes and the amount of activity you desire. For information about Disney's honeymoon packages, call (407) 828-3400.

Inquire with your travel agent about day or overnight cruises leaving from nearby ports in Florida. This is one way to combine two very popular honeymoon options into one!

Other popular and traditional honeymoon plans are as follows:

- Enjoying the beaches and unique treasures of the Hawaiian islands

- Exploring Northern California's romantic wine country

- Ski and snowboard package getaways in Vermont, New Hampshire, Colorado, and Northern California

- Camping and hiking within the beautiful and adventurous National Parks

- Sightseeing, touring, and exploring a variety of points in Europe via the rail system

- Island hopping on a cruise ship around the Greek Isles

- Enjoying a fanciful and adventurous journey on the Orient Express

LESS TRADITIONAL HONEYMOONS

- Bicycling in Nova Scotia while relaxing at quaint Bed and Breakfast Inns

- Participating in a white water river rafting expedition in Oregon

- Mingling with the owners and fellow guests on an Old West Dude Ranch

- Visiting landmarks and parks while enjoying the convenience of a traveling home in a rented RV

- Mustering up the courage and stamina for an aggressive hiking tour of the Canadian Rockies

- Training for and participating in a dog sled race in the brisk tundra of Alaska

- "Roughing it" while enjoying the splendor of a safari in East Africa

CHOOSING YOUR DESTINATION

Maybe your idea of a perfect honeymoon is ten days of adventure and discovery; but for your fiancée, it may be ten days of resting in a beach chair and romantic strolls in the evening. The choices for honeymoon vacations are as varied as the bride and groom themselves. Deciding together on a honeymoon destination is a wonderful opportunity to discover more about each other and negotiate a vacation that will leave both of you relaxed, fulfilled, and even more in love.

First, determine the type of atmosphere and climate you prefer. Then consider the types of activities you would like to engage in.

Do you want the weather to be hot for swimming at the beach... or warm for long guided tours of unknown cities... or cooler for day-long hikes in the woods... or cold for optimum skiing conditions? Keep in mind the time of year in which your wedding falls. Will you be escaping from warm or cool temperatures?

If you have a specific destination in mind, you (or your travel agent) will need to do some research to be sure the weather conditions will be suitable for your planned activities.

Review the previous chapters on traditional and non-traditional honeymoons and note what you feel are the pros and cons of each type of vacation. The two of you should have lots of images and possibilities in your mind at this point! The next step is to determine the most perfect atmosphere to provide the setting for your honeymoon. The following sections, *Creating A Wish List* and *Helpful Resources*, will guide you through this next step and beyond.

CREATING A WISH LIST

Together with your fiancée, complete the following wish list worksheet. You should each check off your preferences even if both of you don't agree on them. There are many locations that provide a variety of activities. Remember, you don't need to spend every minute of your honeymoon together, but your honeymoon destination should be one that intrigues both of you.

This worksheet is divided into 5 sections. You will be considering location, accommodations, meals, activities, and night life.

While completing the worksheet, be as true to your interests as possible; don't concern yourself with finances and practicality at this point. This is your chance to let your mind wander! Think about what you would like to fill your days and nights with. This is the honeymoon of your dreams...

You step out of the plane, train, car or boat that took you to your honeymoon destination. You sigh with satisfaction at the memory of your flawless and enjoyable wedding as your feet touch the ground...

... What type of overall atmosphere do you see yourself stepping into? What is the weather like?

... Do you picture a long stretch of beach, towering mountains, blossoming vineyards, or city skyscrapers? Is the dry sand of the desert blowing around or is everything captured under glistening snowcaps?

... Are there many people walking around (many locals, many tourists), or is it a secluded retreat?

... Are you relaxing indoors in a resort with a pampering environment that caters to your comfort? Do you return to a simple, modest hotel or motel after a long day of sight-seeing, touring, and dining? Are you camping in the middle of your activities --hiking, climbing, fishing, etc.?

... Do you see yourself interacting much with others? Would you like to have these activities be organized? Are there vistas and horizons to gaze endlessly upon, or is there an abundance of visual activity and changing scenery?

... Are you enjoying exotic foods elaborately displayed and available to you at your leisure? Are you testing out your sense of adventure on the local cuisine and dining hot spots? Are you eating fast foods and pizza in exchange for spending your time and money on other items and activities that make your vacation exciting?

... Are your evenings filled with romantic strolls or festivities that run late into the night? Are you staying in for romantic evenings or re-energizing for another busy day of honeymooning?

HOW TO USE THIS WORKSHEET:

Each of you separately should place a check mark next to the items or images on the wish list that appeal to you. After you have finished, highlight those items that both of you feel are important (the items that were checked by both of you).

Next, each of you should highlight, in a different colored marker or pen, 2-3 items in each category that you feel are very important to you individually (even though the other person may not have checked it.)

Your wish lists, after completing this exercise, will probably look like a list of *all* of the positive elements of *all* of your dream vacations combined. This is good, you should list as many things as you can think of. The more information you have, the better the suggestions your travel agent (or yourself if you'll be doing your own research) will be able to make.

Together, using this wish list, you will discover a honeymoon destination and match a honeymoon style that will fulfill your dreams.

The resource leads and exercises provided in the rest of this book will help you get from wish list to reality. Happy planning!

	BRIDE ✓	GROOM ✓
Location:		
hot weather		
mild weather		
cold weather		
dry climate		
moist climate		
sand and beaches		
lakes/ponds		
wilderness/wooded areas		
mountains		
fields		
city streets		
small local town		
large metropolitan area		
popular tourist destination		
visiting among the locals		
nighttime weather conducive to outdoor activities		
nighttime weather conducive to indoor activities		
"modern" resources and service available		
"roughing it" on your own		
culture and customs you are familiar and comfortable with		
new cultures and customs you would like to get to know		
Accommodations:		
part of a larger resort community		
a stand alone building		
lodging amongst other fellow tourists		
lodging amongst couples only		
lodging amongst fellow newlyweds only		

	BRIDE √	GROOM √
lodging amongst locals		
large room or suite		
plush, highly decorated surroundings		
modestly sized room		
modest decor		
balcony		
private Jacuzzi in room		
room service		
chamber maid service		
laundry / dry cleaning service available		
laundry room available		
beauty salon on premises		
workout gym on premises		
gift shop on premises		
pool on premises		
poolside bar service		
sauna, hot tub on premises		
common gathering lounge for guests		
Meals:		
casual dining		
formal dining		
prepared by executive chefs		
prepared by yourself/grocery store		
variety of local and regional restaurants		
traditional "American" cuisine		
opportunity for picnics		
exotic, international menu		
entertainment while dining		

	BRIDE √	GROOM √
planned meal times		
dining based on your own schedule		
fast food restaurants		
vegetarian meals, special diet meals		
delis, diners		
Activities:		
sun bathing		
snorkeling		
diving		
swimming		
jet skiing		
water skiing		
fishing		
sailing		
snow skiing		
snow boarding		
hiking, rock climbing		
camping		
golf		
tennis		
aerobics		
site-seeing suggestions and guidance		
planned bus/guided tours		
ability to go off on your own		
historic tours		
art museums		
theater		
exploring family heritage		

	BRIDE ✓	GROOM ✓
Night Life:		
quiet strolls		
outdoor activities		
sitting and relaxing outdoors		
sitting and relaxing in front of a fireplace		
being alone with each other		
being out with the locals		
being out with other newlyweds		
discovering new cultures and forms of entertainment		
dancing		
visiting bars/pubs		
theater / shows		
gambling		
Other important elements:		

Now that you have a completed wish list, take this list to your travel agent. If you don't already have a travel agent, use the following section for help in selecting a reputable agent.

A good travel agent, especially one who works with a lot of honeymooners, will be able to tell you about several different places that match your wish list while staying within your budget. (The section entitled *Creating A Budget* will prove invaluable in determining exactly what your budget will be). Your travel agent should be able to provide a variety of options which contain different combinations of the elements of your wish list. Discuss with him/her which "lower priority" items you are willing to forego in order to experience the best of your "top priorities."

Helpful Resources

Travel Agents

Hiring the services of a good travel agent will take a lot of unnecessary pressure off of you. In the past, you may have felt that you did not need the assistance of a travel agent when planning a vacation. Planning a honeymoon, however, can often be far more involved and stressful than a "regular" vacation, due to the simple fact that you are also deeply enmeshed in the planning of your wedding!

Therefore, you should take advantage of the professional resources available to you when working out the small details and finding the best values. Keep in mind, though, that you will still probably want to do some research on your own, ask for second opinions, and, most of all, read the fine print.

Since a travel agent can become one of your most valuable resources, you will want to consider a few important things when trying to select one. Ask family, friends, and coworkers for personal recommendations (especially from former honeymooners). If you are unable to find an agent through a personal referral, then select a few agencies that are established nearby (from newspapers, phone books, etc.)

Next, you will want to make an appointment with an agent or speak to one over the phone. Pay close attention to the following and then make your decision.

Find out if they are a member of the *American Society of Travel Agents* (ASTA). Additionally, find out if they are also a *Certified Travel Counselor* (CTC), or possibly a *Destination Specialist* (DS).

ASTA: Members of this organization are required to have at least 5 years travel agent experience. They also agree to adhere to strict codes and standards of integrity in travel issues as established by the national society. In most states, there are no formal regulations requiring certain qualifications for being a travel agent. In other words, any person can decide to call him/herself, and thus advertise as, a travel agent.

CTC: Certified Travel Counselors have successfully completed a 2 year program in travel management.

DS: Destination Specialists have successfully completed studies focusing on a particular region.

For a list of ASTA agencies in your area, call or write:

> **American Society of Travel Agents**
> **Consumer Affairs Department**
> **1101 King Street, Suite 200**
> **Alexandria, VA 22314**
> **(703) 739-8739**

A listing for the local chapter in your area can also be found in your local phone book or visit their web site at **www.astanet.com**.

For a list of Destination Specialists and Certified Travel Agents in your area, call or write:

> **Institute of Certified Travel Agents**
> **148 Linden Street**
> **P.O. Box 56**
> **Wellesley, MA 02181**
> **(800) 542-4282** (press "0" to be connected to a Travel Counselor)
> **www.ITCA.com**

QUESTIONS TO ASK TO QUALIFY YOUR TRAVEL AGENT:

How long has the Travel Agency been in business?

How long has the Travel Agent been with the agency?

How much experience does the Travel Agent have? Any special studies or travels?

Do they have a good resource library?

Does the agent/agency have a variety of brochures to offer?

Do they have video tapes to lend?

Do they have a recommended reading list of travel aid books?

Does the agent seem to understand your responses on your wish list and budget?

Does he/she seem excited to help you?

Does the agent listen carefully to your ideas? Take notes on your conversations? Ask you questions to ensure a full understanding?

Is the agent able to offer a variety of different possibilities that suit your interests based on your wish list? Do the suggestions fall within your budget?

Can the agent relay back to you (in his/her own words) what your wish list priorities are? What your budget priorities are?

Is the agent prompt in getting back in touch with you?

Is the agent reasonably quick in coming up with suggestions and alternatives? Are the suggestions exciting and within reason?

Does the agent take notes on your interests (degree of sports, leisure, food, etc.)?

Does the travel agency provide a 24 hour emergency help line?

Are you documenting your conversations and getting all of your travel plans and reservations confirmed in writing?

Aside from just offering information and arrangements about locations and discounts, a good travel agent should also provide you with information about passports, customs, travel and health insurance, travelers' checks, and any other information important to a traveler.

OTHER SOURCES

National bridal magazines and general travel magazines are a great place to search for honeymoon ideas. But remember, you cannot always believe every word in paid advertising.

In addition to the information your travel agent provides, you can also obtain maps, brochures, and other useful items on your own. At the end of this section, you will find many useful phone numbers to help you in contacting tourist bureaus and travel agencies worldwide. These offices are extremely helpful in acquiring both general information (information about the weather, tourist attractions, landmarks, and even coupons or promotional brochures "selling" the area) and more specific information about reputable hotels, inns, bed and breakfasts, restaurants, etc.

Also provided in this section are phone numbers for sources specializing in information about traveling by train (in the United States as well as abroad) and for camping and hiking throughout the country.

If you have Internet access you can acquire volumes and volumes of information and titillating pictures about your possible destinations. You can even "chat" with other fellow soon-to-be honeymooners or recent honeymooners about their experiences.

If you don't currently have access, local libraries often provide limited free time and user-assistance for their members.

Your local library, the travel section of book stores, and travel stores are also excellent sources for finding information and tips relevant to your travel needs. You will find books on traveling in general as well as books specific to the region or destination you will be visiting. There are numerous tour books, maps, language books and tapes, as well as books about a location's culture, traditions, customs, climate, and geography.

These books are a great source of information since they are independent from the locations they describe and are therefore impartial, objective, and usually contain correct, unbiased information. You can also find books and other resources describing (and sometimes rating) restaurants, hotels, shows, and tours. Books on bargain hunting and finding the best deals are common as well.

SOURCES TO READ

The Ultimate Guide to the World's Best Wedding and Honeymoon Destinations
Written by Elizabeth & Alex Lluch, *A comprehensive resource for planning your honeymoon, including information on popular destinations and information on hotels and resorts.*

The Stephen Birnbaum Travel Guides

Frommer's Guides

Michelin's Green Guides; Michelin's Red Guides

Insight Guides

Let's Go! guides

Fodor's Guides

Fielding Travel Books

AYH Handbook and Hosteler's Manual: Europe and **United States**

The New York Times Practical Traveler

Mobil Travel Guide

Background Notes
U.S. Government notes containing information about the culture, people, geography, history, government, economy, and maps of most countries worldwide.
The U.S. Government Printing Office Cost: $1.00
(202) 512-1800
or download at: www.access.gpo.gov

National Park Service publications:
(202) 208-4747
www.nps.gov

- *National Park System Map and Guide*
- *The National Parks: Index*

National Forest Service publications:
(202) 205-8333
A Guide to Your National Forests
www.fs.fed.us

STATE TOURISM BUREAUS

Alabama Bureau of Tourism	800-ALABAMA	www.touralabama.com
Alaska Travel Industry Assocation	907-929-2200	www.travelalaska.com
Arizona Office of Tourism	866-275-5816	www.arizonaguide.com
Arkansas Dept. of Parks and Tourism	800-NATURAL	www.arkansas.com
California Tourism Office	800-862-2543	www.gocalif.com
Colorado Tourism Board	800-COLORADO	www.colorado.com
Connecticut Vacation Center	800-CT-BOUND	www.ctbound.com
D.C. Convention and Visitors Association	202-789-7000	www.washington.org
Delaware Tourism Office	866-284-7483	www.visitdelaware.com
Visit Florida	850-488-5607	www.flausa.com
Georgia Department of Industry Trade	800-VISIT-GA	www.georgia.org
Hawaii Visitors & Convention Bureau	800-464-2924	www.hawaii.com
Idaho Division of Tourism Development	800-635-7820	www.visitid.org
Illinois Bureau of Tourism	800-2-CONNECT	www.enjoyillinois.com
Indiana Department of Commerce	888-ENJOY-IN	www.enjoyindiana.com
Iowa Tourism Office	888-472-6035	www.traveliowa.com
Kansas Department of Travel & Tourism	800-2-KANSAS	www.travelks.com
Kentucky Dept. of Travel Development	800-225-TRIP	www.kentuckytourism.com
Louisiana Office of Tourism	800-33-GUMBO	www.louisianatravel.com
Maine Bureau of Tourism	888-624-6345	www.visitmaine.com
Maryland Office of Tourist Development	800-MD-IS-FUN	www.mdisfun.org
Massachusetts Department of Tourism	800-447-MASS	www.massvacation.com
Michigan Department of Commerce	888-78-GREAT	www.michigan.org
Minnesota Office of Tourism	800-657-3700	www.exploreminnesota.com
Mississippi Office of Tourism	800-WARMEST	www.visitmississippi.org
Missouri Travel Center	800-877-1234	www.visitmo.com
Montana Travel Promotion Division	800-VISIT-MT	www.visitmt.com
Nebraska Dept. of Travel and Tourism	800-228-4307	www.visitnebraska.org
Nevada Commission on Tourism	800-NEVADA-8	www.travelnevada.com
New Hampshire Division of Tourism	800-FUN-IN-NH	www.visitnh.gov
New Jersey Office of Travel & Tourism	800-JERSEY-7	www.visitnj.org

New Mexico Department of Tourism	800-SEE-NEWMEX	www.newmexico.org
New York Division of Tourism	800-CALL-NYS	www.www.iloveny.com
North Carolina Travel & Tourism Division	800-VISIT-NC	www.visitnc.com
North Dakota Tourism Division	800-HELLO-ND	www.ndtourism.com
Ohio Department of Travel & Tourism	800-BUCKEYE	www.ohiotourism.com
Oklahoma Tourism and Recreation Dept.	800-652-6552	www.travelok.com
Oregon Tourism Commission	800-547-7842	www.traveloregon.com
Pennsylvania Department of Tourism	800-VISIT-PA	www.experiencepa.com
Rhode Island Tourism Division	800-556-2484	www.visitrhodeisland.com
South Carolina Dept. of Parks, Recreation and Tourism	800-346-3634	www.discoversouthcarolina.com
South Dakota Division of Tourism	800-S-DAKOTA	www.travelsd.com
Tennessee Department of Tourism	800-GO-2-TENN	www.tnvacation.com
Texas Travel and Information Bureau	800-888-8-TEX	www.traveltex.com
Utah Travel Council	800-200-1160	www.utah.com
Vermont Travel Division	800-VERMONT	www.travel-vermont.com
Virginia Division of Tourism	800-VISIT-VA	www.virginia.org
Washington Tourism Development	800-544-1800	www.experiencewashington.com
West Virginia Div. of Tourism & Parks	800-CALL-WVA	www.callwva.com
Wisconsin Division of Tourism	800-432-TRIP	www.travelwisconsin.com
Wyoming Travel & Tourism	800-CALL-WYO	www.wyomingtourism.org
U.S. Virgin Islands Division of Tourism		www.usvitourism.vi

*I*NTERNATIONAL TOURISM BUREAUS

Anguilla Tourist Information	800-553-4939	www.anguilla-vacation.com
Antigua Tourist Office	212-541-4117	www.antigua-barbuda.org
Argentina Tourist Information	800-722-5737	www.turismo.gov.ar/eng/menu.htm
Aruba Tourism Authority	404-89-ARUBA	www.aruba.com
Australian Tourist Commission		www.australia.com
Austrian National Tourist Office		www.austria-tourism.at

Bahamas Tourist Office	800-422-4262	www.bahamas.com
Balkan Holidays	800-822-1106	www.balkan-travel.com
Barbados Board of Tourism	800-221-9831	www.barbados.org
Belgian Tourist Office	212-758-8130	www.visitbelgium.com
Belize Tourist Board	800-624-0686	travelbelize.org
Bermuda Department of Tourism	800-BERMUDA	www.bermudatourism.com
Bonaire Tourist Information Office	800-BONAIRE	www.infobonaire.com
Brazil Tourism Office	800-544-5503	www.brazilres.com
Visit Britain	800-462-2748	www.travelbritain.org
Canadian Consulate	613-946-1000	www.travelcanada.ca
Alberta:	800-661-8888	www.travelalberta.com
British Columbia:	800-HELLO-BC	www.hellobc.com
Manitoba:	800-665-0040	www.travelmanitoba.com
New Brunswick:	800-561-0123	www.tourismnewbrunswick.ca
Newfoundland:	800-563-6353	www.gov.nf.ca/tourism/
Nova Scotia:	800-565-0000	www.explorens.com
Ontario:	800-ONTARIO	www.ontariotravel.net
Prince Edward:	800-PEI-PLAY	www.peiplay.com
Quebec:	877-BONJOUR	www.bonjourquebec.com
Saskatchewan:	877-2-ESCAPE	www.sasktourism.com
Yukon:	867-667-5340	www.touryukon.com
Caribbean Tourism Organization	800-603-3545	www.doitcaribbean.com
Cayman Islands Department of Tourism	212-889-9009	www.caymanislands.ky
Chile National Tourist Board	800-244-5366	www.visitchile.com
China National Tourist Office	818-545-7505	www.cnto.org
Colombian Consulate	202-332-7476	www.colombiaemb.org
Cook Islands Tourist Authority	888-994-2665	www.cook-islands.com
Costa Rican Tourist Board	800-343-6332	www.visitcostarica.com
Curacao Tourist Board	800-683-7660	www.curacao-tourism.com
Cyprus Consulate General	212-683-5280	www.cyprustourism.org
CEDOK (Czech Republic and Slovakia)	212-288-0830	www.czechcenter.com
Denmark Tourist Board	212-885-9700	www.visitdenmark.com
Dominican Republic Tourist Info. Center	888-DR-INFO	www.dominica.com.do
Egyptian Tourist Authority	312-280-4666	touregypt.net
Fiji Visitors Bureau	800-YEA-FIJI	www.BulaFiji.com

Finland Tourist Board	800-FIN-INFO	www.gofinland.org
French Government Tourist Office	410-286-8310	www.franceguide.com
French West Indies	877-956-1234	
German National Tourist Office	323-655-6085	www.visits-to-germany.com
Greece National Tourist Authority	212-421-5777	www.greektourism.com
Grenada Department of Tourism	212-687-9554	www.grenada.org
Guam Visitors Bureau	800-US-3-GUAM	www.visitguam.org
Guatemala Tourist Commission	888-464-8281	www.guatemala.travel.com.gt
Honduras Tourist Bureau	800-410-9608	www.honduras.com
Hong Kong Tourist Association	212-421-3382	www.discoverhongkong,com/usa/
Hungary Tourist Board	212-355-0240	www.gotohungary.com
Iceland Tourist Board	212-885-9747	www.icetourist.is
India Tourist Office	800-953-9399	www.tourismindia.com
Indonesian Tourist Office	808-638-8500	www.indonesia2001.com
Ireland Tourist Board	800-223-6470	www.tourismireland.com
Israeli Government Tourist Office	888-77-ISRAEL	www.goisrael.com
Italian Tourist Office	212-245-4822	www.italiantourism.com
Jamaican Tourist Board	800-JAMAICA	www.jamaicatravel.com
Japan National Tourist Office	212-757-5640	www.japantravelinfo.com
Kenya Tourist Office	202-387-6101	www.magicalkenya.com
Korea National Tourist Office	800-868-7567	www.tour2korea.com
Luxembourg National Tourist Office	212-935-8888	www.visitluxembourg.com
Macau Tourist Office		www.macautourism.gov.mo
Malaysian Tourist Centre	213-689-9702	www.tourismmalysia.com
Malta National Tourist Office	212-430-3799	www.visitmalta.com
Mexican Tourist Office	800-44-MEXICO	www.visitmexico.com
Monaco Government Tourist Office	800-753-9696	www.visitmonaco.com
Morocco National Tourist Office		wwww.tourism-in-morocco.com
Netherlands Board of Tourism	416-363-1577	www.goholland.com
New Zealand Tourist Office	800-639-ZEALAND	www.newzealand.com
Norway Scandinavia Tourist Offices	212-421-7333	www.norway.org
Papua/New Guinea Tourist Office	949-752-5440	www.pngtourism.org.pg

Philippine Department of Tourism	213-487-4525	wowphilippines.com.ph
Poland National Tourism Office	201-420-3370	www.polandtour.org
Portugal National Tourist Office	212-354-4403	www.portugal.org
Puerto Rico Tourism Office	800-866-STAR	www.gopuertorico.com
Romanian National Tourist Office	212-545-8484	www.romaniatourism.com
Russian Travel Information Office	877-221-7120	www.russia-travel.com
Singapore Tourist Board	323-852-1901	www.singapore-usa.com
South African Tourism Board	800-822-5368	www.satour.org
Spain National Tourism Office	212-265-8822	www.okspain.org
Sri Lanka Tourist Board	202-483-4025	www.slembassyusa.org
St. Kitts Tourist Board	212-535-1234	www.stkittsnevis.org
St. Lucia Tourist Board	800-4-ST-LUCIA	www.stlucia.org
St. Maarten Tourist Office	800-786-2278	www.st-maarten.com
St. Vincent/Grenadines Tourist Office	212-687-4981	www.svgtourism.com
Sweden Travel & Tourism Board	212-885-9700	www.visit-sweden.com
Switzerland National Tourist Office		www.myswitzerland.com
Tahitian Tourist Board	310-414-8484	www.tahiti-tourisme.com
Taiwan Visitors Association	212-867-1632	www.taiwan.net.tw
Thailand Tourism Authority	212-432-0433	www.tourismthailand.org
Trinidad and Tobago Tourist Board		www.visitTNT.com
Tunisian Tourist Office	202-862-1850	www.tourismtunisia.com
Turkish Tourism Office	212-687-2194	www.tourismturkey.org
Venezuela Tourism Association	415-331-0100	www.venezuela.com

OTHER TOURISM BUREAUS AND SERVICES

American Automobile Association	407-444-8000	www.aaa.com
National Park Service	202-208-4747	www.nps.gov
Amtrak National Railroad Passenger Info.	800-872-7245	www.amtrak.com
Rail Europe	800-438-7245	www.raileurope.com
Via Rail Canada	800-561-3949	www.viarail.ca

CREATING A BUDGET

You want your honeymoon to give you luxurious experiences and priceless memories. But you don't want to return from your vacation to be faced with debts and unnecessary feelings of guilt for not having stayed within a reasonable budget.

This should be the vacation of a lifetime. You can make this trip into anything your imagination allows. Pay attention to which experiences or details you would consider a "must have" and prioritize. As you work with your budget, stay focused on those top priority items and allow less "elaborate" solutions for lower priority items. If you stay true to your most important vacation objectives, the minor sacrifices along the way will barely be noticed.

Perhaps, at this point, you don't know how many days your honeymoon will last. Often, the number of days you'll vacation depends on the type of honeymoon you choose. If you (and your travel agent) are designing your own honeymoon, the typical cost-per-day will most likely determine your length of stay. If you opt for a cruise or another type of prearranged vacation, your length of stay will probably be dependent upon the designated length of the travel package. By determining a basic, overall budget at the start, you will know what your limits are.

Yes, this is a very romantic time... but try to remain realistic! Once you have an idea of your spending limits, your choices will be much easier to make.

Don't be discouraged if you're unable to spend an infinite amount of money on this trip. Very few couples are able to live life so carefree. You can still experience a honeymoon that will leave you filled with those priceless memories... it's all in the planning!

The following budget worksheets will help guide you in creating your honeymoon budget. You may want to make copies of this worksheet so that you can create several budget plans. Keep trying different variations until you are satisfied with how your expenses will be allocated. When comparing your potential honeymoon options, you'll find that laying out a simple budget is an effective, and essential, tool for making decisions.

𝒢ENERAL BUDGET

Traditionally the groom is responsible for the honeymoon. The groom will take on the challenges of gathering information and working through the necessary details of providing a perfect honeymoon for his new bride... and himself! Nowadays, many couples find it necessary for both the bride and groom to contribute to the cost in order to experience the honeymoon of their dreams. (*Today, the average newlywed couple spends $2,500-$3,500 on their honeymoon.*) Many couples, together, determine what each partner will contribute and then shape the budget from there.

Some couples find that including the suggestion of a "Money Contribution towards a Memorable Honeymoon" as a gift in their bridal registry is a great way for friends and family to contribute to the trip. Some couples also include some version of a "Dollar Dance" at their reception. This is a great way for the bride and groom to dance with many of their guests while accepting the dollar "dance fee" as a contribution to their honeymoon. Some couples choose to pursue less romantic options for building up the honeymoon savings... part time jobs, yard sales, etc..

Whatever your methods may be, remember that increasing the amount of money you will spend does not automatically ensure a more pleasurable and enjoyable vacation. Your most important and effective resource is your commitment to planning. You will see that, regardless of what your budget limits may be, your vacation possibilities are endless.

Note: Even if you think you have a good sense of what you will spend (or even if you plan on going with an all-inclusive package) going through this exercise is a smart way to ensure that There will be no surprises later on.

GENERAL BUDGET

**Amount from Wedding Budget set aside
for Honeymoon:** $_____

**Amount Groom is able to contribute from
current funds/savings:** $_____

**Amount Bride is able to contribute from
current funds/savings:** $_____

**Amount to be saved/acquired by Groom
from now until the honeymoon date:** $_____
(monthly contributions, part-time job, gifts, bonuses)

**Amount to be saved/acquired by Bride
from now until the honeymoon date:** $_____
(monthly contributions, part-time job, gifts, bonuses)

> **"GENERAL BUDGET"
> TOTAL AMOUNT:**
>
> $_____

DETAILED BUDGET

BEFORE THE HONEYMOON:

Special honeymoon clothing purchases: $_____

Bride's trousseau (honeymoon lingerie): $_____

Sundries: $_____
(HELPFUL HINT: Make a list of what you already have
and what you need to purchase. You can then use these
lists as part of your Packing List. See *Packing Checklist.*)

Film, disposable cameras, extra camera batteries: $_____

Maps, guide books, travel magazines: $_____

**Foreign language books and tapes,
translation dictionary:** $_____

Passport photos, application fees: $_____
(See *International Travel*)

Medical exam, inoculations: $_____
(See *International Travel*)

Other items: $_____

_____

_____

_____

**BEFORE THE HONEYMOON
TOTAL AMOUNT:**

$_____

DURING THE HONEYMOON:

TRANSPORTATION

Airplane tickets: $_____

Shuttle or cab (to and from airport): $_____

Car rental, Gasoline, tolls: $_____

Taxis, buses, other public transportation: $_____

TRANSPORTATION
TOTAL AMOUNT:

$_____

ACCOMMODATIONS

Hotel/resort room (total for entire stay): $_____

Room service: $_____

Miscellaneous "hidden costs": $_____
Phone use, room taxes and surcharges, chambermaid
and room service tips (see *Tipping Guide*),
in-room liquor bar and snacks.

ACCOMMODATIONS
TOTAL AMOUNT:

$_____

MEALS
(NOTE: Don't forget to include the cost of drinks and gratuities in your meal estimates.)

Breakfast: $_____ *per meal* x _____ *# days* = $_____

Lunch: $_____ *per meal* x _____ *# days* = $_____

Casual Dinners: $_____ *per meal* x _____ *# days* = $_____

Formal Dinners: $_____ *per meal* x _____ *# days* = $_____

Picnics, Snacks, Temptations: $_____ *per meal* x _____ *# days* = $_____

MEALS
TOTAL AMOUNT:

$_____

ENTERTAINMENT

Sport and activity lessons
(tennis, golf, ballroom dancing, etc.): $_____

Day excursions and tours
(boat tours, diving, snorkeling, bus/guided tours, etc.): $_____

Shows, theater: $_____

Lounges, nightclubs, discos:
(don't forget to include the cost of drinks and bar gratuities) $_____

Museum fees: $_____

Pampering
(massages, spa treatments, hairdresser, etc.): $_____

```
ENTERTAINMENT
TOTAL AMOUNT:


$_____
```

MISCELLANEOUS

Souvenirs for yourselves: $_____

Souvenirs and gifts for family and friends: $_____

Postcards (including cost of stamps): $_____

Newspapers and magazines: $_____

Additional film, replacement sundries, other: $_____

```
MISCELLANEOUS
TOTAL AMOUNT:


$_____
```

After the honeymoon:

Film developing costs: $_____

Photo Albums: $_____

> ### AFTER THE HONEYMOON
> ### TOTAL AMOUNT:
>
> $_____

For All-Inclusive Resorts/Cruises and Travel Packages only:

Fill in the entire budget form above (simply put a "$0.00" on items to be included in the total package price), then list the total inclusive package price on the line below. Don't forget to include taxes and surcharges.

Inclusive Package Price: $_____

> ## "DETAILED BUDGET"
> ## TOTAL AMOUNT
>
> $_____

Doing a budget analysis may be one of the most useful things you can do in planning your honeymoon. With all the options available, a good cost analysis will help make the most appropriate decisions very clear to you.

First, create a budget using the above worksheet for what you think allows for an ideal, yet reasonable, honeymoon. Highlight those expenses which are top priorities. For example, a spacious, ritzy hotel room may be the most important element for you. Or, perhaps participating in numerous sports activities and excursions or enjoying fine dining is more important than a spacious room.

Next, as you come across different destinations and options that appeal to you, fill in a new budget worksheet. Compare the results to other potential trips. See how your priority items on each trip compare to one another. Determine the pros and cons of each. This is also an effective way of looking at the pros and cons of an all-inclusive package versus an independently organized trip.

NOTE: Once you've decided on your honeymoon destination and activities, fill in a new budget as accurately as possible and take it with you on your trip. Use it to chart your expenses as they occur so you will have a visual guide of whether or not you are staying within budget.

If you find that you are going over your budget, take a look at those top priority items that you'd still like to keep. See if you can eliminate some lower priority items to free up some money for the favored ones.

If you find you are under budget, celebrate with a special "gift" for yourselves (massages, an extravagant dinner, another afternoon of jet skiing, etc.).

Personal Notes

TIPPING GUIDE

This guide is provided to help you get familiar with customary gratuity standards you may encounter throughout your travels.

Tipping customs vary from country to country. It is advisable to inquire about tipping with the international tourism board representing the country you'll be traveling in. Simply ask for information about tipping customs and social expectations. You will also want to discuss gratuities with your travel agent or planner. Some travel packages include gratuities in the total cost, some leave that to the guests, and some even discourage tipping (usually because they have built it into the total package price) Be sure to discuss this with your travel planner.

SERVICE	GRATUITY
AIR TRAVEL	
Skycaps	$1.00 per bag
Flight Attendants	none
ROAD TRAVEL	
Taxi Drivers	15% of fare (no less than 50 cents)
Limousine Driver	15%
Valet Parking	$1.00
Tour Bus Guide	$1.00
RAIL TRAVEL	
Redcaps	$1.00 per bag (or posted rate plus 50 cents)
Sleeping Car Attendant	$1.00 per person
Train Conductor and Crew	none
Dining Car Attendant	15% of bill

SERVICE	GRATUITY
CRUISE	
Cabin Steward	2.5-7.5% of fare (paid at the end of the trip)
Dining Room Waiter	2.5-7.5% of fare (paid at the end of the trip)
Cabin Boy, Bar Steward, Wine Steward	5-7.5% of total fare (divided proportionately among them)
RESTAURANTS	
Maitre d', Headwaiter	none (unless special services provided, then typically $5.00)
Waiter/Waitress	15% of bill (pretax total)
Bartender	15% of bill
Wine Steward	15% of bill
Washroom Attendant	25-50 cents
Coat Check Attendant	$1.00 for 1 or 2 coats
(NOTE: Some restaurants in foreign countries add the gratuity and/or service charge to your bill. If it has not been added, tip the customary regional rate.)	
HOTEL / RESORT	
Concierge	$2.00-10.00 for special attention or arrangements
Doorman	$1.00 for hailing taxi
Bellhop	$1.00 per bag 50 cents for showing room
Room Service	15% of bill
Chamber Maid	$1.00-2.00 per day or $5.00-10.00 per week for longer stays (no tip for one night stays)
Pool Attendant	50 cents for towel service
MISCELLANEOUS	
Barbershop	15% of cost
Beauty Salon	15% of cost
Manicure	$1.00-5.00 depending on cost of service
Facial	15% of cost
Massage	15% of cost

Things To Pack

TRAVELERS' FIRST AID KIT

Consider the differences in the climates of where you live now and where you'll be visiting. Also consider the air conditions of airplanes, trains and boats. Bring along items that will help in the transition and keep you feeling as comfortable as possible.

- ❑ *Aspirin*
- ❑ *Antacid tablets*
- ❑ *Diarrhea medication*
- ❑ *Cold remedies/ sinus decongestant*
- ❑ *Throat lozenges*
- ❑ *Antiseptic Lotion*
- ❑ *Band-Aids*
- ❑ *Moleskin for blisters*
- ❑ *Breath mints*
- ❑ *Chapstick*
- ❑ *Insect Repellent, Insect Bite Medication*
- ❑ *Sunblock and Sunburn Relief Lotion*
- ❑ *Dry Skin Lotion/Hand Cream*
- ❑ *Eye Drops or Eye Lubricant*
- ❑ *Saline nasal spray, moisturizing nasal spray*
- ❑ *Vitamins*
- ❑ *Prescription drugs*

    NOTE: These should be kept in their original pharmacy containers which provide both drug and doctor information. Be sure to note the drug's generic name. You will want to pack these in your carry on baggage in case the bags you've checked become lost or delayed.

- ❑ *Condoms or prescription birth control*
- ❑ *Physicians' names, addresses, and telephone numbers*
- ❑ *Health Insurance phone numbers*

    NOTE: Be sure to contact your provider to find out about coverage while traveling in the U.S. and abroad.

- ❑ *Names and phone numbers of people to contact in case of an emergency.*

PACKING CHECKLIST

CARRY ON BAGGAGE:

- ☐ Travelers' First Aid Kit (see previous section)
- ☐ Wallet (credit cards, traveler's checks)
- ☐ Jewelry and other sentimental and valuable items that you feel you *must* bring
- ☐ Identification (Passport, Driver's License or Photo ID)
- ☐ Photocopies of the following Important Documents:
  - ☐ Hotel/resort street address, phone number, written confirmation of arrangements and reservations
  - ☐ Complete travel itinerary
  - ☐ Airline tickets
  - ☐ Name, address and phone number of emergency contact person(s) back home
  - ☐ Medicine prescriptions (including generic names) and eyeglass prescription information (or an extra pair); list of food and drug allergies
  - ☐ Phone numbers (including after-hour emergency phone numbers) for health insurance company and personal physicians
- ☐ Copy of your packing list. This will help you while packing up at the end of your trip. It will also be invaluable if a piece of your luggage gets lost, as you will know the contents that are missing.
- ☐ List of your travelers checks' serial numbers and 24 hour phone number for reporting loss or theft
- ☐ Phone numbers to the local U.S. embassy or consulate
- ☐ Any "essential" toiletries and one complete casual outfit in case checked baggage is delayed or lost
- ☐ Foreign language dictionary or translator
- ☐ Camera with film loaded
- ☐ Maps
- ☐ Small bills/change (in U.S. dollars and in the appropriate foreign currency) for tipping
- ☐ Currency converter chart or pocket calculator
- ☐ Reading material

☐ Eyeglasses

☐ Contact lenses

☐ Contact lens cleaner

☐ Sunglasses

☐ Kleenex, gum, breath mints, and any over-the-counter medicine to ease travel discomfort

☐ Inflatable neck pillow (for lengthy, sit down travels)

☐ Address book and thank you notes (in case you have lots of traveling time)

☐ This Book

☐ Your Budget Sheet

Other items to carry-on ...

☐ _____

☐ _____

☐ _____

☐ _____

☐ _____

CHECKED BAGGAGE:

Clothing:

Casual wear

(Consider the total number of each casual outfit item that you will need)

☐ shorts

☐ pants

☐ tops

☐ jackets/sweaters

☐ sweatshirts/sweatsuits

☐ belts

☐ socks

☐ underwear/panties & bras

- ❑ walking shoes/sandals/loafers
- ❑ _____
- ❑ _____

Athletic wear
(Consider the total number of each sporting outfit item that you will need)

- ❑ shorts
- ❑ sweatpants
- ❑ tops
- ❑ sweatshirts/jackets
- ❑ swim suits, swim suit cover-up
- ❑ aerobic activity outfit
- ❑ athletic equipment
- ❑ socks
- ❑ underwear/panties & exercise bras
- ❑ tennis/athletic shoes
- ❑ _____
- ❑ _____

Evening wear
(Consider the total number of each evening outfit item that you will need)

- ❑ pants or pants/skirts/dresses
- ❑ belts
- ❑ dress shirts/blouses
- ❑ sweaters
- ❑ jackets/blazers/ties
- ❑ socks or pantyhose/slips
- ❑ underwear/panties & bras
- ❑ accessories/jewelry
- ❑ shoes
- ❑ _____
- ❑ _____

Formal wear
(Consider the number of each formal outfit item that you will need)

- ☐ dress pants/suits/tuxedo
- ☐ dresses/gowns
- ☐ accessories/jewelry
- ☐ socks or pantyhose/slips
- ☐ underwear/panties & bras
- ☐ dress shoes
- ☐ _____
- ☐ _____

Other Clothing items

- ☐ pajamas
- ☐ lingerie
- ☐ slippers
- ☐ robe
- ☐ _____
- ☐ _____

Miscellaneous items:

- ☐ An additional set of the important document photocopies as packed in your carry on
- ☐ Travel tour books, Tourism Bureau Information numbers
- ☐ Journal
- ☐ Special honeymoon gift for your new spouse
- ☐ Any romantic items or favorite accessories
- ☐ Extra film and camera batteries
- ☐ Plastic bags for dirty laundry
- ☐ Large plastic or nylon tote bag for bringing home new purchases
- ☐ Small sewing kit and safety pins
- ☐ Travel alarm clock
- ☐ Travel iron, Lint brush

- ❑ Compact umbrella, Fold up rain slickers
- ❑ Hand held tape recorder (for recorded memory journal or for bringing along your favorite, romantic tapes) and/or videocamera
- ❑ Copy of *The Ultimate Guide to a Sensuous Honeymoon,* a playful book containing fifty sensual, fun, and exciting games to fill your honeymoon with hot and passionate sex. This book is published by Wedding Solutions Publishing, Inc. and is available at most major bookstores nationwide or on-line in the bookstore section at *www.WeddingSolutions.com.*
- ❑ _____

For International travel:
- ❑ Passports/visas
- ❑ Electric converters and adapter plugs
- ❑ Copy of appropriate forms showing proof of required vaccinations/inoculations
- ❑ _____

Other items to bring ...
- ❑ _____
- ❑ _____
- ❑ _____
- ❑ _____
- ❑ _____

ITEMS TO LEAVE BEHIND (with a trusted contact person):
- ❑ Photocopy of all travel details (complete itineraries, names, addresses, and telephone numbers)
- ❑ Photocopy of credit cards along with 24 hour telephone number to report loss or theft. (Be sure to get the number to call when traveling abroad. It will be a different number than their U.S. 1-800 number.)
- ❑ Photocopy of travelers checks along with 24 hour telephone number to report loss or theft
- ❑ Photocopy of passport identification page, along with date and place of issuance
- ❑ Photocopy of drivers license
- ❑ Any irreplaceable items

*I*NTERNATIONAL *T*RAVEL

There are over 250 U.S. embassies and consulates around the world. After contacting the Tourism Bureau for the area you will be traveling to, it is also a wise idea to contact the U.S. Embassy or Consulate for that region. With assistance from both of these sources you will be able to determine the travel requirements and recommendations for your chosen travel destination. Within this section you will find numerous resources to assure all of your questions and concerns are addressed before you travel.

Call for a list of U.S. embassy and consulate locations with emergency phone numbers:

(202) 647-5225 or visit http://travel.state.gov

*P*ASSPORTS AND *V*ISAS

Your travel agent should be able to provide you with information to adequately prepare you for your international travels. Additional information (and possibly more detailed and current information) can be obtained by contacting the appropriate sources listed in this section.

As a U.S. citizen, you generally need a passport to enter and to depart most foreign countries and to reenter the United States. Some countries also require Visas. A Visa is an endorsement by officials of a foreign country as permission to visit their country. You first need a passport in order to obtain a Visa. Inquire with the resources listed in this section for requirements of your specific destination.

As mentioned, you will be required to prove your U.S. citizenship upon reentry to the United States. If the country of your destination does not require you to possess a current passport, you will still need to produce proof of citizenship for U.S. Immigration. Items that are acceptable as proof of citizenship include a passport, a certified copy of your Birth Certificate, a Certificate of Nationalization, a Certificate of Citizenship, or a Report of Birth Abroad of a Citizen of the United States. Proof of identification can include a driver's license or a government or military identification card containing a photo or physical description.

NOTE: The bride should have her passport and airline tickets reflect her maiden name for ease in proof of identification while traveling. Name changes can be processed after returning from the honeymoon with your marriage certificate.

Your passport will be one of the most important documents you will take with you. Contact the local U.S. Embassy immediately if your passport becomes lost or stolen. Have a photocopy of your passports' data page, date and place of issuance, and passport number to be kept with a contact person at home. You should also travel with a set of these photocopies in addition to an extra set of loose passport photos for speed in attaining a replacement.

Passports can be obtained from one of the 13 U.S. Passport Agencies (listed later in this section) or one of the thousands of authorized passport locations, such as state and federal courts as well as some U.S. Post Offices (check in the Government Listings section of your phone book).

Currently, the cost to obtain a passport is $65.00 (in person; Form DSP-11) or $55.00 (through the mail; Form DSP-82). If you have had a passport in the past, contact a passport agency to find out if you are eligible to apply through the mail. You will want to apply for your passport several months before your trip, keeping in mind that January through July is a busier time and the process may take longer.

In addition to calling the U.S. Passport Agencies for personal assistance, you can also call their 24-hour recorded information lines for information on agency locations, travel advisories and warnings, and Consular Information Sheets pertaining to every country in the world.

Travel Advisory Updates are also available 24 hours a day by calling:
The Department of State's Office of Overseas Citizens' Services at: (202) 647-5225

Additional, and very helpful, official information for U.S. citizens regarding international travel can be found at:
http://travel.state.gov

Foreign embassies and consulates located in the U.S. can provide current information regarding their country. You can locate phone numbers and addresses in the following:
The Congressional Directory
Foreign Consular Offices in the United States
(both available at your local library)

UNITED STATES PASSPORT AGENCIES

http://travel.state.gov/passport_services.html   800-688-9889

Boston Passport Agency	Inquiries:	617-565-6990
	24-hr info line:	617-565-6698
Chicago Passport Agency	Inquiries:	312-341-6020
	24-hr info line:	312-341-6020
Honolulu Passport Agency	Inquiries:	808-522-8283
	24-hr info line:	808-522-8283
Houston Passport Agency	Inquiries:	713-751-0294
	24-hr info line:	713-751-0294
Los Angeles Passport Agency	Inquiries:	310-235-7075
	24-hr info line:	310-235-7070
Miami Passport Agency	Inquiries:	305-859-2705
	24-hr info line:	305-859-2705
New Orleans Passport Agency	Inquiries:	504-412-2600
	24-hr info line:	504-512-2600
New York Passport Agency	Inquiries:	212-374-0615
	24-hr info line:	212-374-0615
Philadelphia Passport Agency	Inquiries:	215-597-7480
	24-hr info line:	215-597-7480
San Francisco Passport Agency	Inquiries:	415-744-5627
	24-hr info line:	415-538-2700
Seattle Passport Agency	Inquiries:	206-808-5700
	24-hr info line:	206-808-5700
Stamford Passport Agency	Inquiries:	203-969-9000
	24-hr info line:	206-969-9000
Washington Passport Agency	Inquiries:	202-647-0518
	24-hr info line:	202-647-0518

*Some private sources offering assistance in obtaining a passport
(usually offering expedited service):*

International Visa Service   1 (800) 627-1112

World Wide Visas   1 (800) 527-1861

Travel Document Systems   1 (800) 874-5100 or www.traveldocs.com

HEALTH CONCERNS

In the United States the National Center for Infectious Diseases (NCID) and the Centers for Disease Control (CDC) provide the most current information pertinent to international travel. The World Health Organization (WHO) concerns itself with general and specific health issues for almost every part of the world. Health and safety issues as related to international travel are the basis for the International Heath Regulations adopted by the World Health Organization.

Your travel agent should be fully informed about current conditions and requirements. Your personal physician should also be able to provide you with health-related information and advice for traveling in the region you visit. You can personally obtain very useful (and very thorough) information from the Center for Disease Control and Prevention (CDC). The CDC's Travelers' Health Section has the following useful resources:

Health Information for International Travel (*"The Yellow Book"*)
> available from:
> The Superintendent of Documents
> U.S. Government Printing Office
> Washington, D.C. 20402
> 202-512-1800
> or download a free copy at www.cdc.gov

Summary of Health Information for International Travel (*"The Blue Sheet"*)
> A biweekly publication available by fax: 404-332-4565
> (request document 220022#)

For updates and changes by phone or fax, call 404-332-4559 or visit www.cdc.gov.

OTHER CONCERNS

TRAVELERS' HEALTH INSURANCE COVERAGE:
If your health insurance policy does not cover you abroad, consider acquiring a temporary health insurance policy. Travel agencies, health insurance companies, travelers' check companies, and your local phone book should be able to provide names of relevant companies for you. In addition to health insurance coverage, many policy packages also include protection in case of trip cancellation and baggage loss.

Keep prescription medications in their original pharmacy containers with the original labels. Bring a copy of your prescriptions and note the drug's generic name. You may consider getting a letter from your physician warranting your need for the medication.

CUSTOMS
The following list contains some useful publications regarding customs and custom policies when travelling internationally:

Know Before You Go; Customs Hints for Returning U.S. Residents
   U.S. Customs
   P.O. Box 7407
   Washington, D.C. 20004
   202-566-8195

Travelers' Tips on Bringing Food, Plant and Animal Products into the United States
   U.S. Department of Agriculture
   613 Federal Building
   6505 Belcrest Road
   Hyattsville, MD 20782

An Unwanted Souvenir; Lead in Ceramic Ware
   U.S. Food and Drug Administration
   HFI-40
   Rockville, MD 20857

Personal Notes

_____

_____

_____

_____

_____

_____

_____

_____

_____

_____

_____

_____

_____

_____

_____

_____

_____

_____

_____

_____

_____

_____

_____

_____

_____

_____

_____

*T*ELL US ABOUT YOUR WEDDING

We would greatly appreciate your writing to us after your honeymoon to let us know how your wedding went and how much the *Easy Wedding Planning Plus* helped you in planning your wedding. We will use this information to continue improving this extensive wedding planner, and we may even use your story in our upcoming book about wedding experiences. We might even ask you to participate in some of our future radio and TV tours where you can tell your own story to the public! Feel free to use additional sheets, if necessary.

Dear Alex & Elizabeth:

I want to tell you that your book: (helped a lot), (helped a little), in planning my wedding. I especially liked your section on _____. My wedding was on _____ and it was: (a complete success), (a wild party), (a boring event), (a complete disaster), (the most stressful day of my life).

My comments about your book are: _____

_____
_____
_____
_____

I wish your book had given me information about: _____

_____
_____
_____
_____

The best thing about my wedding was: _____

_____
_____
_____
_____
_____

The worst thing about my wedding was: _____

_____
_____
_____
_____
_____

The funniest thing about my wedding was: _____

_____

_____

_____

_____

_____

What made my wedding special or unique was: _____

_____

_____

_____

_____

_____

My wedding would have been much better if: _____

_____

_____

_____

_____

This is to authorize Wedding Solutions Publishing to use our story in any of their upcoming books. Wedding Solutions Publishing (can), (cannot) use our name when telling our story. I also (am), (am not) interested in participating in a radio/TV interview tour.

Bride's Name _____   Bride's Signature _____

Groom's Name _____   Groom's Signature _____

Address _____

Home Number _____   Email _____

Fold in three and mail to Wedding Solutions Publishing, Inc.

Place
Stamp
Here

Wedding Solutions Publishing, Inc.
6347 Caminito Tenedor
San Diego, CA 92120

KAREN FRENCH

WEDDING SOLUTIONS

The largest and most respected wedding publishing and consulting company in America

Proudly Presents

WEDDINGSOLUTIONS.COM

FOR ALL YOUR WEDDING NEEDS

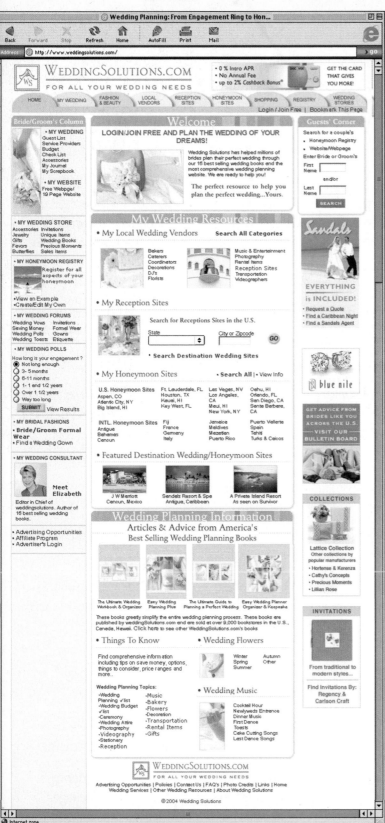

*E*verything you need to plan the wedding of your dreams!

- 🎀 Wedding Planning Tools
- 🎀 Search for Wedding Dresses
- 🎀 Create Your Own Website
- 🎀 Free Photo Gallery
- 🎀 Largest Online Wedding Store
- 🎀 Thousands of Resources:
  - •Local Vendors
  - •Reception Sites
  - •Honeymoon Destinations
- 🎀 Gift Registry
- 🎀 Honeymoon Registry
- 🎀 Book Your Travel
- 🎀 Chat Room
- 🎀 Bulletin Board
- 🎀 Free Newsletters
- 🎀 Fashion and Beauty Tips
- 🎀 And Much More

*C*ome and see how easy wedding planning can be!

Log on to *www.WeddingSolutions.com* for details

Voted the most comprehensive and easy-to-use website by brides nationwide!

WeddingSolutions.com
FOR ALL YOUR WEDDING NEEDS

Voted the most comprehensive and easy-to-use website by brides nationwide.

Why use **WeddingSolutions.com?** Because *WeddingSolutions.com* has features not offered by any other wedding website on the market. From the moment of engagement to your honeymoon, we offer resources, helpful hints, and wedding planning tools to make wedding planning as easy as it can be.

Bride's Community

Our wedding community is a place where brides across the U.S. can come together to lend support to each other:

- Chat Room
- Newsletters
- Featured Articles
- Advice Column
- Bulletin Board
- Fashion & Beauty

Karen French Photography

Register for Your Honeymoon

Register for monetary gifts toward your honeymoon. Your guests will appreciate this convenient way to contribute towards your:

- Airfare
- Meals
- Tours
- Hotel Accommodations
- Recreation & Activities
- Entertainment
- Rentals
- Spa Treatments
- & More

Karen French Photography

Wedding Website

Easily create your very own wedding web site. Share with your guests what you are planning for your wedding and beyond!

- Home Page
- Our Story
- Photo Gallery
- Details of Events
- Wedding Party
- Local Information
- Wedding Journal
- R.S.V.P.
- & Much more

Karen French Photography

Book Your Travel

Take care of all your travel arrangements, from locating the perfect destination, to booking tickets, hotels and more.
We offer the lowest prices on:

- Cruises
- Resorts
- All Inclusives
- Private Villas
- Unique Places
- Golf Packages
- Car Rentals
- Special Offers

Log on to *www.WeddingSolutions.com* for details

WEDDINGSOLUTIONS.COM

FOR ALL YOUR WEDDING NEEDS

Voted the most comprehensive and easy-to-use website by bride's nationwide!

What is **Wedding Solutions Publishing?** Wedding Solutions is the largest and most respected wedding planning and publishing company in America. We have been in business for over ten years and have helped millions of brides and grooms plan the wedding of their dreams through our best selling wedding planning books.

Easy Wedding Planner
Organizer & Keepsake
U.S. $29.95

The Ultimate Wedding
Workbook & Organizer
U.S. $24.95

Easy Wedding
Planning Plus
U.S. $ 19.95

The Ultimate Guide
to Planning the
Perfect Wedding
U.S. $23.95

Easy Wedding
Planning
U.S. $9.95

The Very Best
Wedding Planner & Organizer
U.S. $26.95

The Very Best
Wedding Planning Guide
U.S. $26.95

Wedding Party
Responsibility Cards
U.S. $9.95

The Ultimate Guide to the
World's Best Wedding
& Honeymoon Destinations
U.S. $17.95

The Ultimate Guide
Wedding Music
U.S. $19.95

The Ultimate
Groom's Guide
U.S. $9.95

The Ultimate Weddiing
Planner & Organizer
U.S. $29.95

The Ultimate Wedding
Name & Address Change Kit
U.S. $19.95

The Ultimate Guide to a
Sensuous Honeymoon
U.S. $17.95

The Ultimate Weddi
Planning Calendar
U.S. $19.95

Wedding Solutions Books are sold at all major book stores, such as Barnes & Noble, Borders, Waldenbooks, B Dalton, and Books-A-Million. You can also see complete details on these books when you log onto *www.WeddingSolutions.com*.

Log on to *www.WeddingSolutions.com* for details